UNDERSTANDING & TEACHING PRIMARY HISTORY

Sara Miller McCune founded SAGE Publishing in 1965 to support the dissemination of usable knowledge and educate a global community. SAGE publishes more than 1000 journals and over 800 new books each year, spanning a wide range of subject areas. Our growing selection of library products includes archives, data, case studies and video. SAGE remains majority owned by our founder and after her lifetime will become owned by a charitable trust that secures the company's continued independence.

Los Angeles | London | New Delhi | Singapore | Washington DC | Melbourne

UNDERSTANDING & TEACHING PRIMARY HISTORY

JAMES PERCIVAL

SAGE

Los Angeles | London | New Delhi
Singapore | Washington DC | Melbourne

Los Angeles | London | New Delhi
Singapore | Washington DC | Melbourne

SAGE Publications Ltd
1 Oliver's Yard
55 City Road
London EC1Y 1SP

SAGE Publications Inc.
2455 Teller Road
Thousand Oaks, California 91320

SAGE Publications India Pvt Ltd
B 1/I 1 Mohan Cooperative Industrial Area
Mathura Road
New Delhi 110 044

SAGE Publications Asia-Pacific Pte Ltd
3 Church Street
#10-04 Samsung Hub
Singapore 049483

First published 2020

Editor: James Clark
Assistant editor: Diana Alves
Production editor: Imogen Roome
Copyeditor: Sarah Bury
Proofreader: Leigh C. Smithson
Indexer: Elizabeth Ball
Marketing manager: Dilhara Attygalle
Cover design: Naomi Robinson
Typeset by: C&M Digitals (P) Ltd, Chennai, India
Printed in the UK

Library of Congress Control Number: 2019946509

British Library Cataloguing in Publication data

A catalogue record for this book is available from the British Library

ISBN 978-1-5264-2082-4
ISBN 978-1-5264-2083-1 (pbk)

CONTENTS

ABOUT THE AUTHOR

James Percival studied history and philosophy as an undergraduate, and subsequently trained as a primary teacher with history as his specialist subject. After a 10-year teaching career in several Oxfordshire schools, having taught in both Key Stages, acted as curriculum coordinator and mentored teacher trainees and Newly Qualified Teachers, he transferred into teacher training at Oxford Brookes University in 2004. James has subsequently worked with trainee teachers across several programmes while developing a research profile in primary history pedagogy. His doctorate centred on the curriculum management of history in primary schools.

ACKNOWLEDGEMENTS

I would like to thank my employers, Oxford Brookes University, for continuing to support staff research and scholarship. Thanks also to my family, H, S and J, who have endured the sound of typing in lieu of family fun.

CHAPTER 1

INTRODUCTION

HOW WILL THIS BOOK HELP MY PRACTICE?

The book is essentially written for primary teacher trainees, or early career teachers, who entered teaching through a Postgraduate Certificate in Education (PGCE) or school-based routes and who may not have studied history in any form since they were in Key Stages 3 or 4. It is also equally useful for teachers and those who have studied history to 'A' level, and possibly continued to study the subject at university, who are unlikely to know the content and concepts covered by the National Curriculum, and who may appreciate an opportunity to think more deeply about the nature of the subject they have studied for several years. It also contains some useful content for subject coordinators who may wish to find out more about curriculum design and implementation, including assessment practices.

The reduction of university-based training for prospective primary teachers *may* be based on sound pedagogical reasons, but it does mean that to learn 'on the job' requires high levels of dedication and independent study from trainees. A related point is that in times of uncertainty, especially given the new powers available to state-funded schools to determine differentials in terms of pay and conditions, it is arguably ever more important that qualified teachers can demonstrate the 'value-added' they bring to the classroom in terms of subject knowledge and pedagogical expertise. State-funded primary schools have always been required to deliver a 'broad and balanced' curriculum in which history should play a full part. It is surely not coincidental that several of the world's top-performing educations systems, for example Finland, South Korea and Singapore, have very competitive and highly regarded teacher recruitment and training systems; and certainly, in the case of Finland, a commitment to a broad and balanced curriculum.

A further impetus in support of the previous point is the consideration that at the time of writing, in the summer of 2019, Ofsted (Office for

Standards in Education, Children's Services and Skills) have revised their school 'Inspection Framework'. Under the direction of Chief Inspector Amanda Spielman (Ofsted, 2018, 2019), the focus has changed from an emphasis on the core subjects and educational standards to a broader remit concerning the whole curriculum, including teachers' planning skills and children's progress. Given that Ofsted can be described fairly as the tail that wagged the educational dog and is therefore more responsible than any other organisation for the obsession with standards in literacy and mathematics, this shifting focus might legitimately be viewed rather cynically. However, the principal outcome of the revised Inspection Framework is that state-funded primary schools will now have to demonstrate a deep-rooted commitment to the whole curriculum, including history, based on sound and original planning and delivered by skilled teachers.

Although there are several well-regarded primary history texts in print, none of the established books deals directly with the revised National Curriculum (DfE, 2013) for history, which was introduced relatively recently and without the level of support and official guidance that the early forms of the National Curriculum received. Although it is argued in Chapter 2 that an overview of the requirements for primary history demonstrates high levels of continuity rather than change, nevertheless there are important differences. Essentially, the main distinctions can be found in ideological beliefs in the primacy of transformative forms of knowledge, and in the importance of children knowing a chronological overview of British history.

It is also the aim of this book to attempt to re-establish some of earlier debates about the nature of history, particularly the often heated discussions from the 1970s. There is a danger that some of the important discussions that took place, often based on lengthy research projects, will be lost and replaced with a passive acceptance of decisions made by career politicians and civil servants, almost all of whom lack personal experience and knowledge of teaching and primary education. If this sounds a little hyperbolic, would doctors, for all the current scrutiny of the National Health Service, allow politicians to determine how they carry out their professional practice?

This book therefore aims to summarise, in a readable and informed style, the main findings from the research base into the teaching and learning of history in the primary (or elementary) years. A related aim, and one arguably under-emphasised in earlier primary history texts, is to supplement the research into history pedagogy through the inclusion of reflections and debates from within the philosophy of history. In some chapters the underpinning philosophical foundations, aimed at supporting professional practice, are relatively extensive. This essentially means that a considerable amount of time is dedicated to introducing and explaining the main concepts of history, and how these might be introduced at primary level to shape and support children's historical understanding.

RECENT CHANGES: SOCIAL REALISM, POWERFUL KNOWLEDGE AND THE PLACE OF CHRONOLOGY

The primacy of knowledge has deep roots, some of which will be explained in Chapter 2, but in terms of influence on the former Secretary of State for Education, and chief architect of the revised National Curriculum, Michael Gove, one name stands above all others: E.D. Hirsch. In many respects Hirsch has become a polemic and misunderstood figure, and his arguments are certainly more robust and nuanced than his many critics would allow, but his principal concern, accepted by Gove, was that students from poorer, culturally deprived backgrounds were often unable to engage with challenging texts or high-level discussions because of their lack of specific forms of knowledge (Abrams, 2012). Thus, in his landmark text, *Cultural Literacy* (1988), Hirsch argued that schools have neglected to teach the knowledge that could possibly unlock the path to academic success for disadvantaged children. While some critics have attacked Hirsch for his increasingly entrenched position, arguably more credence should be given to the position of Michael Young, who has accepted that his former belief in the efficacy of teaching for understanding, rather than teaching for knowledge, was simply misguided. In several publications (e.g., Young, 2008, 2011), Young has moved to a social realist position and now accepts the transformative potential of what he has termed 'powerful' and specialist forms of knowledge and the importance of disciplinary boundaries, such as history.

Michael Gove certainly heeded this positional shift from experienced academics: in a 2009 speech to the Royal Society of Arts (RSA), when he was shadow Secretary of State, he not only acknowledged the influence of Hirsch and the libertarian historian and philosopher, Michael Oakeshott (1962), he outlined his belief in the efficacy of important and hierarchical forms of culturally rich knowledge, and that this aim was correlated with the promotion of social justice. Once in power and in a position to carry out his stated policies, Gove unquestionably took a particularly keen interest in the history curriculum, which bolstered the status of the subject; indeed, the proposed reforms to primary history generated much comment and considerable attention.

The second major change, which was also linked to knowledge, but also predominately associated with ideology, has been the introduction of a chronological (time-ordered) overview of British history in Key Stage 2, presumably based on Gove's own personal beliefs and the practices of the private school sector. In the 2008 Conservative Party conference, Gove criticised state schools for not teaching children 'our Island story' (Edgar, 2013); and it became increasingly clear that his aim was that publicly funded schools should teach a broadly factual overview of British (principally English) history in chronological order and with few elements of

European or World history. Although predominately ideological in origin, the debate around the efficacy of covering history in a chronologically coherent way generated support from several eminent historians, such as Niall Ferguson and David Starkey in an open letter to *The Times* (Sellgren, 2013), yet also admiration from liberal journalists such as Kettle (2012) and Jenkins (2011).

The background to this debate can be found in the deliberations of the History Working Group, which was formed to determine the nature of history within the first iteration of the National Curriculum. The History Working Group (DES, 1990, pp. 9–10) discussed many possible approaches regarding the teaching of chronology. They considered several alternative ideas, including teaching chronology in reverse order so contemporary history would be taught to the youngest pupils, and they also considered the main objections to starting with ancient history, not least the assumption that the younger children would find the content of earlier periods more accessible, a point reinforced by Chris Husbands (Sellgren, 2013) in his critique of chronological approaches. Nevertheless, until the final draft of the National Curriculum was approved and published in 1991, the History Working Group was still recommending that the history units with the National Curriculum would be taught in a broadly chronologically way. For mostly practical and organisational reasons this did not happen, and from that point onwards there were several critical voices, mostly from senior politicians. To be scrupulously fair to the critics, the fact that children might be learning about the 'Ancient Greeks' unit in Year 3 followed by 'Britain since 1930' in Year 4 before hopping backwards to the 'Egyptians' in Year 5, the so-called 'Dr Who' approach to the past (Burns, 2012), with the classroom presumably acting as a metaphorical Tardis, prevented many children from gaining a coherent overview of historical time and change. Ofsted reports (2007, 2011), which had largely been complimentary about history in primary schools, noted that chronology was often inconsistently covered and one of the weakest aspects of primary practice.

Once in power, during the coalition government of 2010, Gove acted quickly to drive through his educational reforms. He consulted several eminent historians, notably Simon Schama and Niall Ferguson, even if he did largely ignore wider consultation from the world of education. It would be an understatement to suggest that the early proposals were controversial, but rather than getting diverted into the detail and heat of the debate, which featured strong criticism from equally eminent historians, such as David Cannadine (2013) and Richard Evans (2013), over its narrow and selective content, it is simply necessary to state that the counter-arguments had some success because the final version of Gove's curriculum overview was considerably revised. The detail, of course, will be explained in Chapters 2 and 8–10, but in summary, primary-aged children in Key Stage 2 are now required to learn a chronological overview of British history from the Stone Age to 1066. The introduction of ancient British history was a new element, and the decision to end at 1066 received widespread criticism due to the fact it removed some of the most popular Key Stage 2 history units, such as the Tudor and Victorian periods. Almost certainly as a form of compensation, schools are able to select a theme in British history 'Beyond 1066'. However, the reason for this seemingly puzzling and arbitrary decision to end at 1066 and the death of Edward the Confessor is because secondary schools are required to continue to teach 'this Island story' from 1066 to the end of the twentieth century. The strongest analogue can be found in National Curriculum geography where three continent studies in Key Stage 2, Europe and North and South America, are completed by the remaining four continents in Key Stage 3.

Nevertheless, there are several key questions that have not been systematically researched or answered:

- Since state-funded academies and free schools are not required to follow the National Curriculum, to what extent is adherence to the National Curriculum being followed?
- Are secondary history departments following on from the work of primary schools? If not, why should primary schools keep to their side of the bargain?
- The new elements, such as ancient British history, have not been funded or resourced, nor have schools received resources for training (for example, compared with the extensive levels of support for the literacy and numeracy strategies of the late 1990s).
- The revised National Curriculum is meant to be trimmed down to allow schools to develop their own detailed curriculum, but there is no convincing evidence to suggest that primary schools have the subject expertise or resources to develop the non-core subjects to the extent that they must cover literacy and mathematics.
- Has history received enough development time and funding to teach the subject thoroughly and consistently?

Quite apart from these important organisational elements, the decision to begin Key Stage 2 with ancient British history can be questioned on sound pedagogical and educational grounds. The practical considerations that initially thwarted the introduction of a chronological approach in primary classrooms remain. The principal barrier is that in smaller primary schools, or in larger schools that may choose to combine year groups in one class, often termed 'vertical grouping', it is not always possible to cover the content chronologically due to the necessity of a two- or three-year rolling programme. For example, if a child beginning Year 3 were introduced to the earliest period, and subsequently followed this chronologically into Year 4, the newly joining Year 3 children would necessarily start at the later time. To go back would result in repetition for the Year 4 children. In medium-sized schools and above, with clearly delineated year groups, the History Working Group was concerned that all children studying the same unit at the same time would place a strain on resources. This is arguably less of a consideration now due to virtual resources.

The chronological overview of British history is important, but arguably it ought to have been introduced in Key Stage 3, thus allowing primary schools to concentrate on the things they have done very well, which are essentially working with children's natural curiosity and enthusiasm about the past and challenging them with creative and conceptual approaches to each historical unit of study. However, this did not happen, and so primary schools will have to make necessary adjustments to make the content accessible for younger children.

THE CASE FOR HISTORY

History is an important subject, not least because of the significance of historical knowledge in terms of the cultural literacy argument outlined above. The brief introduction to the background to the National Curriculum, and the importance afforded to history, involving scrutiny from the senior politicians, rather reinforces Robert Phillips' (2000, pp. 15–17) point that the extensive debate around the form and content of history reflected the 'battle for the big prize' of determining Britain's heritage and cultural legacy. This point is discussed further in Chapter 3, but it is worth considering that this discussion involves a lot more than just what children ought to know. I quoted from Gove's RSA speech in 2009; in it he also stated that he was disappointed that children were 'taught to put Britain in the dock' (Edgar, 2013) rather than celebrating British achievement. History is undoubtedly an important curriculum subject, but it can be used for narrow and questionable aims. A counter-argument for the importance of open and critical forms of history is that the training of the mind in historical forms of enquiry will act as one of the main bulwarks against the increasingly contentious use of 'spin' and propaganda. This emerging period of 'post-truth' (Coughlan, 2017) is resulting in several trends and outcomes, but the evidence is often available if one knows where to find it, and how to interpret it.

A related justification for history, linked to the idea of powerful and transformative knowledge, is that historical perspectives are an essential element in full contextual understanding of almost any aspect of human endeavour. Whatever your main hobbies are, whether ballet, a genre of music or literature, motion pictures, crochet, a sport or motorcycles, etc., it is highly likely that you will know something about the history and background of your interest. A further argument is that, whatever the efficacy of powerful knowledge, one of the strongest educational rationales for history is the level of intellectual challenge it requires of children of all ages, and the inclusion of high-level concepts which promote higher-order thinking skills and overall cognitive development. Consider these few points:

- History can be a hard subject for children, particularly if investigation and reasoning are included, principally because it is an introduction into understanding the world of adults and adult decision making.
- Given that there is no direct relationship with the past, history is an activity of the present which relies on traces from the past that have survived through the ages.
- Fragmentary and incomplete evidence requires high levels of imagination and reasoning to fill the gaps and to interpret the evidence.
- The lack of direct relationship requires children to develop high levels of abstract and imaginative thinking to be able to place themselves into the past. This was one of the arguments Copeland (1998, p. 21) employed when he described history as the 'most overtly constructivist subject in the primary curriculum, and the reason for this lies in the subject's relationship with "the past"'.

The final justification is that most children appear to enjoy the subject. There is convincing recent evidence that history is now a popular subject with primary-aged children. Ofsted (2011, p. 9) reported that pupils' attitudes to history were generally high in the schools they surveyed, and the independent Cambridge review of the Primary Curriculum (Alexander et al., 2010, p. 213) similarly claimed that history was often singled out by pupils as a subject they enjoyed partly because of its enquiry-based approach. This should not be assumed; however, drawing from extensive years of university-based training, there are many young teachers who cannot recall studying the subject very much or were put off by secondary school approaches. Equally, it can also be the case that teachers can reawaken a love of the subject through planning and teaching history. The Historical Association's (HA) survey of teachers (Historical Association, 2011) provided convincing evidence that history is a popular subject among primary teachers.

THE LEARNING OUTCOMES FROM HISTORY

In terms of the high-level concepts, linked to generic reasoning skills, that rival any other subject in the National Curriculum in terms of challenge and differentiation, the importance of chronology has already been outlined in the account of recent reforms. Additionally, there is the place of enquiry, which aligns with constructivist accounts of learning, including the use and interpretation of a range of historical evidence. Interpretation itself, the way in which the past can be understood and represented in different ways, remains both controversial and under-researched, but it is certainly one of the most important historical concepts. Significance, or understanding that some events and periods are more important or influential than others, is also under-researched but equally important. Then there are a range of other concepts linked with historical explanation, such as understanding 'change and continuity', the troubling inclusion of 'cause and consequence', and the much more accessible idea of 'similarities and differences'. All of these will be discussed in detail in subsequent chapters.

There are also other concepts linked to the elements of chronology and historical imagination. Academic historians often seem uneasy about the links between history and narrative, principally because they understandably wish to distinguish their work from historical fiction, but many published accounts are undoubtedly narrative in form, particularly overviews of historical epochs. A distinction can be made between the academic forms of history, which may not share many elements with popular forms of the subject, and narrative accounts of children's learning from psychology, principally those of Bruner (1996) and Egan (1997), which are concerned with pedagogy and practice rather than disciplinary questions. Thus, for the primary teacher, models of learning may be much more important than the nature of the subject. Narrative approaches can legitimately include stories set in the past and thought experiments such as the 'what ifs' of history: the use of historical counterfactuals. This concept introduces the idea of alternative outcomes which offer tests of plausibility and causality in history. Counterfactualism remains a controversial form of academic history, but arguably its usefulness for teaching and learning has been underestimated.

A key claim in this book will be that true forms of historical reasoning involve immersion into history topics far beyond the acquisition of knowledge. With contributions from idealist forms of history, and constructivist models of teaching and learning, the role of imagination, insight and 'insider' perspectives – including a developing children's theory of mind – will be considered. Of course, realistic expectations must be considered in the primary school, and are conditional on the age, maturity and experience of individual children, not to mention the constraints of curriculum time; but it can be argued that it is better to be ambitious than to place low expectations of children's attainment, not least reductionist approaches which relegate history to trivial, quiz-level facts, which are not always based on sound research.

It has also been claimed, for example in the Her Majesty's Inspectorate (HMI) guidance booklet *Curriculum Matters* (DES, 1988a, p. 25), that history is 'well placed to enrich the school curriculum' in terms of broader civic and citizenship aims and contains natural links with many other subject domains. Indeed, Cooper (2012, p. 72) described history as an 'umbrella' subject because of this attribute. Of course, this claim should also not be accepted uncritically, but one of the aims of this text is to examine the research into the efficacy of history at the centre of cross-curricular planning and teaching.

WHAT IS HISTORY?

When this subject is introduced to non-specialist primary trainees there is generally surprise that history is a relatively new academic subject, established in university departments only towards the end of the nineteenth century. The surprise is understandable: the subject is centrally concerned with the past; therefore, it must have long and deep roots. Naturally, there were some early historians. Thucydides (460–395 BC/BCE and Herodotus (484–c.425 BC/BCE) are generally agreed to be the first historians, although they generally drew from oral traditions rather than written sources. As the early civilisations crumbled, much of their knowledge was lost for several centuries until the Renaissance and the rebirth of classical knowledge. During the so-called Dark Ages there were some accounts of the past, for example from the English perspective, the Anglo-Saxon Chronicles, and key religious writers such as the Venerable Bede, but these naturally tended to focus on ecclesiastical and political aspects and are far from complete or unbiased. Later, there were many printed chronicles and almanacs which attempted to list key historical events and dates. However, the key event that resulted in the modern form of history was the revolutionary Enlightenment period at the end of the eighteenth century, which heralded the beginning of the modern approach to knowledge and understanding. In European universities several burgeoning social sciences emerged, for example sociology and political science, which attempted to match the advances made in the natural sciences. Thus, in many respects the growth of academic history began as a reaction to the emergence of the social sciences.

For those primary trainees, possibly history graduates, who are interested in the early development of history, there are two highly recommend key texts: Marwick's *The Nature of History*, especially the more detailed second edition (1981), and Tosh and Lang's *The Pursuit of History* (2006). Both texts outline how the early academic development of the subject was divided between the science-orientated positivists – such as Comte and Lord Acton, who were concerned with generating historical knowledge and theory through empirical means utilising the raw materials of history, namely archival, written documents, and the idealists – such as Von Ranke and Collingwood, who emphasised history from the inside, through thought rather than action and events. Collingwood will appear in detail later in this book because his ideas influenced a generation of academics and teachers, but both sides of the debate accepted the scientific aspects of enquiry and the central importance of questions (and hypotheses) tested against the available evidence. The early pioneers were also concerned with the elements of history so far introduced, such as the role of creativity and imagination and the importance of adopting a critical attitude when reconstructing the past.

However, this still does not define history. The key element is that history is not everything that has existed in the past; essentially, it is concerned with human civilisation, and especially the raw materials of written documents – historical archives. This also means that the work of historians only goes back to the cradle of civilisation and the birth of writing. While a precise definition is not possible, 33,000 years is an extreme figure for the earliest development of symbols; more conservative estimates would be around 6,000–8,000 years before the present time (6000–4000 BC/BCE). But these are still extreme figures in the sense that they refer to the first literate societies: in the case of the British Isles, there were no written records until the Roman conquest; therefore, British history, in this narrow and strict sense, begins with the Roman occupation in the first century (Smith, 2016).

Thus, when primary teachers have occasionally stated that they enjoy covering history, and that they recently studied a topic on the dinosaurs, this cannot count as history. Palaeontology, although a fascinating and important academic discipline, is a different form of enquiry into the past, and one with much closer links to the natural sciences. That stated, there have been school projects on dinosaurs which have included the history of palaeontology, which is a branch of history, and in certain counties, such as Oxfordshire and Dorset, it would also act as an example of local history.

The nature of the raw materials of study can be further employed to distinguish between history and archaeology. For the archaeologists, the approach and questions may be very similar, but here the evidence is based on human artefacts and bones, and thus the timescales are considerably longer. It might be asked whether this distinction matters. Given that the primary curriculum now covers several ancient history units, it probably does matter. Even if the distinction between archaeology and history is not made to children, and it can be questioned why these definitions could not be discussed with upper juniors, teachers ought to know this debate to support their own understanding. It is also the case that archaeology is increasingly drawing from pioneering research from the natural sciences, for example DNA (deoxyribonucleic acid) analysis from bone fragments. Thus, while historians can expect to add very little to the sum of knowledge about ancient British history, due to the limits of Roman written archives, archaeologists allied to palaeontology are making many new breakthroughs which are receiving high levels of general interest, and Chapter 9 draws on some of these recent publications.

There is another reason for providing this brief overview. It is principally because professional history is a relatively new academic discipline, and also because historians have not always been very analytical or reflective about their methods (Jenkins, 1991, pp. xv–xx; Evans, 1997, pp. 10–12; Marwick, 2001, pp. x–xvi), with Hobsbawm (1997, p. 89) going so far as to describe history as an 'immature discipline', that historians can sometimes appear defensive when challenged. Several historians have been critical, even hostile, when they have considered the aims and outcomes of school history. For example, the Tudor historian Geoffrey Elton (2002) was summarily dismissive of the ability of any pupils, even sixth-formers whom he had taught as an unqualified teacher, to engage in genuine forms of historical reasoning; Hilary Cooper (1995, pp. xi–xii) wrote movingly of the way the outstanding work of primary practitioners was ridiculed by an academic colleague from a 'prestigious' university; and David Sylvester (in an interview with Sheldon; see Sheldon, 2009b) discussed the difficulties of getting academic historians involved in the School Council History Project compared with other subjects like physics and geography. History can be a hard subject for children to understand, and it certainly contains challenging elements, but are historical concepts any more challenging that the conceptual aspects of mathematics, science or English grammar? John West (1978) made a strong case that history is not a uniquely hard subject discipline and that this point, namely the difficulties and challenge of history, has been overplayed.

The final point in this section is to make a distinction between history and heritage. In Chapter 4 the foundations of history in enquiry and evidence will be addressed, reflecting the nineteenth-century developments outlined earlier. For many historians, for example Tosh (1991) and Evans (2013), the importance of history is its willingness and ability to challenge stereotypes, mythologies and the accounts representing powerful elites. Not all academic historians are radical liberals, let alone Marxists, but a characteristic they all tend to share is a willingness to ask probing questions and let their opinions be shaped by the evidence rather than shaping the evidence to fit the historian's ideology or previous beliefs. Of course, the mind of the historian, or as Hexter (1971, p. 80) termed it, the 'second record', is impossible to remove fully, but critical historians attempt to account for, and limit, the influence of their personal beliefs and biases. Indeed, bias is a term that seems to have fallen into disuse within educational debate, and arguably it had a very limited role in the primary school, but primary teachers should be aware of E.H. Carr's oft-quoted advice: 'study the historian before you begin to study the facts' (Carr, 1961/2001, p. 23).

By contrast, heritage, as Lowenthal (2007) defined it, is an aspect of the privileges of wealth and power and largely concerned with venerating and ossifying their inheritance. Although heritage was identified as one of the outcomes of history in the early HMI guidance (DES, 1988a, p. 1), the booklet also contained a strong account of the problematic nature of heritage, not least the importance of adopting a critical approach towards the idea of cultural inheritance. Essentially, heritage is the opposite of the probing and critical forms of history, and the danger is that it can distort and misrepresent how things really were, particularly for ordinary people. Naturally, there must be a place for the democratisation of nostalgia, including things like heritage railway lines, organisations such as the National Trust, and the promotion of historic centres in ancient towns and cities. A case can be made that museums at least partially reflect aspects of heritage rather than history; but equally, many museums also challenge comfortable assumptions. Perhaps the greatest danger lies with period dramas, such as *Downton Abbey*, and their frequently unrealistic presentation of the past. The point, however, is that heritage, though important for generating interest in the past, is not true history, and that good forms of primary history should begin with questions and not assumptions based on privilege.

CLARITY CONCERNING TERMINOLOGY

Every writer has the challenge of varying the vocabulary through the employment of synonyms but trying to retain clarity and consistency. In one key respect, accuracy regarding the descriptions to describe the occupants of the British Isles requires historical as well as geographical accuracy. This has added relevance now that the relationship between the four countries of the United Kingdom (UK) are part of the geography curriculum (DfE, 2013, pp. 184–7). From a purely geological point of view, the islands that comprise the politically neutral concept of the 'British Isles' number about 4,400, of which 210 are inhabited, and several of these are not part of the UK. It is difficult to be precise about the number of islands due to natural changes in sea levels as a result of tidal forces, and longer-term changes in sea levels. One of the main concepts for children to understand in the ancient history element is that a land bridge between Europe and the east coast of present-day England existed until approximately 8,000 years ago – hence the importance of understanding the origins of our 'island story'. Historically, the political term 'Britain' emerged from Roman times long before any concept of England. Celtic tribes such as the Scots (who lived in Ireland) and the Hibernians account for some of the more ancient names that are associated with these islands. Following Roman times, the various Anglo-Saxon settlements and kingdoms led to the concept of England, land of the Angles, by the ninth and tenth centuries. The kingdoms of England and Wales were formally united during Tudor times, thus despite the clear cultural and linguistic differences, the unification of England and Wales has long (but possibly shallow) roots. The kingdoms of England and Scotland were united under the Stuarts: James VI of Scotland became James I of England, but the two countries were not politically united until the Act of Union in 1707 to create Great Britain. The Act of Union in 1801 formally united Great Britain with Ireland to create the United Kingdom of Great Britain and Ireland, and from 1922, Northern Ireland. Thus, the text will endeavour to use the historically accurate term for the period of history under review. If nothing else, this brief overview, and the elements that are now under question, such as the possibility that Ulster and Scotland will cede from the UK, is a powerful reminder of the importance of historically informed knowledge.

STRUCTURE OF THE BOOK

Several aspects of this book have already been introduced. Chapter 2 covers the background to the National Curriculum for history and some of the earlier disciplinary debates; in short, the contextual information of a history of primary school history. Chapters 3 to 7 outline the concepts that define historical understanding, including chronology, interpretation, enquiry and evidence. Chapter 8 covers the curriculum for Key Stage 1, while Chapters 9 and 10 outline the statutory and optional requirements for Key Stage 2. Chapter 11 discusses the research into creative and cross-curricular approaches to subject management and implementation. The final chapter, Chapter 12, covers the research into assessing children's historical understanding. To help readers prioritise the most useful and beneficial chapters for study, especially given the fact that all teachers are time poor, a self-audit has been created below.

SELF-AUDIT

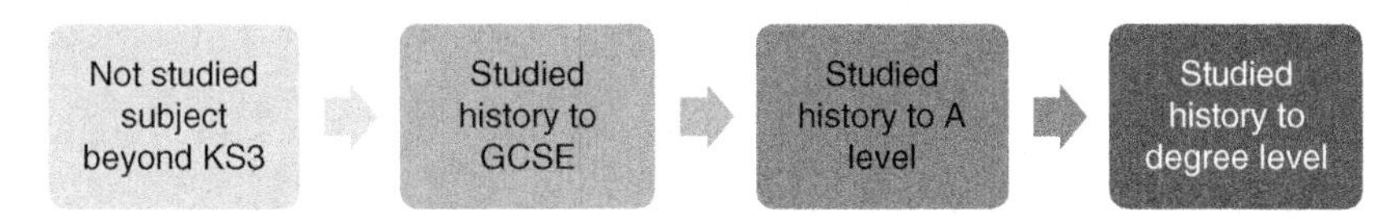

Figure 1.1 Have you studied history since the end of Key Stage 3?

For those trainees or early career professionals without recent experience of studying history, and possibly the retention of bad memories of having studied it at secondary school, then the most useful sections will be Chapters 8, 9 and 10, which outline the history that you need to know in sufficient detail in order to teach well. That stated, Chapter 12 on assessment is also recommended as it attempts to summarise the key concepts and evidence for learning, and therefore will help to evaluate the effectiveness of teaching approaches. Beyond these chapters, a study of the nature of history in Chapters 3, 4, 5, 6 and 7 should also repay careful study.

Trainees who have some experience of taking examinations in history ought to feel more confident and enthusiastic to teach primary history. It is unlikely that exam syllabuses will act as a full preparation for teaching all the primary units, but greater confidence when approaching planning and preparation could be anticipated.

For graduates, and even post-graduates, the early chapters outlining the history of the National Curriculum and the underlying concepts will be most interesting and informative. It would be rare for a history graduate not to have been introduced to the key approaches and the use of archives, so these formative debates should prove interesting.

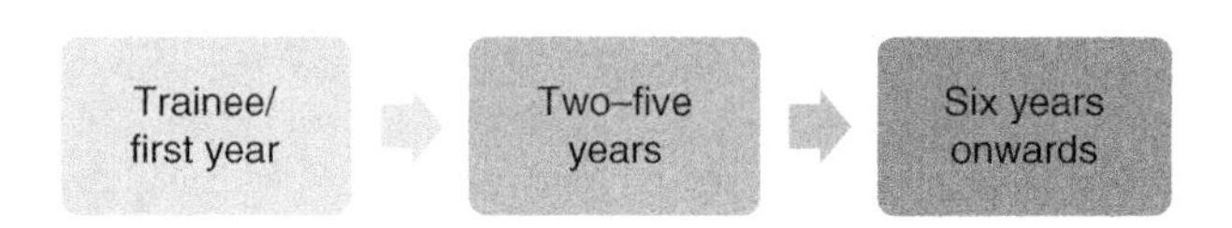

Figure 1.2 How long have you been teaching in primary schools?

As stated, the text is designed principally for trainees, who will probably learn something from all the chapters. Similarly, for teachers who have not studied the subject at a high level, the most immediately useful chapters will be those outlining the requirements of the National Curriculum, followed by assessment and the key concepts. For more experienced teachers, especially those who have already taught several history units and therefore have spent time planning and preparing them, the most useful chapters will be those concerned with curriculum management and assessment (Chapters 11 and 12). More experienced teachers ought to focus on Chapters 3, 4, 5, 6 and 7, which discuss the underpinning concepts, thus providing an opportunity to reflect on how far these are embedded in current practice, and how they might be used to engage children in higher-order thinking skills.

DO YOU HAVE A SUBJECT COORDINATOR ROLE FOR HISTORY OR THE HUMANITIES?

In the very early days of the National Curriculum all subjects had coordinators, even in the smallest schools, often resulting in early career teachers taking on multiple roles. The long-term trend towards the domination of literacy and mathematics changed schools at a fundamental level and therefore the leadership of non-core subjects is now something of an afterthought. However, the rise in multi-academy chains, and the revised Ofsted Inspection Framework (Ofsted, 2019), may provide opportunities for talented individuals to make important decisions. This book can aid history (or humanity) coordinators in three ways. Chapters 3, 4, 5, 6 and 7 can challenge subject coordinators to think more seriously about coverage of historical concepts and skills and thus act to promote higher-order thinking skills – which should benefit all forms of learning. Chapter 12 can then offer advice about assessment to chart children's progress. Chapter 11's discussion of cross-curricularity, and the content covered in Chapters 9 and 10, could theoretically help coordinators to design a curriculum map for history in Key Stage 2, and offer guidance towards more creative and embedded forms of history throughout the school.

FURTHER READING

Bruner, J.S. (1960) *The Process of Education*. Cambridge, MA: Harvard University Press.

One of the most influential texts from educational psychology, outlining Bruner's constructivist model of learning. It also contains relatively extensive discussions about the importance of history and the nature of historical reasoning.

Carr, E.H. and Evans, R.J. (2001) *What is History?* Basingstoke: Palgrave Macmillan.

The classic and controversial text on the nature of history read by many history undergraduates in their first year of study. It has a very readable style but asks probing and challenging questions about the nature of history and the indirect study of the past. This version contains an introduction from Richard Evans.

Lowenthal, D. (1985) *The Past is a Foreign Country*. Cambridge: Cambridge University Press.

One of the most thought-provoking and accessible general texts on the nature of history and historical reasoning.

Marwick, A. (1981) *The Nature of History* (2nd edn). Basingstoke: Macmillan.

Marwick's text went through several iterations, and arguably the most balanced and thorough was the second edition. This is one of the most comprehensive texts for those teachers who would like to know more about the development of academic history and the key debates and schools of thought.

Ofsted (2019) *Education Inspection Framework 2019: Inspecting the Substance of Education*, 14 May. London: Her Majesty's Inspectorate. Available at: www.gov.uk/government/publications/education-inspection-framework

The consultation document can be found at:

www.gov.uk/government/consultations/education-inspection-framework-2019-inspecting-the-substance-of-education/education-inspection-framework-2019-inspecting-the-substance-of-education

CHAPTER 2

HISTORY IN THE NATIONAL CURRICULUM

What this chapter will cover

This chapter demonstrates the ability of history to provide a contextual understanding of key events. In this example, the subject under review is the place of history in the primary National Curriculum. It will account for early research and thinking into the pedagogy of school history, including the identification of key concepts essential for developing historical forms of reasoning. The debate between progressives and traditionalists, frequently termed the 'new' versus 'old' approaches to the subject, is discussed, and how this debate led to a middle way which synthesised the best elements of both approaches, specifically a combination of essential knowledge with vital skills and concepts linked to understanding. This debate was influential not only on the professionalisation of the subject discipline; it also unquestionably influenced the first version of history in the National Curriculum. The final consideration is to explain the extent of political interference surrounding the teaching and learning of history, and how this should encourage professional vigilance and awareness from all teaching professionals. By the conclusion of the chapter you should have a good understanding of the key debates within history pedagogy, and a sense of its overall continuity.

INTRODUCTION

When I begin my university seminars with primary trainees, I invariably ask the students to hold small group discussions and to come up with a list of the history 'topics' they can remember studying while at primary school. Despite the vagaries of memory – although often mitigated by recent experiences in schools and the inclusion of several privately educated students who often provide an interesting point of departure – most groups can manage to come up with a reasonably complete list. By contrast, shared memories of historical concepts, including students who went on to study history at A-level or university, are much less successful. I use these collective memories to provoke discussion about what ought to be included in primary history, essentially the case for powerful, transformative forms of historical knowledge, before introducing the revised content of the 2014 curriculum. If you went to a state primary school after 1991, and if you attempt this activity before reading on, you might recall studying most of the following topics:

- World War II and the Home Front (British history since 1930);
- The Victorians;
- The Tudors (especially Henry VIII);
- The Egyptians (or Aztecs);
- The Ancient Greeks;
- The Invaders (and probably the Romans and Vikings above the Anglo-Saxons);
- Local history study (possibly in conjunction with geography).

These have been ranked in terms of frequency of recall based on many years of informally surveying students in the form outlined above. If you have a good memory and had dedicated primary history teachers, you may also recall carrying out timeline activities, and using some forms of historical evidence such as artefacts and pictures; but I would make the bold claim that you cannot recall too much coverage on forms of historical explanation, comparing different accounts of the past, or trying to explain the causes of historical events. After all, this is probably why you are reading this book.

This chapter starts with the important statement that, despite all the fear and trepidation outlined in the introduction, a systematic overview of the history of primary history in the National Curriculum demonstrates much higher levels of continuity than change. There are several elements that are recognisably the same over the last quarter-century. The principal purpose of this chapter, therefore, is to provide the historical and contextual background, a key justification for the importance of history, of how and why the National Curriculum was introduced, and just how difficult it was to achieve agreement on the nature and purpose of primary history. The second aim, as indicated above, is to provide contextual information to understand both the continuities and changes found in the 2014 National Curriculum in England (DfE, 2013). The third purpose for this chapter is to provide a reasonably brief overview and summary of the confusing origins of the concepts that underpin children's historical understanding, not least because these will be used as a framework for the early chapters of this book.

It might be questioned how important these considerations are, particularly the foundations of the National Curriculum for history, but as Cannadine, Keating and Sheldon (2011) and Phillips (1998) argued, only the content and form of English, particularly the teaching of reading, created as much controversy and debate as history; and certainly, the subject has resulted in more direct political interventions than almost any other curriculum subject. In short, it is important that primary practitioners consider the potential dangers of political and ideological influences on the National Curriculum for history, forces which unquestionably shaped the current history curriculum, and understand the importance of democratic and professional forms of curriculum design. More on this point at the end of the chapter.

THE ELEMENTS AND CONCEPTS OF HISTORY: THE BACKGROUND DEBATE

It would be an egregious mistake to think that early forms of primary or elementary history were just uncritical facts and stories about Britain's illustrious past, and indeed, as Cannadine et al. (2011) outlined in their important overview of history pedagogy as part of the 'History in Education' project, there is evidence from a raft of official reports and documents to suggest that there were thoughtful and creative approaches from the beginning of the state system. Nevertheless, perhaps reflecting the comparative newness of history as an academic subject, the identification of the key historical concepts related to teaching and learning has a relatively recent history, and one that predated the National Curriculum by approximately two decades.

One of the earliest and arguably most influential attempts was Coltham and Fines' Historical Association publication (1971), which challenged teachers in both primary and secondary sectors to think more analytically about their practice and included an embryonic list of suggested elements. An important delineation that emerged from this period of exploration and experimentation in the 1970s was the distinction between the *substantive*, or *first-order*, concepts of history, linked to knowledge, such as 'parliament', 'democracy' or 'reform', and *organising* (also described as *second-order* or *procedural*) concepts, such as 'causality', 'interpretation' or 'change'. Historical concepts were further developed and refined by the Schools Council History Project (SCHP) (Shemilt, 1980), and they have been discussed in detail by Guyver (1997) and Lee and Shemilt (2004, p. 14).

In many ways the SCHP became the centre of the discussion that raged between the educational traditionalists, who defended the '*old* history' and who favoured historical knowledge and synthesis of key information, and the progressives, who promoted the 'new history' (Cannadine et al.,

2011, pp. 165–6), which emphasised historical skills and understanding incorporated into teaching approaches based on enquiry, investigation, and an extreme form of interpretation – empathy. For the *new* historians, it was the '*old*' or traditional history's concentration on information and memorisation that was the problem. According to Sheldon (2011, pp. 12–13), for the traditionalists, it was the emphasis on understanding at the expense of breadth and knowledge that was the critical weakness, and by the late 1980s, some prominent historians, notably Robert Skidelsky, had started to campaign against the '*new*' history, notably the over-emphasis on students' responses.

Table 2.1 Comparison between two schools of history pedagogy

'*New*' History	'*Old*' History
• Understanding as the main learning outcome • Conceptual approach linked to active forms of learning (e.g., investigations and enquiry) • Teachers as facilitators working alongside and guiding children • Questioning and interpretive approach to the past	• Knowledge as the main product of history • Passive forms of learning linked to discussion and written outcomes • Teachers in position of authority and broadcasters of knowledge • Synthesis of ideas and explanatory accounts, based on a predominately fixed sense of the past

In some respects, this educational conflict reflected the long-standing debate in the philosophy of education surrounding the balance between content and skills, often reflecting the distinction that theorists such as Ryle (1949) have made between procedural (knowing how) and propositional (knowing what) knowledge, or Schwab's (1964) categorisation of substantive and syntactic understanding. However, from the vantage point of several decades of reflection and experience, it is arguable that neither position was truly reflective of what eventually emerged in schools, particularly in secondary schools, where history tended to be viewed as more of a synthesis between understanding and knowledge. Indeed, few theorists accepted the extreme version of the skills approach to pedagogy over the transmission of knowledge, and there were many powerful critiques of a predominately skills-based approach. Rogers (1987) and Lee (1994) argued for the importance of historical information, essentially as a form of reference to help children scaffold their understanding, and the desirability of synthesising skills with knowledge. Lee (1991, pp. 43–8) was particularly vocal against the 'vicious relativism' that sometimes emerged from predominately skills-based approaches.

Counsell (2000, p. 65), too, has been a vocal and powerful advocate for the re-establishment of 'substantive knowledge' as an 'organising device' in children's engagement and understanding of history. She further advocated a 'fingertips' approach where patches of detailed knowledge are taught to help children with specific historical questions or problems. Similarly, Husbands (1996) and Turner-Bisset (2005) independently argued that the processes and products of history should always be planned and taught together, while Fines (1987) described this synthesis as the essential 'craft' of teaching primary history.

Another important point when considering the conflict between the two historical positions is that this was essentially a secondary stage issue; for primary schools, the main point of contention for educational traditionalists was the move towards integrated, or cross-curricular, approaches to teaching and learning where history might be one of several subjects combined within an overarching theme or class topic. This point will be discussed more thoroughly in Chapter 11, but it was indicative of the move towards child-centred learning that followed the landmark Plowden Report (CACE, 1967).

GOVERNMENTAL INTERVENTIONS

Her Majesty's Inspectorate's (HMI) muted support for integrated approaches was noticeable in the slew of official reports that emerged from the late 1970s onwards. The influential survey of primary schools (HM Inspector of Schools, 1978), apart from including powerful criticisms of integrated approaches, identified the need for improved planning at the whole-school level, and specialist subject leadership. It also argued that a 'framework is required to provide some ordering of the content being taught' (HM Inspector of Schools, 1978, p. 73) to provide greater coherence and consistency throughout the primary sector. The HMI report on first schools (DES, 1982, pp. 30–2) highlighted the strengths and 'immediacy' of early years' history that included educational visits, access to artefacts and an active learning approach. According to some writers, for example Phillips (2000, p. 13) and Sheldon (2011, pp. 4–5), HMI's official position had been influenced by elements of the 'new' history. The report *History in the Primary and Secondary Years* (HMI, 1985), under the direction of John Slater, contained a lot of advice for good practice that including conceptual approaches such as enquiry, empathy and interpretation. Nevertheless, there was still official and growing dissatisfaction about the inconsistencies of coverage, lack of subject leadership, clear planning and assessment practices in primary history (HMI, 1985, 1989).

One result of this process was the HMI publication *History from 5 to 16* (DES, 1988a), one of the so-called 'raspberry ripple' books because of their binding colour, which contained a great deal of advice that eventually found its way into the National Curriculum. This was due in part to Roger Hennessey's role as senior inspector for history, and his advisory position in the History Working Group (Sheldon, 2011, pp. 5–8).

The booklet essentially contained a synthesis of the new history, which Hennessey was sympathetic to, with traditionalist views about the importance of historical knowledge, which he also held. Thus, alongside advice over suitable topics designed to develop a sense of national heritage (Sylvester, 1994, pp. 20–22), there was a long concatenation of historical attributes that provided a rationale for history, including criticality towards historical interpretations, and the identification of concepts such as cause and consequence, and the skills of enquiry and the testing of hypotheses (DES, 1988a, pp. 1–2).

The introduction of the National Curriculum was unquestionably a response to the inconsistencies and weaknesses in teaching and learning for all subjects, found in most state schools, specifically curriculum coverage, subject leadership, planning and assessment practices which resulted in growing governmental dissatisfaction. By the early 1980s the then Secretary of State for Education, Keith Joseph, announced his intention to create a National Curriculum, but it was his successor, Kenneth Baker, who finally began its implementation, beginning with the landmark 1988 Education Act (DES, 1988b). The history curriculum, alongside all the other National Curriculum subjects, was ultimately to be determined by a working group. As with other subjects, the History Working Group was composed of a mixture of teachers, educationalists, academics and other professionals, and was advised by HMI inspectors and civil servants (Slater, 1991, p. 12).

Their remit was to come up with a broadly British-based history curriculum, and to identify progression in understanding and knowledge that could fit into the 10-point assessment scale devised by Paul Black (Sheldon, 2011, p. 6), which was to be used for all subjects. From the outset, the group demonstrated a broader frame of reference, and decided that since historical knowledge is not cumulative – for example compared to science or mathematics where prior knowledge is often essential – and therefore unlike other disciplines, assessment would be based on skills and understanding rather than knowledge. The History Working Group's interim report (DES, 1989) included an outline of the suggested content, which included European and world topics alongside British history, and addressed citizenship issues that had not always been consistently taught by schools (Sheldon, 2011, pp. 8–9). Other themes that emerged included recognition of the intellectual challenge of history, its unique methodology, and its importance in preparing children for adult life (DES, 1989, pp. 5–6).

The political reaction to the interim report was considerable; and although it is unnecessary to recount the details, the controversy surrounding the proposed history curriculum and direct political interference, approached, as indicated above, only by those for English, was proof of the importance of history. The result was that the History Working Group was asked to reconsider. Although the final report was resubmitted with some minor amendments (Phillips, 2000, pp. 16–17), overall, they remained true to their principles, and showed a considerable degree of courage and independence (Sheldon, 2011, p. 8). Phillips' (2000, pp. 15–17) view was that the History Working Group produced a very 'shrewd' and politically wise report, which met the remit yet challenged the boundaries.

The History Working Group's final report (DES, 1990) was a landmark document, and well worth seeking out for those teachers who are genuinely curious about how curricula are and were derived. It has essentially shaped state education of history for almost three decades, and therefore deserves a reasonably detailed analysis and examination. To begin with, the History Working Group defined the aims of the subject as an educational discipline: history was to 'arouse interest in the past', help children to understand the present in the 'context of the past' and allow them to develop a 'sense of identity' (DES, 1990, p. 1). The domination of British history (rather than English) was to be supplemented with 'knowledge and understanding of other countries and other cultures in the modern world', and the methodology of history was recognised as both 'distinctive' and able to 'train the mind by means of disciplined study' (DES, 1990, p. 1). Finally, a case was made for history as a framework for preparing 'pupils for adult life', including a recognition of the importance of history in understanding current affairs (DES, 1990, p. 2). Considerable space was given over to defining historical knowledge as more than just the recall of information, and progression was defined as a spiral – clearly borrowing from Bruner's concept of the spiral curriculum (1960, pp. 52–4) – with understanding and skills advancing in step with historical knowledge (DES, 1990, p. 6). Once again, the synthesis between knowledge and understanding was observable.

The principal controversy that emerged after the publication of the report concerned the place of chronology, with ministers wanting an essentially chronological framework of British history, which is what the History Working Group recommended, but without the amount of complexity contained in the final report. The addition of the Political, Economic, Social, Religious and Cultural (PESRC) formula (DES, 1990, p. 16) for the different 'dimensions' of history was a significant decision because it acknowledged that history could not simply be a parade of kings, queens and battles, but had to incorporate a broader definition of history, and more accurately represent the work of academic historians (DES, 1990, pp. 183–5).

Unquestionably, academic forms of history have broadened to include new subject areas and approaches: economic history, social and cultural histories were undoubtedly influenced by the burgeoning social sciences, such as sociology and psychology, and as Stephens (1977) described, local history became more accepted by professionals from the 1960s onwards. What was initially a lesser concern to academic historians, namely the promotion of less visible aspects of history such as the silent voices of women, children and minority groups, has certainly been reflected in the growing inclusion of citizenship themes and the active promotion of the history of minorities, including the history of women and black Britons. It seems to be generally accepted by educationalists that history in schools should reflect broader perspectives, both national and international, and this strengthens the case for the importance of history as a socially inclusive subject discipline.

The History Working Groups' final report then went off for consideration by the National Curriculum Council (NCC). At this consultative stage several important revisions were made (NCC, 1993a, 1993b). One of the most significant was the decision to allow primary schools to teach the history study units in non-chronological order. Very little explanation was given for this decision and, considering ministerial interference at the report stage in favour of a chronological approach, it appears puzzling and inconsistent, but was probably due to anticipated difficulties with school-based resources.

PROGRAMMES OF STUDY FOR KEY STAGE 1 AND KEY STAGE 2

Perhaps reflecting the two cultures debate outlined above, the first iteration of the National Curriculum contained two overlapping elements: Programmes of Study that outlined the content to be studied, and Attainment Targets (AT) that identified opportunities for assessment and understanding, and therefore contained more historical skills and concepts. Incidentally, this was true for all subjects and not restricted to history. This first version of the National Curriculum deserves a reasonably detailed introduction, partly because it was the most thoroughly debated and planned, and second, because it has understandably remained the benchmark by which later versions have been compared.

The single Programme of Study for Key Stage 1 was predominately topic based, including narrative accounts, myths and stories set in the past, the use of historical sources such as artefacts, pictures and photographs, and more detailed studies on famous people and events. In Key Stage 2, the only changes to the History Working Group's final report were the previously mentioned removal of the chronological order of topics and the removal of Egypt from the Ancient Civilisations unit. The Programme of Study for Key Stage 2 included the core units of Invaders and Settlers, Life in Tudor and Stuart times, and either Victorian Britain or Britain since 1930. The non-British core units were the study of Ancient Greece and Exploration and Encounter 1450–1550 (including the Aztec civilisation). The optional units included broad topics such as food and farming and ships and seafarers, which were designed to be predominately British.

Additionally, schools were given the discretion to develop their own study units, which had to include local history. The 'Supplementary study units' adopted broad themes, such as transport and domestic life as category A. Category B included at least one local history study, and category C included ancient non-European societies, including Ancient Egypt or the Maya, to balance its omission from the core unit (DES, 1991a, pp. 11–32; NCC, 1993c).

The full list of category A topics was: Ships and seafarers; Food and farming; Houses and places of worship; Writing and printing; Land transport; and Domestic life, families and childhood. Category C topics included: Ancient Egypt; Mesopotamia; Assyria; The Indus Valley; The Mayan civilisation; and Benin (DES, 1990, pp. 31–2).

ATTAINMENT TARGETS FOR ALL KEY STAGES

Equal emphasis should be given to the Attainment Targets since these not only defined progress and assessment in history, but also contained the historical elements and concepts identified by the History Working Group and included in the National Curriculum. Attainment Target 1, 'Knowledge and Understanding of History', concentrated on the development of chronological awareness and understanding, particularly the ability of children to sequence events or retell events from history. As children progressed, chronology would include explanations of historical change; in other words, a link with explanation and the concept of cause and effect, and the identification of differences between past and present times. It further stated that by the end of primary school most children should be able to understand ideas such as historical causes and consequences (DES, 1991a, pp. 3–4). Attainment Target 2, 'Interpretations of History', was clearly harder to define and delineate. Essentially, children would show progress by developing their understanding that stories may be about real or fictional people (level 1) to an 'understanding that deficiencies in evidence may lead to different interpretations of the past' (level 4), which might include explaining why illustrations of Ancient Egypt vary so much (DES, 1991a, p. 7). Attainment Target 3, 'The Use of Historical Sources', clearly based on the principles of enquiry and evidence, defined progression as 'communicating information acquired from an historical source' (level 1) to putting together 'information drawn from different historical sources' (level 4), such as information from old newspapers, photographs or maps (DES, 1991a, p. 9).

Nevertheless, despite all the thought and innovation that went into constructing the National Curriculum, its implementation was far from smooth. As Sheldon noted, two issues quickly stood out: the 'overloaded content and the problem of assessment' (Sheldon, 2011, p. 18). The response was the 1995 Dearing Review, which set up a new history working party, which ultimately trimmed a little of the content, for example dropping the Stuarts from the Tudor unit, but more significantly reduced assessment to a single Attainment Target, containing very broad, and arguably largely meaningless, overall level descriptors (DfE, 1995, pp. 73–83), and abandoned any idea that history could be tested in the primary years. It additionally promoted chronology to a more prominent position, thus addressing one of the main concerns of senior politicians.

The third iteration of the National Curriculum began with the 1999 History Task Group review in preparation for the Curriculum 2000 (DfEE, 1999). It resulted in few significant changes other than the broadly welcomed addition of citizenship (Arthur, 2000, pp. 2–5), which did have some impact on the provision of history, and the aim to give schools greater autonomy over the curriculum. The Dearing Review (Dearing, 1994) had introduced key elements in lieu of the lost Attainment Targets, and these were now defined as 'Knowledge, skills and understanding' to be taught and assessed as part of the study units. In the Curriculum 2000 (DfEE, 1999, p. 104) the key elements were:

- 'Chronological understanding';
- 'Knowledge and understanding of events, people and changes in the past';
- 'Historical interpretation';
- 'Historical enquiry';
- 'Organisation and communication'.

The study units were also recognisably the same as the recommendations from the History Working Group's final report: in Key Stage 1 they included changes in their own lives and in those of their family, people in the past, including the locality, and the study of significant people and events from the past (DfEE, 1999, p. 104). For children in Key Stage 2, the key elements contained the same titles but included more detail to reflect children's progression. The study units included very similar ideas to both the History Working Group's final report and earlier versions of the National Curriculum, although with some trimming:

- 'A Local History Study';
- British History to include:
    - Romans, Anglo-Saxons and Vikings in Britain;
    - Britain in the wider world in Tudor times;
    - Victorian Britain **or** Britain since 1930;
- A 'European History Study' (Ancient Greece);
- A 'World History Study' (virtually the same list as the 1991 document with the addition of the Aztecs).

(DfEE, 1999, pp. 106–7)

The main significance of this version of the National Curriculum was that it lasted from 1999 to 2014 and therefore became far more embedded in school culture than the previous iterations, hence the success of the collective memory test outlined at the beginning of this chapter. There are a couple of points to note, however. Few practitioners seemed to be aware that schools were asked to make a choice between the 'Victorians' or 'Britain since 1930'. In practice, some schools made the decision to place the Victorian topic in Year 2, thus ensuring that famous people and events could be studied as part of the Key Stage 1 curriculum, while increasing the coverage of British history. Although the 'Britain since 1930' unit suggested studying the 'impact of the Second World War', this element tended to dominate and so the study unit was arguably narrowly interpreted by many schools. A similar concern was the introduction of exemplar plans produced by the Qualification and Curriculum Authority (QCA). These were meant to act as templates for guidance. However, a considerable number of primary practitioners viewed them as either welcome time-savers or official instructions for action, and so the Tudor topic often became solely an examination of Henry VIII's private life, while in Key Stage 1 the significant people and events was reduced to the Great Fire of London and Florence Nightingale, with many teachers seemingly unwilling to take control of planning decisions.

In conclusion, arguably the best way to account for the development of history in the National Curriculum is to see it as a tension, or alternatively a synthesis (Counsell, 2000, p. 70), between the traditionalists – defenders of the 'old' history informed by historical content and information, against the progressives – the vanguard of 'new' history, which emphasised skills and processes such as interpretation, insight and empathy. In many ways what emerged was a compromise between 'knowledge, skills and concepts' (Phillips, 2000, p. 16). Informed opinion, for example Culpin (1994), defined effective historical learning as the synthesis of historical concepts, skills and knowledge, and this was essentially what the National Curriculum eventually prescribed.

Given the paucity of history in primary schools prior to the National Curriculum, the outcome was almost certainly going to be improved teaching and learning. Ofsted's first main review (Ofsted, 1999) suggested just this. The report began by stating that prior to the National Curriculum there 'was relatively little systematic teaching of history in primary schools', just the occasional 'rubies in porridge', but 'a decade later, history is prospering in primary schools', even if many schools were failing to stretch the most able pupils, and concentrating on knowledge in lieu of skills and enquiry (Ofsted, 1999, 12.7). Research carried out for the 'History in Education' project (Cannadine et al., 2011, pp. 202–6) reported broadly similar findings, not least the greater and more consistent provision of learning time allocated to history.

THE INTRODUCTION OF THE 2014 NATIONAL CURRICULUM IN ENGLAND

Since the purpose of this book is also to provide clear and practical guidance on planning and teaching the revised National Curriculum, there is arguably little purpose in discussing it in detail here. But since a reoccurring theme has been the overall continuity, it is necessary to provide a brief comparison between the requirements for Key Stage 1 and Key Stage 2 in the Curricula 2000 and 2014. In Key Stage 1, presented in Table 2.2, the National Curriculum 2014 (DfE, 2013) has fewer obvious references to skills and concepts, but with a few minor adjustments in order, the high level of continuity can be detected. The table also demonstrates how the intention to 'return' to a knowledge-based curriculum discussed in the Introduction is something of a misrepresentation and oversimplification.

Table 2.2 Continuity in the Key Stage 1 National Curriculum for history

National Curriculum 2000	National Curriculum 2014
Knowledge, Skills and Understanding	
• Chronology (especially language of time and timelines)	• Awareness of the past • People and events placed in a chronological framework
• Historical Interpretation	• Understand how we find out about the past and the different ways it is represented
• Historical Enquiry (from a range of sources including ICT); asking questions about the past	• Ask and answer questions
Breadth of Study (Content)	
• Changes in their own lives, etc.	• Changes in living memory
• The way of life of people in the more distant past who lived in the local area or elsewhere in Britain	• Know key features of historical events • Significant events and people in their locality
• The lives of significant men, women and children drawn from the history of Britain and the wider world (e.g., Florence Nightingale)	• The lives of significant individuals in the past (nationally and internationally)
• Past events from the history of Britain or the wider world	• Events beyond living memory that are significant nationally or globally

Finally, presented below is an introduction to the revised Key Stage 2 content for primary history in the National Curriculum 2014:

- Changes in Britain from the Stone Age to the Iron Age;
- The Roman Empire and its impact on Britain;
- Britain's settlement by Anglo-Saxons and Scots;

- The Viking and Anglo-Saxon struggle for the Kingdom of England to the time of Edward the Confessor;
- A local history study;
- A study of a theme in British history the extends knowledge beyond 1066;
- The achievements of the earliest civilisations;
- Ancient Greece;
- A non-European society to provide a contrast with British history.

The first four elements unquestionably reflect Michael Gove's determination to include a chronological overview of British history. While the first section (changes from the Stone Age) was new, the following three are essentially an expansion of the former 'Invaders' unit, and arguably resulted in high levels of continuity. Equally, the retention of local, world and European units has retained the former breadth and range of coverage. As stated at the start of this chapter, fundamentally it is not so different from the versions that preceded it. However, there is more emphasis on historical knowledge rather than skills, concepts and understanding. More detailed links between the National Curriculum 2014 and earlier forms of the primary history curriculum will be explored in the relevant chapters.

HISTORICAL CONCEPTS CONTAINED WITHIN THE NATIONAL CURRICULUM

The important point is now to consider how the National Curriculum helped to shape and define the components of history beyond the subject matter of the study units. However, it is probably fair to state that in many ways the discussion surrounding historical concepts becomes overly confusing and therefore self-defeating, and thus one of the aims for this text is to simplify this debate and to produce a more understandable and workable list, specifically the most important and useful *organising* concepts of history included in all versions of the National Curriculum.

To begin with, one of the most significant aspects of the first iteration of the National Curriculum was the fact that the Attainment Targets – in other words, the historical concepts used to gauge children's understanding and therefore assessment – were the same for Key Stage 1 all the way up to Key Stage 4. This was Bruner's spiral curriculum in action, but in theory as well as practice it also implied that non-specialist primary teachers should have a working knowledge of historical forms of understanding that mirrored subject specialists working in secondary schools. While this might have some intellectual merit, and in the core subjects of English, mathematics and science, some validity, for non-core subjects taught by non-specialists, this was clearly problematic.

The most important concepts have already been identified clearly enough in the account of the history of the National Curriculum, and each demands a separate and detailed discussion, hence the focus of the following two chapters of this book: chronology and change (Chapter 3) and enquiry, interpretation and significance (Chapter 4).

At this point, however, it is worth discussing what is meant by the term '*organising* (or *procedural*) concepts', and further, what are concepts and why they are considered so important? First, the rather pretentious word 'concept' is merely a synonym for an abstract idea. It could be argued that graduate teachers should not shy away from words that partially define teaching as a profession. If the activity of being a primary teacher does not rely on specialist forms of knowledge (like the practice of law), or is not combined with highly skilled procedures (like medicine), then teachers should not reject the ideas that help to define the skilled and reflective forms of practice that underpin learning in primary classrooms. If primary history is simply the telling of stories and imparting some knowledge about the past in uncritical and unreflective ways, then what is the value of maintaining standards for qualified teachers? In the neo-liberal climate that schools are now experiencing, the 'value-added' that qualified teachers allegedly bring to the classroom is increasingly under scrutiny, particularly from financial considerations. An understanding of the concepts that underpin each curriculum subject is arguably an essential foundation for professional practice and standards.

To support the important claim above, let us examine an illustration of the importance of the concepts that support and define historical understanding. During recent consultation work with an Oxfordshire primary school, specifically a pair of upper-junior classes, there was clear evidence that the teacher and most of the children held a deep and longstanding interest in history. Upon questioning the class, it was evident that to a certain extent this had been fuelled by the 'Horrible Histories' series of books and other texts, and was reinforced by several televisions series. During the work carried out with both classes, many of the children knew a considerable amount of information about the past. However, when faced with their school homework project – World War II Theatres of War – it became evident just how fragmentary and episodic this knowledge often was. For example, a sizeable minority chose to write about the Battle of Britain, and when challenged to frame their points of reference (in terms of what preceded and followed the Battle of Britain), the children were frequently confused between events as disparate as Dunkirk and D-Day. Overall, it was concluded that many of the class had no sense of when the Battle of Britain occurred within the full context and overview of World War II, and therefore understandably did not recognise its significance. To help this group of children gain an essential chronological perspective, the class worked on a collaborative timeline from the beginning of the conflict in Western Europe in 1939, the evacuation of the British army from Dunkirk in June 1940, and the position that the UK faced in the mid-summer of 1940 with no real land army, few allies, shipping supplies under attack by German U-boats, and a confident German army ostensibly preparing for invasion across the narrow English Channel. By the end of the project there was considerable evidence that this group had a much better historical overview of this early period of the World War II. It was partially based on a sequence of key events (chronology), which helped the children to organise and connect the many bits of disembodied information they had gained up to this point. It is arguable that this example illustrates why concepts such as chronology – an understanding of time linked to sequencing and connections between key events, a process termed colligatory reasoning by some historians – rather than the reductive learning of historical dates, are important, and why the term 'organising concept' is a useful and accurate one. Two examples of timelines linked to this project are reproduced in Chapter 3.

Hidden within the layers of the early guidance documents, and the first iteration of the National Curriculum, is a further series of concepts that arguably deserve a little more exposure because they are useful in providing a more complete description of children's developing understanding of history. As outlined above, many of these concepts were identified and formerly linked to Attainment Target 1 (DES, 1991a, pp. 3–4), and then incorporated into 'Knowledge and understanding of events, people and changes in the past' (DfEE, 1999, pp. 104–5). The clearest account of these important concepts was provided by the relatively recent Programme of Study for Key Stage 3 history (QCA, 2007, pp. 112–13), and it is ironic that history specialists in secondary schools previously received clearer and more integrated guidance than their non-specialist primary colleagues. However, despite its trimmed-down, skeletal nature, the revised National Curriculum outlines a series of historical concepts linked to understanding:

> ... historical concepts such as continuity and change, cause and consequence, similarity, difference and significance, and [to] use them to make connections, draw contrasts, analyse trends, frame historically-valid questions and create their own structured accounts, including written narratives and analyses. (DfE, 2013, pp. 189–90)

This is the limit of the current guidance, merely the inclusion of a list and an indication that they support historical reasoning and work outcomes such as written accounts and (verbal) forms of reasoning. Hence the purpose of this book is to unravel all these complex elements of history. The list of concepts covered in the early chapters is the following:

- 'Change and continuity', including historical comparisons within and across periods of history (Chapter 3);

- 'Significance', which has often been partially linked to interpretation and historical judgement (Chapter 4);
- 'Cause and consequence', involving the analysis and explanation of historical accounts (Chapter 5);
- 'Similarities' and 'differences' between past and present times, formerly in the History Working Group's final report and then within Attainment Target 1 in the first version of the National Curriculum because it is arguably the first level of historical analysis for younger children (Chapter 6).

Additionally, three further key concepts are included in this book:

- A more elusive concept, linked strongly with the philosophy of history, namely the promotion of historical 'imagination' as a form of historical reasoning and engagement (Chapter 5);
- 'Narrative' as a model of historical learning and as an outcome of history, and linked to historical explanation, using 'counterfactual' reasoning. Both are controversial within the philosophy of history, but more accepted by educationalists (Chapter 6);
- Colligation as a mode of historical reasoning (Chapter 5).

THE CONTROVERSIAL NATURE OF HISTORY

Since the introduction of the Education Act 1988 and the introduction of the National Curriculum (DES, 1991a), UK governments have increasingly centralised both what is taught and how it is taught in English and Welsh state schools. The National Curriculum 2014 (DfE, 2013), although 'trimmed down' to allow more practitioner and school-level decision making, is prescriptive in terms of the curriculum knowledge or content that should be covered in state schools. Increased government control of both curriculum and pedagogy has arguably emasculated successive generations of new teachers, and resulted in a loss of professionalism, status and autonomy (themes mentioned previously), and it is therefore important that preparing teachers to cover the curriculum should not be at the cost of wider academic and professional understanding. With this point in mind, two defining aspects of professionalism – self-regulation and autonomy – can be identified. There is also the danger that uncritical teachers, particularly non-specialist primary practitioners, may unwittingly transmit government policies aimed at creating national mythologies and even social control. This was the 'battle for the big prize' of determining Britain's heritage and cultural legacy, as Phillips (2000, pp. 15–17) described it.

For example, the previous Secretary of State for Education, Michael Gove (2010–15), the chief architect of the National Curriculum 2014, indicated that he was tired of 'British history' being placed on the rack and for failing to celebrate British achievement, including the British Empire. One of Gove's first actions as Secretary of State was to invite Niall Ferguson, a noted defender of the British Empire, to help draft the new curriculum for history. This form of ideological input and control was an important concern of the History Working Group and, as reported by Boffey (2013), drew strong criticism from a range of professional historical organisations and bodies. In their final report, the History Working Group argued that there were four main reasons why history should not be controlled by politicians and should include an understanding that historical reasoning and knowledge was conditional and open to interpretation. To begin with, the History Working Group argued that the study of history *necessarily* includes interpretations, and that students should have an acquaintance with the writings of historians and knowledge of historical controversies. Their second argument was that students should understand that the past has been represented in many ways, including written forms, songs, oral traditions, art, film and drama, and not always for academic reasons. They were also concerned that students should have an understanding that some histories have a high profile and others are hardly known, and that this was a justification for promoting the history of minorities and echoed by wider and more recent initiatives such as 'black history month'. Their final reason was a warning that:

> many people have expressed deep concern that school history will be used as propaganda: that governments ... will try to subvert it for the purpose of indoctrination or social engineering. (DES, 1990, p. 11)

This extract explains not only why *interpretation* is considered such an important organising concept in history, but also that these aims seem equally relevant more than a quarter of a century since they were expressed.

If the claims of the History Working Group are thought to be hyperbolic, one must study the lengthy and bitter conflict between China and South Korea on one side and Japan on the other – the so-called 'textbook' disputes (Masalski, 2001) – to realise that the way history is selected and taught in a nation's schools has wide and important consequences. In brief, the Chinese and Korean governments resent the way that alleged war crimes committed by the Japanese during the second Sino–Japanese war (1937–1945) are ignored in officially recognised Japanese school textbooks. Arguably, all nations are guilty to some extent of transmitting simplistic and jingoistic elements in their national narratives. It is reasonable that prospective and current primary teachers realise the importance of the choices behind the content of what they teach and how they teach it.

CHAPTER SUMMARY

- There has been more consistency than change regarding the units or topics within primary history, including a concentration on popular elements of British history alongside World and European units.
- However, the revised curriculum does require a chronological overview of British history to be taught in Key Stage 2, beginning with ancient history.
- Historical concepts are arguably essential for genuine and deeper forms of historical understanding, and therefore it is important that primary practitioners have a working knowledge of how these can be included in planning, teaching and assessing children's understanding and lesson evaluations.
- The early division between knowledge, skills and understanding (notably key concepts) has not been maintained in the later iterations of the National Curriculum, but the elements still exist as part of its general aims.
- The pioneering work from the 'new', or progressive, history educators ultimately found its way into the National Curriculum, and although recent educational reforms have returned to historical knowledge as the main outcome of primary history, the concepts are now so embedded that it has resulted in a clearer union between the 'new' and 'old' approaches to teaching and learning history.

FURTHER READING

Department for Education (2013) *The National Curriculum in England Key Stages 1 and 2 Framework Document*. London: HMSO. (This can be found online as a pdf document from the following link: www.gov.uk/government/publications/national-curriculum-in-england-primary-curriculum)

Clearly, no teacher can understand the full context of this text without examining the actual document itself. It is important to note that this trimmed-down curriculum does not contain lengthy sections on each subject.

Phillips, R. (1998) *History Teaching, Nationhood and the State: A Study in Educational Politics*. London: Cassell.

This is the clearest and most complete and questioning account of the tense conflict to determine the nature of school history.

History in Education Project website: www.history.ac.uk/history-in-education

For those interested in primary data on the developments in history pedagogy, this site contains a wealth of invaluable information.

CHAPTER 3

CONCEPTS OF CHRONOLOGY AND CHANGE

What this chapter will cover

This chapter introduces the crucially important historical concept of time, which has received more emphasis in the 2014 National Curriculum in England. The chapter begins with a definition of historical timeframes and outlines many of the challenges of covering chronology with primary-aged children, principally the complexity of the language and the conventions used to describe historical periods. Chronology is further defined in terms of the concept of change, which can be developed through sequencing and ordering activities. The chapter then outlines the importance of timeline activities, including the use of computers. Several examples are included which help to illustrate the dimensions of primary history. The remainder of the chapter examines the closely related concepts of change and continuity and examples of activities that can help to develop children's 'sense of time'.

INTRODUCTION

Having stated in Chapter 1 that the 2014 National Curriculum (DfE, 2013) has resulted in the 'return' of overall chronological or narrative approaches to the past, specifically British history, it is important to explain exactly what is intended. Under the opening paragraph entitled 'The Purpose of Study', there is a sentence which outlines that history is to 'help pupils gain a coherent knowledge and understanding of Britain's past and that of the wider world' (DfE, 2013, p. 188). This is followed by a list of aims for primary history, in which the first is that children should:

> Know and understand the history of these islands as a coherent, chronological narrative, from the earliest times to the present day: how people's lives have shaped this nation and how Britain has influenced and been influenced by the wider world. (DfE, 2013, p. 188)

However, these learning outcomes should not be accepted uncritically, and therefore this chapter will introduce several important claims. To begin with, although history is fundamentally associated with an understanding of time, this challenging and elusive concept is not restricted to history. Mathematics introduces children to the concepts of recorded time and duration. Science, especially physics, is concerned with the fundamental nature and definition of time. Languages rely on a sense of time, for example verb tenses and prepositions associated with time which relate objects in terms of temporal relationships. Additionally, there is the chronological underpinning of narrative structures to which the National Curriculum statement alludes. Music is also fundamentally concerned with time as one of the parameters of musical form. In geography there is now more emphasis on the human and physical changes to landscape and settlement, now termed 'processes' in the new National Curriculum, and while the human aspect of geography mirrors historical timescales, geological timeframes (4.54 billion years in the case of the Earth) dwarf human history. Therefore, there is nothing unique or especially challenging about historical timeframes, especially since the parameters of historical time (roughly 11,000 years, as outlined in Chapter 1 of this book) are miniscule compared to geological or scientific concerns. That stated, in one sense history is different in that its parameters of study are almost entirely defined by the concept of time.

However, the second point is that historical timeframes are still extremely challenging for primary-aged children – indeed, for many adults – especially since the revised National Curriculum now places much more emphasis on chronology and requires that the oldest aspects of British history are taught first. So, what are these challenges? First, the language: Key Stage 1 colleagues should not assume that children in this key stage are confident users of the prepositions and language linked to time. Terms like 'before', 'after', 'yesterday' and 'last year', etc., must be discussed and explained. At the very least, the language associated with the past and past events needs some form of systematic coverage. Second, within Key Stage 1, any use of historical timelines should mirror work in place value. If children are not comfortable with numbers up to a thousand, they will struggle with any understanding of longer timeframes. As children move into Key Stage 2 the challenges remain. The first consideration is the complication over the language used in historical timescales. While the western calendar may predominate, it is not the only system for counting years. More recently, there has also been a tendency to use Common Era (CE) in place of Anno Domini (AD), a term that requires a translation from Latin, and Before Common Era (BCE) in place of Before Christ (BC).

A second important consideration is that historical timeframes do not fully match the integers children will use in mathematics. The western calendar does not have year zero, and the earlier sequence employs positive numbers travelling in the opposite direction rather than negative numbers. Thus, to find the age of Stonehenge since its construction (which might be covered in Year 3), one must add the BCE time (2500 BCE) to our current CE date (2000 CE) to find the total duration (4500 years). By any standards this is challenging for most primary-aged children, and certainly for Year 3s, some of whom may be acquiring an understanding of larger numbers and place value.

There is also the related difficulty in understanding the language of the centuries. Most adults, it would be fair to state, probably rarely question why a date such as 1789 is described as the eighteenth century. As a child, I found this confusing, and like most children simply accepted the practice without fully understanding why. The explanation is quite simple when one thinks about it: the first century AD/CE began with year 1 and so the century between 1 and 99 AD/CE became the first century in the western calendar.

Finally, consideration must also be given to the complexity of the concepts under review. Historical concepts are complex, and they do become proportionately less challenging the further back in time one studies through some mysterious transmogrifying process. Husbands (cited in Sellgren, 2013) was most vocal, arguing that 'if you teach chronologically you end up with a seven-year-old understanding of the Saxons, a 10-year-old understanding of the Middle Ages and a 14-year-old understanding of the industrial revolution', and that history 'is more complex than that'. Husbands also outlined some of the alternative ideas. One seriously considered alternative explored by the History Working Group (DES, 1990, pp. 9–10), and mentioned in Chapter 1, was to teach history in reverse order, thus beginning with more relatable contemporary issues and gradually working backwards towards ancient history. However, this idea was rejected.

CHRONOLOGICAL UNDERSTANDING

Having outlined some of the challenges, and having discussed in Chapter 2 how chronology can be defined as one of the core *organising* concepts underpinning historical understanding, this section requires a reasonably clear explanation of the nature of time, as defined by science, in order that its importance, and the challenges of introducing this concept, can be fully understood. What we measure when we calculate time is essentially based on the notion of change in a dynamic, not static, universe. Prior to the Renaissance, most understanding followed Aristotle's argument that all bodies would come to a rest unless moved by a force. Copernicus, and then Galileo, argued the opposite: that objects are in motion unless modified by force. This concept of inertia would later come to be refined, modified and codified by Newton as the first of his Laws of Motion (first published in 1687). Thus, without a concept of change, whatever the scale, time would not be measurable, and therefore this chapter will also consider the role of the related concepts of 'change and continuity'. The term 'chronology' is derived from the rather unpleasant Greek legend of the Titan, Kronos (and can therefore be legitimately studied in primary schools as part of an Ancient Greece unit), which acts as one of the Greek foundation myths, and so there is no extra significance in the term other than it now acts as a synonym for time and the study of time.

In terms of guidance for teachers, this began with the recommendation of Her Majesty's Inspectorate that children 'develop a knowledge of chronology within which they can organise their understanding of the past' (DES, 1988a, p. 3), and that children 'should develop a "sense of time" which enables them to put historical events in the correct order, to acquire an historical perspective and to avoid anachronism' (DES, 1988a, p. 7). Hence the final part of this chapter will consider what a 'sense of time' might mean as a learning outcome. While chronology has always featured in the National Curriculum guidance for primary history, the National Curriculum 2014 currently states very clearly that one of the main outcomes of primary history is that:

> Pupils should continue to develop a chronologically secure knowledge and understanding of British, local and world history, establishing clear narratives within and across the periods they study. They should note connections, contrasts and trends over time and develop the appropriate use of historical terms. (DfE, 2013, p. 189)

Therefore, this chapter will also act as a foundation for the discussion of narrative approaches in Chapter 6. Finally, while it is possible to sympathise with Turner-Bisset (2005) when she argued that too much emphasis has been placed on developing children's chronological understanding, this chapter follows Stow and Haydn's (2000) persuasive argument for the importance of chronology in underpinning *all* understanding of historical change and development, an argument supported by Thornton and Vukelich (1988) and their concept of 'developmental-historical' time, even if they also acknowledged that chronology was a necessary but not sufficient element for full historical understanding. For those not used to the language of formal logic, this essentially means that, although an understanding of time cannot be the whole of historical reasoning, it is an essential component and therefore cannot be ignored. And this is surely right: in what sense can genuine historical thinking occur without a concept of historical dates, sequences of historical events and the concept of duration?

RESEARCH INTO CHILDREN'S UNDERSTANDING OF TIME

Although, as argued above, the concept of chronological understanding is an important part of pedagogic approaches to history, it has largely been ignored by academic historians. Hobsbawm argued that an understanding of time is 'essential to the modern, historical sense of the past, since history is [concerned with] directional change' (Hobsbawm, 1997, p. 29), but he appears to have been a rare exception. Structuralists such as Lévi-Strauss (1963) and Braudel (1980) have tended to place more attention on it, while simultaneously adding a more critical approach, such as identifying differing rates and perceptions of time and change according to region, class or status. This may have some relevance to primary pedagogy in the sense that sometimes children (and trainee teachers) are confused about the varying rates of human civilisation – for example, when the old world (European colonisers) met the new world, still largely existing in the Stone Age in North America (but not in South America where metallurgy had started), or to begin to understand that for some people in the world their mode of living may have changed little in centuries.

It is arguable that the more important consideration for primary pedagogy relates to the research that has been conducted into children's understanding of time and chronology. Fortunately, this has been reasonably extensive, though often with a broader remit than just historical understanding. Early research often required children to answer several questions and challenges associated with a range of different timescales and involving real-world problems (such as estimating how long it would take to complete certain tasks like walking around a playground). The overall conclusion was that a full understanding of time includes several different concepts, some more historical than others, all of which were difficult to develop and not easily separated from linguistic and mathematical understanding. If nothing else, these fascinating, and still widely cited, studies rebut uncritical claims that children were more advanced in their understanding of time in the past.

Piaget's (1946) work on time has also been widely cited. He demonstrated how children's understanding of time developed in line with his ontogenetic theory of development stages, but with some interesting subtleties such as the concept of age, which he demonstrated was often confused in children's minds. Children frequently struggled to explain why a younger sibling would always be younger (due to order of birth), and children under seven often struggled to understand that their parents and grandparents were once young, because they tended to associate adults with roles disassociated from time and change. Again, the overall sense was that chronological understanding was, and remains, challenging for young children, and that we should not be surprised if they take time to develop a meaningful understanding of this complex and elusive concept.

If there is any lesson to be taken from the evidence on the nature of time and children's understanding of chronology, it is not to assume that children of any age have a satisfactory or working knowledge of any aspect of historical time; but equally, it is not to assume that this challenge is unique to history.

TEACHER INTERVENTIONS AND SEQUENCING ACTIVITIES

Although the research evidence may be daunting, this does not mean that teaching approaches cannot accelerate and guide the development of children's understanding of chronology. For example, in terms of the development of language associated with time, Hodkinson (2007) carried out extensive research that indicated that teacher intervention could accelerate children's understanding; and his research, echoing Wood's (1995) earlier studies, reinforced the importance of clear modelling and explanation of temporal terminology. Teachers can make a difference if they take the time to explain, and reinforce, key terms associated with historical time and change, and if they do not begin with assumptions about what children of any age know and understand. As indicated above, by the end of primary school children should be introduced to the language of periodisation, including decade, century and the conventions of the western (Christian) calendar through progressive, consistent and effective teaching.

Many writers cite West's (1981a) work as influential in promoting the development of chronological understanding in primary schools. West was keen to emphasise that Key Stage 1 and lower Key Stage 2 children should initially and predominately carry out sequencing activities, drawing upon their wider contextual knowledge and reasoning skills, rather than focus on complex historical dates and periods. Many other researchers have adapted West's picture sequencing work, including studies by Harnett (1993), Lynn (1993) and Stow (1999), with sequencing and chronology often underpinning wider research into children's historical understanding. All these works repay further study because they demonstrate how sequencing can also help the assessment of children's historical understanding, and the common misconceptions they display.

Comparing objects and pictures, which obviously links with the concepts of 'similarities and differences', can begin at the start of Key Stage 1, possibly including the foundation stage. A direct comparison should ideally begin with two commonplace objects, for example home appliances linked to common Early Years Foundation Stage/Key Stage 1 themes such as the 'home' or 'when granny was a girl' (refer to Chapter 8 for more details of these units). For example, compare Figures 3.1 and 3.2, two photographs of domestic irons.

Figure 3.1 Flat iron

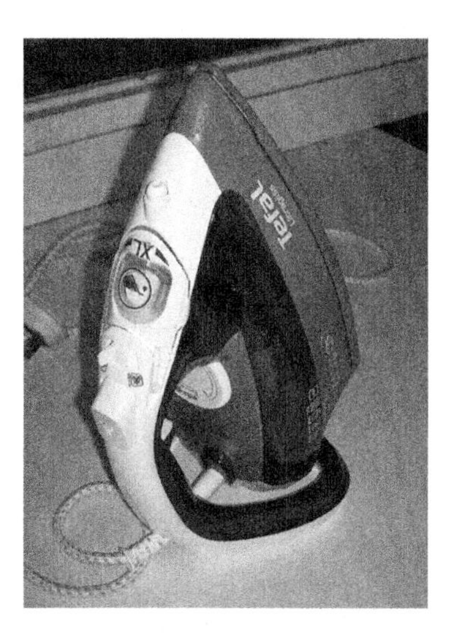

Figure 3.2 Modern electric steam iron

Both irons have an identifiable design, or basic shape in common, principally linked to the flat plate and the location and function of the handle. Beyond these important similarities (in other words, points in common), there are very profound and important differences which could result in follow-up lines of enquiry. The mode of heating the plate is very different, namely direct transference, or conduction to use its technical term from science, compared with an electrical element. The other main difference is also associated with science, namely chemistry and the study of materials, and references the replacement of largely iron (and wood) components with aluminium (and its alloys) and plastics. Any teacher who has carried out comparisons of this sort will quickly realise that similarities and differences can often be reduced to design, materials and, less commonly, a slightly different function. Of course, for younger children some of the complexities of technological change may be beyond their understanding. For example, consider early dial phones compared with modern mobile cellular technology. But here the differentiation, or outcomes, should be limited by children's observational skills and prior knowledge rather than preconceived ideas of what children ought to know. It could be argued that the main role for the teacher is to initially model the process of close observation and comparison so that children have had an example from which to base their own observations and language of analysis.

The next stage, ideally by the end of Key Stage 1 and then into the early stages of Key Stage 2, is the sequencing of a range of historical objects and pictures. Thus clothes, toys, household objects – indeed, almost any form of technology which can enter the classroom through artefacts or photographs/illustrations – can be sequenced. Once again, whatever the teaching level, teachers should model at least some of this process and explain their reasoning, thus illuminating the forms of analysis and prior knowledge they are using. Fundamentally, it is about understanding clues such as materials and design, or obsolescence, and therefore what we use instead today. In the example in Figure 3.3, to continue the theme of domestic irons, the introduction of the first electrically heated iron (second on the left) produced an exceptionally heavy object weighing around 10kg, followed by much lighter, partially plastic models and, finally, the very light and efficient steam irons most of us are familiar with.

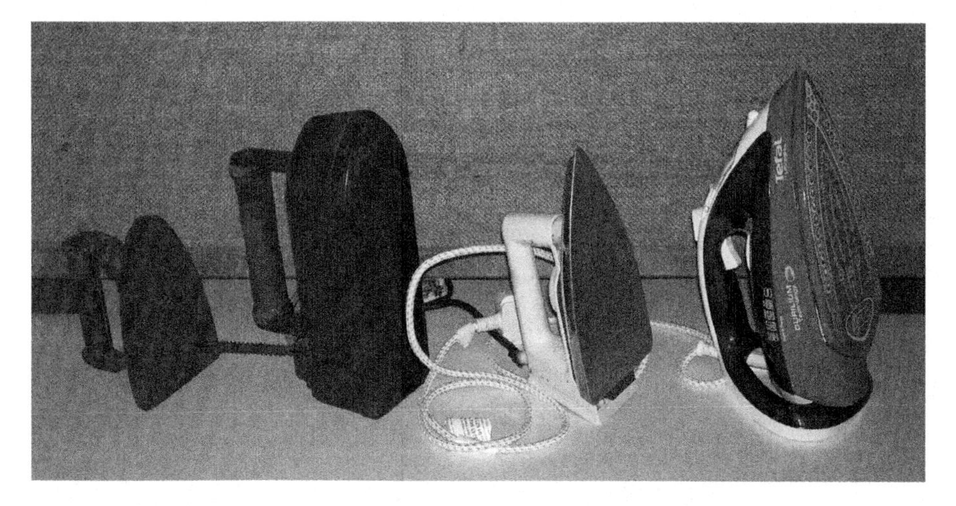

Figure 3.3 Sequencing domestic irons from earliest to most recent

Any sequencing activity can be made more challenging, and therefore extended to almost any level, by the addition of dates, or research into sequence and dates. Some forms of reasoning, and certainly aspects of history linked to technology and manufacturing, have a definite logic in the order (although the same cannot be said of cultural trends such as fashion, which are partially cyclical). For example, with primary trainees, often including mature students, I ask them to sequence several illustrations of important inventions, such as the steam engine, the first powered flight, and electronic computers. I have observed that when this is carried out by reasonably large groups there is a collective wisdom that usually gets the sequence reasonably accurate, although the dates are often wayward. But this should not mean that children's ability to sequence historical objects and images should be underestimated; research has tended to reveal the importance of wider, out-of-school knowledge and context (West, 1981a, 1981b; Stow, 1999). Levstick and Barton's (1996) work deserves a brief discussion: their use of images from twentieth-century American political and social history supported West's belief that there is a widely distributed knowledge of historical imagery, often gained from non-traditional sources that children continue to develop throughout their lives.

Another aspect of culturally shared knowledge was Stow's (1999) observation that children often become confused if recent images or objects are damaged or dirty, and the association of age with monochrome images: it seems that cultural stereotypes can also cause confusion in many young children's minds. Yet rather than a barrier to understanding, examples of pristine older objects compared with damaged modern items can reveal the importance of deeper clues than superficial condition. The same is unquestionably true when creating opportunities to discuss how the past may be misrepresented by grainy, monochrome images, and that the people in old photographs (and it is worth noting that photographic images are now almost 200 years old) would have viewed their world just as vibrantly and viscerally (more so in the case of smell) as children do today.

THE USE OF TIMELINES

Arguably, the most influential teaching approach is the development and use of timelines. If any more evidence is required about the challenge of understanding historical (and geological timeframes) one only need think of the well-known metaphor of the history of the Earth being compressed into a calendar year, with *homo sapiens* emerging at five minutes to midnight on New Year's Eve. Indeed, any adult could be challenged to honestly claim that they can mentally conceive a thousand-year duration, let alone a million years, or the 4.54 billion years since the Earth was formed. It is doubtful whether human experience can relate to such timescales. And in this sense, certain aspects of popular culture, and even quite well-regarded children's books, add to the difficulty by hugely compressing and distorting longer time periods. I often show students a book written for children which relates British history to roughly two decades on every page, but then uses the first two pages to cover the formation of the Earth and the appearance of modern humans (over 4 billion years in two pages). This cannot be helpful for children's understanding of historical timescales.

The initial guidance from the first iteration of the National Curriculum, and some practitioner research (White, 1997), recommended the use of personal timelines in Key Stage 1. Two comments immediately need to be made: first, this approach will ultimately be unsuccessful without the cooperation of parents, guardians and even the wider family; second, it is a potentially dangerous activity to carry out with some children and safeguarding issues must always be considered. Nevertheless, I used this approach as a Key Stage 1 teacher, and always with personal photographs which the children ordered themselves and then displayed, usually in the form of a washing line. One thing to note is that the distinction between sequencing and timelines at this level is not easy to make, but it could be argued that the introduction of dates and labels (with information gathered from their families) made this activity a timeline. The usual events the children remembered, or had photographic evidence of, included the birth of siblings, pets, moving to a new house, starting school, family holidays and birthday parties. The potential risk is when young lives also encompass family deaths or relationship problems, etc. Equally, one can understand why this was a suggested approach because it aligns with Piagetian ideas about the importance of personal experience as a starting point for ordering and sequencing events in time.

The next stage is also linked to the sequencing activities outlined above. Following a sequencing activity, linked to objects, images or both, research could be carried out to find out the accurate order, and then dates used to develop a sense of duration and time intervals. This last point deserves a little thought. If dates are to be used, unlike the example given above, the intervals must be roughly accurate if children's understanding of historical time periods is to progress. Thus a 100-year period should take roughly twice the distance covered by 50 years. Therefore, progression throughout Key Stage 2 ought to correspond with increasingly accurate mathematical timescales and a sense of proportion.

A key argument is that throughout Key Stage 2, each classroom should have a prominent timeline linking together all history topics, and indeed, all other forms of learning involving historical timescales. Consider some of the likely scales:

- A 10-metre wall could encompass 10,000 years of human history at roughly a metre for every thousand years, but this would result in a very compressed format.

- 10 metres to cover 2,000 years could result in a relatively useful scale, with each metre covering 200 years. This would still result in a rather compressed last section, but at least this would indicate the rate of development in the modern world.
- A 20-metre class timeline to account for 2,000 years would result in 1 metre for each century, and this would allow enough space for the inclusion of many important events.
- The ideal would be a 40-metre timeline using the 1 metre per century (or 10 cm per decade) scale, encompassing the whole classroom. Such a timeline could represent a significant amount of ancient history. If used carefully, and in conjunction with interactive virtual timelines, Key Stage 2 children would begin to understand the scale of the less reported aspects of history, for example the 600 years of Anglo-Saxon Britain, compared with the relatively brief length of more favoured eras, such as the Victorians, Tudor Britain and the two World Wars.
- The latter point can currently be demonstrated with the archived BBC overview of British History: www.bbc.co.uk/history/interactive/timelines/british/index_embed.shtml
- Or this alternative archived example: www.bbc.co.uk/schools/primaryhistory/timeline/timeline.shtml

This is not meant to be overly prescriptive, but the importance of retaining an accurate and proportionally consistent scale must be emphasised, and arguably 10 cm for each decade is a more realistic scale. If this results in long sections when not much seems to have occurred, then this is still an extremely important and valuable teaching point.

Examples from practice and research reveal that timelines can be demonstrated to children as vertical as well as horizontal, while Cooper (1995, p. 34) argued that with very young children circular time lines may be more appropriate due to their developing understanding of the cyclical nature of astronomical time, such as the pattern of the day and the year (refer to ICT examples below). For older children, the PESRC formula introduced in Chapter 2 can be applied through developing overlapping timelines to extend children's understanding of the differing dimensions to history (Haydn, 1995). This might mean looking at parallel developments in culture, economics, science and technology alongside political changes. In the revised version of the National Curriculum, the general statements introduced above reiterated the importance of the different strands of history, thus allaying the fears that the focus would solely be placed on political history, with the inclusion of the statement that contextual studies should include 'cultural, economic, military, political, religious and social history; and between short- and long-term timescales' (DfE, 2013, p. 188). Thus, the remit is now broader with the inclusion of military themes (see Table 3.1).

Table 3.1 The dimensions of history

Political	Timelines of monarchs, prime ministers, key political events, etc. In many respects the most obvious and common forms of timelines.
Economic, Technological and Scientific	Arguably the most interesting aspect of history in the sense that technology and science generally progress, often with simultaneous inventions. This could also include key scientific and mathematical discoveries as well as the more obvious key inventions. The scope could include continental and world themes, including intellectual movements such as the Renaissance and Enlightenment. An example, the development of radio waves, is included in this chapter.
Social	Here the potential scope is endless. The focus could include citizenship themes, such as timelines demonstrating women's rights, or key legislation that has improved the lives of children and minorities.
Religious	The addition of religion was a later amendment, and it is fair to state that this theme has received less attention in primary schools than the other dimensions, but it would be possible to produce a timeline illustrating key religious events, such as the establishment of the main world religions and key moments, such as the Reformation, and possibly events at the local level.
Cultural and Aesthetic	Here the scope is vast and can be adapted to fit virtually all history units. I have produced examples linked to fashion, music and sporting events, such as the modern Olympic Games.
Military (introduced in revised National Curriculum)	The examples included in this chapter demonstrate how useful timelines can be in terms of organising children's understanding of complex events.

A further extension to challenge upper Key Stage 2 children would be to demonstrate or develop simultaneous timelines on a range of geographical scales, for example contrasting local, national and international events over the same period (Chapman, 1993). In the latter case, books that demonstrate timelines can be useful. The publisher Dorling Kindersley continues to produce a range of beautifully illustrated history textbooks that often overlay several timelines, some comparing continental developments over the same time periods. An excellent example is the American publication *The Timetables of Science* (Hellemans and Bunch, 1988), which is now available as an online book. This text vertically overlays six timelines associated with mathematics, science and technology. One of the main virtues of this book is its emphasis on how synoptic and interdependent most scientific knowledge is. It is a European or western conceit to think that most world events and principal discoveries happened in 'our' continent. More accurately, parallel developments were happening throughout the world. China retained an overall technological advantage over Europe until well into the second millennium CE/AD, and while North America remained technologically in the Stone Age until European settlement, in South America it was a different story with full metallurgy, including smelting and casting in some cultures. Equally, the Mayan civilisation independently developed the concept of zero, something not achieved by either the Greek or Roman civilisations. In summary, throughout Key Stage 2 either children should be exposed to timelines in a range of scales and forms or they should be sequencing events and developing their own timelines and contributing to class ones – at every opportunity.

AN EXAMPLE FROM SCIENCE AND TECHNOLOGY

The timeline presented in Figure 3.4 provides a brief and rather under-developed example, due to space restrictions, of the logical progress inherent in the development of technology. It begins with the discovery and identification of radio waves, their initial application in domestic radio broadcasts, followed by the invention of television once a way to convert light into an electrical signal had been discovered. Each subsequent development was dependent on the inventions that came before it. In this example, there is a clear sense of scientific and technological progress and the logical development of ideas, which is not true of other forms of historical change.

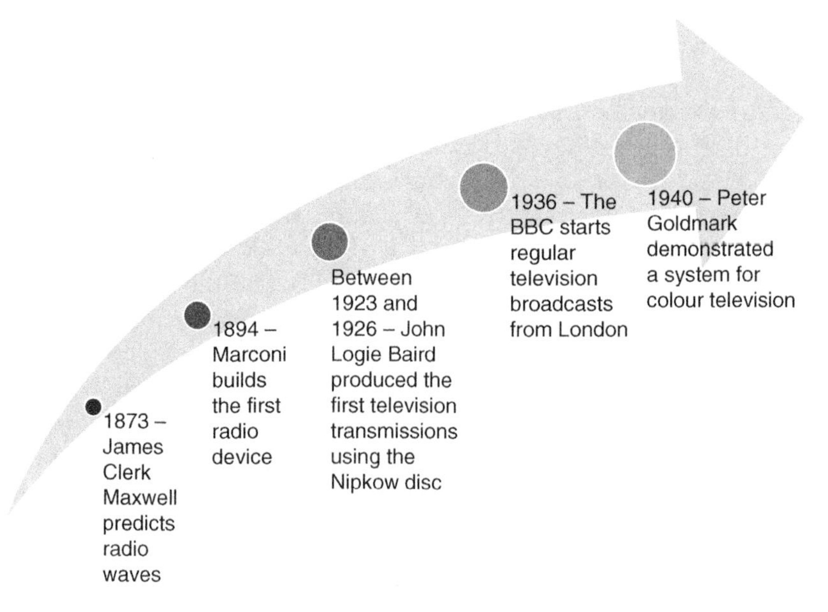

Figure 3.4 A synoptic timeline demonstrating the evolution of broadcasting using radio waves

THE APPLICATION OF COMPUTING/ICT

Information and communication technology (ICT) can support children through exposure to a wider range of timelines as well as guiding them in their development of their own chronological work. I am hesitant to provide current examples of useful timelines suitable for the primary school. Examples that I provided several years ago (Percival, 2012) are not all currently available, or, in the case of the BBC, have been archived. Nevertheless, the overall technological trend is ineluctably moving towards online teaching resources, and so it would be reasonable to assume that online and interactive examples will ultimately triumph over physical resources (even if the latter are never wholly supplanted).

The timelines produced by the BBC Education and History Departments should also be considered (and it should always be remembered that part of the BBC's charter is to support education, so these are in no sense an unexpected bonus), or the publicly funded British Museum and British Library. Indeed, there are many organisations producing reasonably interactive, online timelines, to the extent that teachers are often spoiled for choice.

However, the more significant potential of ICT is in the range of software that can help children to develop their own timelines. Commonplace software such as Microsoft PowerPoint or Word can help children to sequence historical events, but with limitations such as a sense of historical scale and proportional representation of time. The timeline created by an 11-year-old boy during a recent consultation exercise linked to a focus on World War II and the 'Theatres of War' project discussed in Chapter 2, and presented in Figure 3.5, was time-consuming and difficult to complete, but

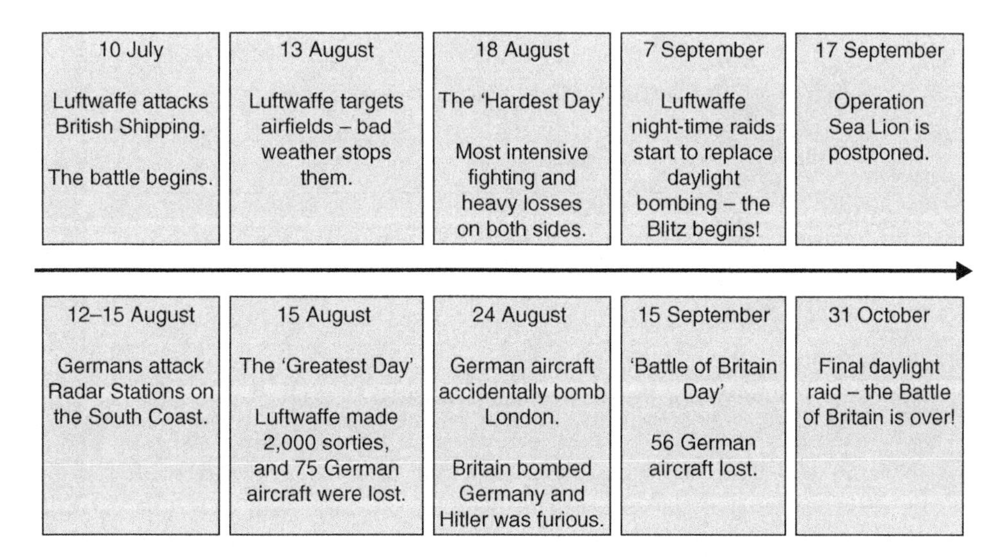

Figure 3.5 Timeline of the 'Battle of Britain': summer and autumn 1940

it allowed him to develop a more comprehensive overview of how the Battle of Britain began, developed and transmogrified into the Blitz.

By contrast, the use of pre-formatted diagrams within Word (see Figure 3.6) allowed a 9-year-old girl, working on the same project, to order the main events in the Battle of the Atlantic more as a sequencing activity, restricted to one main event each year, rather than creating an accurate and proportional timeline.

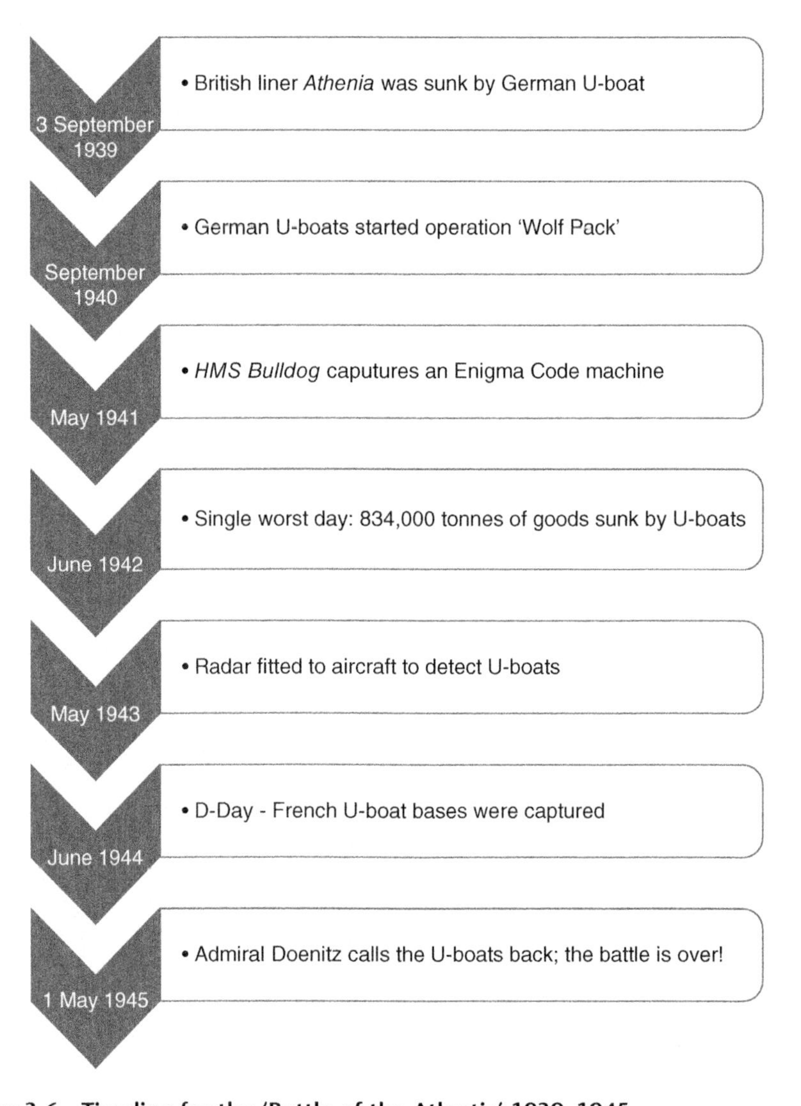

Figure 3.6 Timeline for the 'Battle of the Atlantic' 1939–1945

Other software, such as TimeToast, will allow this. A timescale can be entered when using this program, or the timeline will develop proportionally depending on the dates added, but either way a virtual timeline can be created with accurate time intervals. Compared with software routinely covered in the primary school, it is relatively easy to access and use.

Another powerful piece of software is Prezi, now often used by educators as an alternative to PowerPoint. The ability to link text and photographs is an ideal platform for timelines, although unlike TimeToast it will not create the parameters. One important aspect is Prezi's flexibility, including the ability to create a circular timeline as recommended by Cooper (1995).

CHANGE AND CONTINUITY

According to the Qualification and Curriculum Authority (QCA, 2007, p. 112), 'Change and Continuity', as a related yet contrasting pair of concepts, should be closely linked to a 'sense of period', a theme identified by Turner-Bisset (2005, p. 20) as important in developing young children's burgeoning understanding of the past, and linked to overarching themes, including consideration of the pace of change. Despite their recent prominence, this pair of concepts has rarely been discussed by philosophers of history, and Counsell (2011) noted that there is also far less educational research about these concepts compared with other historical terms. Early research into young children's accounts of change found that this concept was often misinterpreted by young children in personal terms, such as substitution, for example related to changes in personal circumstances such as clothes or friends, although by the end of primary school a more mature understanding of historical change and transference often started to emerge. More recent evidence of primary-aged children's ability to understand change was provided by Sampson, Grugeon and Yiannaki (1998) as part of a research project that linked discussion and teacher exposition to key historical concepts and language.

In terms of pedagogy, Counsell (2011, pp. 10–20) advocated making stronger links with narrative to engage pupil interest, developing clearer questioning strategies and allowing enough time for children to develop their ideas and reflections. There has also been some agreement that the concept of change is linked to observation and comparative analysis, particularly with younger children. Hodgkinson (1986) was typical of many primary practitioners who asked children to compare artefacts and to consider how their design and use has changed. Thus, any form of comparison or ordering activity, as outlined earlier in this chapter, should cover these concepts in enough detail.

Where the concept of change becomes more challenging, and arguably beyond most primary-aged children, is in accounting for the reasons for change – in other words, causality in history – especially when combined with an attempt to explain why some things have remained the same. Change and continuity can also occur in several scales and dimensions, mirroring the timeline activities outlined in this chapter. A 'theme beyond 1066', for example, might look at the history of the British Parliament and contrast the retention of conventions and traditions alongside the major changes to political representation and voting rights that have occurred. The centenary of the rights of woman to vote in the UK (November 1918) is an obvious contemporary example of how a Key Stage 2 project might be aligned with a major anniversary and studied alongside a popular unit, such as the Great War, establishing the relationship between women's crucial work during the war and the added pressure that gave to the strong logical and moral case for voting equality. The fact that full equality for women is still being fought for in several contemporary spheres also demonstrates the ongoing relevance and importance of contextual historical knowledge.

DEVELOPING A 'SENSE OF TIME'

I have a conceit: it is a minor conceit, perhaps, but a conceit all the same. I believe I can watch any motion picture I have not seen before and guess its year of production to within three to five years, even within a couple of years for the 1960s and 1970s. And I am usually quite accurate. The question is therefore: what knowledge, contextual clues and cultural cues am I using to date the films? It is made harder when older films are representing the past, so in these cases there is also a layer of historiography to consider – the past as it was represented in the past.

I principally use my knowledge of fashion, slang and the technology represented to date films set in their own time. Soundtracks can also offer important clues if they accurately represent musical trends at the time of production. Films are often culturally significant in the sense that they help to determine contemporary fashions, and so these are important signifiers. I also use some more technical clues, such as the dyes used in film stock. Unquestionably, the use of certain film dyes and processing techniques can help to identify most post-war decades – think of the browns and pastels in early 1970s films – and this I combine with knowledge of directorial styles. I would argue that the previous examples are a kind of folk knowledge. I have never formally studied film-making, nor attempted to analyse it before. But it does raise an important consideration. Children self-evidently are not born with any knowledge about the past, so if a 'sense of period' or a 'sense of time' have been identified by bodies such as Her Majesty's Inspectorate and the QCA as markers of historical understanding, a theme returned to in Chapter 12 on assessment, then our role as educators is surely to build up children's bank of knowledge, particularly historical imagery, but also to help them to question and analyse the clues and knowledge they are using, and to identify the main indicators of the historical periods they are studying.

Many of the citations in this chapter, notably the work of West, Stow and Harnett from the UK, and Levstick and Barton from the USA, support the claim that children begin to build up their personal 'bank' of historical imagery from quite a young age, and often from non-academic sources. The role of primary educators is surely to build upon these foundations, to introduce criticality (for example, is it true that Vikings wore horns on their helmets?) and analysis to enable children to think more carefully about the signifiers of the past. These are themes that I will return to in Chapters, 4, 5, 6 and 7.

CHAPTER SUMMARY

- Chronology is one of the key organising concepts in history and is essential for the development of children's historical understanding at any age:
  - In the Early Years curriculum, teachers should consider the accurate and careful use and explanation of language associated with time, especially the propositions before, after, yesterday, tomorrow, etc.;
  - In Key Stage 1, children should have the opportunity to develop personal timelines;
  - In Key Stages 1 and 2, there should be increased links with mathematics and time: days, weeks, months, seasons, years, etc.;
  - Children should be given the opportunity to carry out sequencing activities that link historical evidence and reasoning;
  - Teachers should include opportunities for children to experience the different dimensions of history;
  - Above all, history projects should include the creation and use of timelines, including books and class displays;
  - In the use of ICT, including virtual timelines and programs like Prezi or Time-Toast;
  - In opportunities for historical reasoning based on accounts of historical change;
  - The ultimate learing goal should be to develop children's burgeoning 'sense of time'.

FURTHER READING

Cooper, H. (2018) *History 5–11: A Guide for Teachers* (3rd edn). Abingdon: Routledge. Chapter 4 on Chronology.

The oldest and best general text on primary history which contains an important chapter on chronology (Chapter 4).

Harnett, P. (1993) Identifying Progression in Children's Understanding: The Use of Visual Materials to Assess Primary Children's Learning in History. *Cambridge Journal of Education*, 23(2): 137–54; and Lynn, S. (1993) Children Reading Pictures: History Visuals at Key Stages 1 and 2. *Education 3–13*, 21(3): 23–9.

(Continued)

Both of these articles sprang from an extensive and fascinating empirical research project into children's ability to sequence historical images.

Hodkinson, A. (2007) The Usage of Subjective Temporal Phrases within the National Curriculum for History and its Schemes of Work – Effective Provision or a Missed Opportunity? *Education 3–13*, 31(3): 28–34.

Hodkinson carried out doctoral research into the development of chronological understanding and published widely on this subject.

CHAPTER 4

ENQUIRY, INTERPRETATION AND SIGNIFICANCE

What this chapter will cover

In many respects, this is one of the most challenging chapters of the book. It introduces some of the key debates within the philosophy of history, namely the importance of evidence and historical enquiry associated with the generation of new knowledge from archival sources. However, due to gaps in evidence and the approach and beliefs of the historian, this is never a neutral or complete activity and consequently the study of history necessarily produces contested accounts. This is what is meant by historical interpretation. The subject matter under review also needs to be considered: historical enquiries can focus on trivial questions, and it is important that students select the most important, or significant, aspects of learning. The chapter attempts to blend key theorists from the philosophy of history with important research into pedagogy. Examples of how enquiry, interpretation and significance might be developed throughout the primary school are included towards the end of the chapter.

INTRODUCTION

Having introduced the overview of the development of primary history pedagogy and the National Curriculum in Chapter 2, it is now necessary to discuss three of the key *organising* or *procedural* concepts in more detail. The inclusion of enquiry, essentially an investigatory approach towards historical understanding linked with evidence, reflected the growing influence of constructivist models of learning, principally the ideas of Piaget and Bruner, on educational theory and practice. Enquiry, as a core component in child-centred approaches to learning, was an important part of the Plowden Report's (CACE, 1967, pp. 225–30) recommendations for primary schools, although it is important to note that the recommendation was for all subjects and not just history. Nevertheless, the 'new' approach to history pedagogy placed an emphasis on the role of enquiry and the importance of questions rather than the passive acceptance of uncritical accounts, which are often narrative in form.

The 'new' history also emphasised the limits of historical knowledge and the fact that history is an evolving and partial form of knowledge, in contradistinction to a fixed view of the past favoured by traditionalists. This, in short, is what is meant by interpretation; that our understanding of the past is conditional, shaped by fragmentary evidence and by the mind of the historian. Due to the nature of historical evidence, enquiry-based approaches necessarily introduce the idea of historical interpretation, not least how historical evidence is selected and used by the historian. The place of interpretation was, and remains, one of the most controversial aspects of the National Curriculum and its place was contested. Finally, the concept of significance has been less discussed, but it deserves inclusion because it is now a clearly stated aim of the revised National Curriculum and there was a tendency for enquiry-based approaches to engage in relatively trivial pursuits. Given the pressures on each subject for learning time, it is important that teachers direct children towards the most fruitful forms of enquiry and acquisition of knowledge.

ENQUIRY-BASED LEARNING AND THE NATIONAL CURRICULUM

Let us start by recapping the previous discussion. After the recommendation of the Plowden Report, the early work of the Schools Council History Project (SCHP) and Her Majesty's Inspectorate's guidance (DES, 1988a), the first iteration of the National Curriculum contained many elements based on enquiry and investigation. Attainment Target 3, 'The Use of Historical Sources', was clearly based on the principles of enquiry and evidence. The Dearing Review (Dearing, 1994) had introduced key elements in lieu of the lost Attainment Targets, and these were now defined as 'Knowledge, skills and understanding'. They were to be taught and assessed as part of the study units, which included enquiry and the use of evidence. In the Curriculum 2000 (DfEE, 1999, p. 105) this included 'historical enquiry', which recommended that children should find out about the past from a range of sources, including information technology, artefacts, images and educational visits. It further recommended that pupils should 'ask and answer questions' as well as selecting information. A related point was the 'organisation and communication' of children's findings as an outcome of their investigations.

Despite the widely held fears that the National Curriculum 2014 would simply advise schools to concentrate on the acquisition of knowledge, the final document clearly acknowledged the place of organising concepts. The general 'Purpose of study' statement contains the following sentence: 'Teaching should equip pupils to ask perceptive questions, think critically, weigh evidence, sift arguments, and develop perspective and judgement' (DfE, 2013, p. 188). Not only does this statement recognise the place of enquiry and investigation, it also makes explicit the link between investigation and broader understanding. This is followed by a list of subject-specific aims, which includes the desire that children should:

> understand the methods of historical enquiry, including how evidence is used rigorously to make historical claims, and discern how and why contrasting arguments and interpretations of the past have been constructed. (DfE, 2013, p. 188)

THE PHILOSOPHICAL FOUNDATIONS OF ENQUIRY-BASED APPROACHES

Given the relatively shallow roots of academic history outlined in the Introduction, the debates about the form and practice of history are similarly recent compared with other subject disciplines. Regarding the specific place of historical enquiry and investigation, the most influential voice, certainly in terms of influence on history pedagogy, has been that of R.G. Collingwood (1939, 1946), and to a lesser degree Michael Oakeshott (1962, 1983). They both described history as a 'special form of research or enquiry' (Collingwood, 1946, p. 9) that required historians to follow Acton's advice to 'study problems not periods' (Collingwood, 1939, p. 124).

Since this is the first discussion on Collingwood's influence, he deserves a brief introduction. R.G. Collingwood was an archaeologist and ancient historian as well as a philosopher, and one of his self-declared aims was to create a rapprochement between history and philosophy, while also establishing the foundations of history as an independent and autonomous subject. In his *An Autobiography* (Collingwood, 1939, pp. 22–8), he described his growing disillusionment with the prevailing logical positivist approach to history in Oxford at the start of the twentieth century and his growing acceptance of idealism as an epistemological model. Collingwood's arguments were shaped by the ideas of earlier philosophers of history and sociology, namely Giambattista Vico and Benedetto Croce, and, above all, F.H. Bradley. Another powerful influence, as Van der Dussen (1994) explained, was the Baconian method of 'question and answer', which he adopted in his archaeological research as a more 'scientific' form of historical enquiry.

Collingwood's idealist epistemology did not result in a rejection of empirical science, or the importance of historical sources – indeed, he emphasised archival or archaeology evidence as the foundation of historical study – but he did make two important points that are now largely accepted by historians. The first is that history is an activity of the present in that the historian studies 'traces' that survive in the present, thus adopting from Croce (1960, pp. 12–14) the idea of history being a 'contemporary' activity based on a continuous source of knowledge from a past that is 'in some sense living in the present' (Collingwood, 1939, pp. 96–8). Second, in a rejection of eighteenth-century 'scissors and paste' antiquarianism, he described how he followed Vico's arguments for adopting a critical approach to sources (Collingwood, 1946, pp. 257–9).

It is hard to argue against the claim that the activity of being a historian is necessarily abstract and cerebral, especially given the relationship between the present and the past. Perhaps more significantly, Collingwood made very bold statements about the nature of history which coincide closely with constructivist theories of learning. Throughout his work, the importance of historical imagination and the mental construction of historical knowledge are emphasised. For example, Collingwood discussed at considerable length the nature of historical reasoning, which he principally defined as inferential, based as it is on an incomplete or fragmentary evidence base, hence the importance of creative and imaginative reasoning to interpolate, or fill in the gaps, and sometimes to go 'beyond' the statements in the sources (Collingwood, 1946, pp. 237–41). Equally, history should also be a highly self-reflective and critical form of reasoning, and should always be verified against historical sources.

This may seem unduly complex, and more than primary practitioners require, but it can be argued that the foundations of the study of history are an important consideration. Nor are the ideas prohibitively complex: in short, Collingwood was merely observing that history should be based on asking key questions based on the evidence that has survived to the present, that this should be an active and constructivist form of learning rather than passively rearranging existing material, and that the forms of historical reasoning involve high levels of imagination. In terms of Collinwood's criticism of 'cut and paste', not only was this a frequent criticism of children's work post-Plowden, but the current danger is the even more prevalent one of children uncritically copying and pasting images and texts from questionable internet-based sources of information. Collingwood's important point is that unless the historian, of whatever age, is engaging with and interpreting the source material in a questioning manner, it cannot be true historical work.

There is an excellent example from Collingwood's autobiography (1939, pp. 128–31) which illustrates his approach in practice. During some of his pioneering archaeological work of Roman Britain in Northumbria, he began to question the fundamental purpose of Hadrian's Wall. The uncritical, 'common-sense' view was, and remains, that the wall was simply a formidable barrier to keep out the troublesome Pict tribes from the north of the British Isles. Collingwood reasoned that the wall could not have been high enough nor sufficiently defended at every point along its full length for it to act as a genuine deterrent. Collingwood further reasoned that a wall would not prevent attacking tribes from sailing around the coast and thus avoiding the wall altogether. Therefore, its role must have been equivalent to a modern-day state border in terms of controlling the passage of people and goods, and as a form of reconnaissance. He further speculated that this should have resulted in a series of look-out posts at each coastal end to observe boats sailing southwards. Having posed a question based on existing knowledge, Collingwood discovered that previous archaeological digs had unearthed the foundations of coastal towers, but that without a question to answer, this evidence had simply been ignored.

Collingwood was not alone in his belief in the primacy of enquiry. Karl Popper contributed the useful metaphor of shining a searchlight into the dark places of the past, guided by a hypothesis, and based firmly on his post-positivist, falsification theory of knowledge in which ideas are tested against the available evidence (Popper, 1966, pp. 260–9). Thus, there is very little disagreement from academics that questions and hypotheses should guide historians' work. Historians also tend to agree that the foundations of history are firmly based on primary sources.

ENQUIRY, EVIDENCE AND PRIMARY PEDAGOGY

It is because the sources and uses of historical evidence are so important that Chapter 7 will discuss this in much more detail. The intention in this section, therefore, is simply to outline some of the research and scholarship conducted to investigate children's use of objects, images, text and educational visits as sources of historical enquiry. There is evidence that pedagogical approaches using enquiry and evidence began in the late nineteenth century (Levesque, 2008, p. 26), and so we should always beware of calls to 'return' to traditional forms pedagogy. However, contemporary accounts tend to begin with the work of the aforementioned Schools Council History Project (SCHP) in the 1970s (Shemilt, 1980). Within this project, children from the early 1970s onwards were introduced to the aims and methods of professional historians, principally through enquiry and exposure to primary sources, while their progress and understanding were measured against *organising* concepts such as significance, continuity and change, and understanding. Evidence of the triumph of the 'new' approaches to history can be seen in the way that virtually all the main primary history theorists advocated that children should engage with history through enquiry. Similarly, Cooper (1995, 2012) argued for the use of primary sources in the classroom, and the importance of an evidence base for children's work. Husbands, writing principally about older pupils, favoured an active model strongly based on children learning history not as a 'cipher', but as an 'active participant in the dialogue between present and past' (Husbands, 1996, p. 53).

Following Collingwood's example from Hadrian's Wall, Ashby (2004, 2011) made a distinction between sources and evidence, and suggested that children need to be introduced to the idea that a source only becomes evidence when it is used to answer a question, and therefore children should understand that evidence is an idea and not a 'thing'. For younger children, Blyth (1989, p. 113) made an interesting argument for a hierarchy of resources, with the teacher acting as the 'first resource' for children, thus emphasising the importance of subject knowledge and confidence when introducing history topics. Nevertheless, beyond the teacher, the most immediate and visceral form of evidence is physical, particularly objects, but also images, buildings and other physical remnants from the past. The local study is an important aspect of historical evidence, and discussed in considerable detail in Chapter 7.

THE PLACE OF INTERPRETATION IN THE PRIMARY CURRICULUM

At this stage the relationship between enquiry, evidence and interpretation should be a little clearer. According to the educationalist John Fines (1994), competing and evolving accounts of the past have resulted from the lack of direct experience of the past, fragmentary and unrepresentative forms of historical evidence that have survived into the present, and not least the cliché that history is written by the 'winners'. He also argued that historical evidence has nearly always received at least one layer of interpretation from the original writer or archivist.

The example Fines used was to challenge the reader to take arguably the most famous date in English (British) history, the Battle of Hastings in 1066, and to consider how much is really known about this seminal event. There are a few eyewitness accounts, naturally written after the event and very much from the perspective of the victors; there is the famous tapestry, which lacks a clear provenance and has been subject to many different interpretations; and there is some archaeology, though even with this form of 'hard' evidence there are ongoing debates and uncertainties. If this seminal historical event lacks a clear evidence base, then it is unsurprising that competing theories emerge. Added to this is the fact that science, and unexpected discoveries, add new information that frequently necessitates revised accounts to be written. In short, historical knowledge is always incomplete, subject to different interpretations and almost certainly will evolve in some way.

Thus, despite the fierce ministerial opposition it received, it was surely right that the first iteration of the National Curriculum included Attainment Target 2, 'Interpretations of History' (DES, 1991a, p. 7). Progress against this outcome was clearly harder to define and delineate than other attainment targets. In essence, children would show progress by developing their understanding that stories may be about real or fictional people (level 1) to an 'understanding that deficiencies in evidence may lead to different interpretations of the past' (level 4), which, they suggested, might include explaining why illustrations of Ancient Egypt vary so much. By the time of the introduction of the National Curriculum 2000 (DfEE, 1999), there was merely a general requirement that children in both Key Stages would be required to cover the third element, entitled 'historical interpretation', which stated that 'Pupils should be taught to recognise that the past is represented and interpreted in different ways, and to give reasons for this' (DfEE, 1999, p. 105), but no detail was provided to illustrate how this was to be carried out. Despite initial fears, interpretation has been retained in the Curriculum 2014, although Cooper (2018, p. 32) has warned that the potential for an uncritical 'grand narrative' of British history should be firmly exposed and contested.

It is worth repeating the short section contained in the statement concerning enquiry, which includes the clause that pupils should 'discern how and why contrasting arguments and interpretations of the past have been constructed' (DfE, 2013, p. 188). However, irrespective of the fact that it remains part of the overall aims within the National Curriculum, the strongest argument for the inclusion of interpretation is that it incorporates high-level thinking skills and the corresponding opportunity to intellectually challenge children who are capable of engaging with increasingly abstract forms of reasoning.

KEY DEBATES WITHIN THE PHILOSOPHY OF HISTORY

Understandably, the question of historical interpretation has been widely discussed within the philosophy of history. According to Marwick (1981, pp. 54–7), the preoccupation of the pioneering nineteenth-century empiricists was to create objective forms of history based on scientific principles which would enable history to be equally acceptable to both sides of a debate. In the twentieth century, eminent historians, notably Elton (2002), continued to argue that rigorous forms of historical enquiry demonstrate an objective truth of historical knowledge, often as a bulwark against charges of overt relativism. However, few, if any, contemporary historians believe in a naïve definition of objective forms of history, but the aim to respect the boundaries of evidence is still adhered to by virtually all academics and philosophers of history. For example,

Evans (1997, pp. 238–53), in his critique of postmodernism and extreme relativism, argued persuasively that historical enquiry demands high levels of imagination from the historian in the form of a 'conversation' with the past, but is circumscribed by a complex set of rules that historians adhere to in implicit forms (Evans, 1997, pp. 115–16) and which produce recognisably historical forms of reasoning.

However, there are several further theoretical arguments that have also questioned the reliability of historical knowledge. Structuralists such as Lévi-Strauss (1963) have questioned the possibility of describing accurately the potentially infinite number of individual perspectives and interpretations as a unitary historical event. Lévi-Strauss (1962) frequently used the example of the French Revolution to demonstrate the overwhelming multiplicity of equally real interpretations: whether Jacobin or aristocrat, etc., all must be accepted as equally real. Therefore, there cannot be an 'account' of the French Revolution, and to believe in a definitive interpretation of history, certainly an account that claims totality, is to transform history into 'myth' (Lévi-Strauss, 1963, pp. 254–5). Lowenthal (1985, pp. 214–15) and Jenkins (1991, pp. 13–14) have made a similar argument about the complexity of past events due to the potentially infinite number of possible perspectives, interpretations and events, while Braudel (1980, p. 15) further noted that historical explanations invariably became 'increasingly complex when actively investigated'. In short, the deeper the historian probes, the more complicated accounts tend to become.

From a postmodernist position, discussed in relation to narrative theory in Chapter 6, theorists such as White (1978, 1999) and Jenkins (1991) have argued that historians inevitably select, shape and interpret their ideas in the form of their political and philosophical belief systems, an argument supported by Hexter's (1971, p. 80) concept of the historian's 'second record'. The outcomes of history are then shaped using literary devices, including narrative and 'emplotment' (White, 1999, pp. 7–10) – in other words, writing approaches that inevitably shape the way history is written. E.H. Carr, in his controversial text *What is History?* (Carr, 1961, p. 23), similarly emphasised the importance of theory and ideology in shaping historical accounts, and his advice to 'study the historian before you begin to study the facts', echoing the argument from postmodernism, remains important. Finally, hermeneutical approaches to history, advocated by historians of ideas such as Skinner (1976), described how anachronism and other contemporary misunderstandings routinely occur in the work of historians. Historians should therefore concentrate on understanding the context and milieu of the historical period under review, sometimes termed historicism, thus allowing a more complete and accurate understanding of historical beliefs and interpretations from the perspective of the time under review. This point has rather naturally been felt to be beyond the powers of almost all primary- (and secondary-) aged children, although it was unquestionably the foundation of the now discredited approach within secondary history to engage with historical 'empathy'.

Other considerations included the representativeness of data. For example, Stone's (1987, pp. 57–9) argument that the rich and powerful (and literate) nearly always predominate in any given time or society is qualified by Bloch's (1954, pp. 73–6) point regarding the question of uneven survival, with chance and fragmentation creating unintentional biases as much as deliberate destruction. Carr (1961) identified the cumulative nature of historical reasoning and the fact that historical knowledge does progress, if only in the sense of layers of interpretation. Naturally, this consideration is of lesser importance to primary practitioners, but the History Working Group did argue that teachers – and they were thinking more in terms of Key Stage 3 – ought to introduce extracts from key texts rather than relying on the main textbooks. (Recall the controversy around Japanese textbooks mentioned at the end of Chapter 2.)

RESEARCH INTO PEDAGOGY: CHALLENGING PUPIL PRECONCEPTIONS AND MISCONCEPTIONS

Chapter 2 included an account of the determination of the History Working Group (DES, 1990, p. 11) to retain interpretation in the face of ministerial hostility (Sheldon, 2011, p. 10) due to their fear that history would be used as 'propaganda' or for the purposes of 'social engineering'. Despite its prominent place within the National Curriculum, academics such as Williams and Davies (1998) and Counsell (2000) argued that historical interpretation remains an organising concept in history which has been infrequently discussed by educationalists or narrowed down to a rather sterile debate about bias in secondary schools (for example, Lang, 1993).

One principal concern, with good reason, was the anticipated difficulty of introducing interpretation to young or 'less able' (sic) children in primary schools (for example, McAleavy, 2000). McAleavy (1993) also advocated using pupils' existing knowledge as a starting point. He emphasised the long and careful road to historical judgement rather than rushing to conclusions, and ensuring that pupils understand the hermeneutical distinction between contemporary viewpoints and perspectives from the past. This point was also explored by Chapman (2011), who advocated the use of rigorous discussion and dialogue to explore the weight of evidence when assessing competing claims.

It should be noted, however, that projects led by Pendry et al. (1997) and Husbands (1996, pp. 73–7) revealed the 'startling' range of pupil preconceptions, including some that were 'astonishingly inaccurate', when children were introduced to history topics. At the very least it means that teachers should consider beginning lessons by addressing likely or anticipated preconceptions around a given aspect of history and should be prepared to challenge misconceptions while simultaneously allowing that history cannot be fixed. If nothing else, this balancing act demonstrates the considerable challenge of covering this core historical concept.

Research into introducing interpretation in the primary classroom may be limited, but it has taken some interesting forms. With very young children, Cooper (1995) advocated making links with English through the coverage of myths, legends and different story accounts – such as the many versions of Cinderella – with suitable outcomes taking place through drama. Indeed, drama and film have often been suggested as ways of exploring different perspectives, hence the rather obvious and important links with narrative. Haydn et al. (2001) recommended looking at different historical presentations on film. For example, Cunningham (2001) used a technique of editing television programmes, leaving just the historians and their interpretations to demonstrate vividly how they produced contrasting accounts and explanations. In both cases, the authors strongly advocated encouraging pupils to adopt a critical stance towards accounts, and to consider why they might differ so much. Other examples, addressing the theme of hidden or less promoted accounts of the past while challenging the orthodoxy of powerful white men, include Wrenn's (2002) account of the black Briton Equino from primary and secondary sources, leading to deep questions about hidden black history and more generic questions about some of the inconsistencies within the evidence base. Visram (1994) carried out research that advocated more attention towards black and Asian perspectives on British history, while Bourdillon (1994) made a similar case for the hidden role of women in political and economic history, and considerations of how and why official accounts deliberately distorted women's roles outside the home.

SUGGESTED TEACHING APPROACHES

To develop these ideas further, here are some approaches taken from research or practice, both as a teacher or in teaching-training and consultancy work. These examples are presented in a roughly hierarchical order.

DIFFERENT REPRESENTATIONS OF THE PAST

From the Foundation Stage onwards, songs, rhymes, stories, images and objects can be introduced to demonstrate the range of ways in which the past can be represented and understood. By the end of primary school this can include critical examinations of the accuracy of stories, illustrations and film.

ALTERNATIVE STORIES (SET IN THE PAST)

The next level is almost certainly the inclusion of stories that show an alternative perspective. *The True Story of the Three Little Pigs* (Scieszka and Smith, 1989) or *The Three Little Wolves and the Big Bad Pig* (Trivizas and Oxenbury, 1993) are two texts that demonstrate how changing the protagonist allows very young children to engage with the idea of different perspectives and accounts.

COMPARISON OF IMAGES

Comparing images, whether photographs, paintings or illustrations, is one way to engage with the nature of historical evidence and to begin to understand the range of representations. For example, when covering events and figures from Victorian Britain with Year 2s, I frequently compared images of street and factory children with middle-class children in their nurseries. Both representations have become clichés, and so the accuracy of each representation was explored, with Victorian childhood acting as an accessible portal for discussion and opinion.

COMPARATIVE BIOGRAPHIES

A similar activity with Year 2 (or Year 3) children is to research and compare the lives of two famous figures. Given the promotion of Florence Nightingale in the QCA sample plans to support Key Stage 1 planning, she has proven a popular choice in Year 2. The inclusion of Florence allows an opportunity to contrast her life and achievements with the Jamaican-born and mixed-race nurse Mary Seacole, who, like Florence, took a team of nurses to the Crimean War (more on this in Chapter 8 where Key Stage 1 requirements are discussed in detail). This example allows the promotion of black history, coverage of minorities and the inclusion of citizenship themes, as well as an opportunity to explore historical interpretation in action since Seacole's work is the subject of contemporary research and publication.

FACT/OPINION DISTINCTION

At the beginning of Key Stage 2 it is possible to explore some more challenging ideas. An early project was Scott's (1994) proposal to adopt a more workable three-phase model based around the fact/opinion distinction. This is the idea that children, in pairs or groups, can be given statements that contain examples of either historical facts or opinion, and they are required to sort them into two groups. This can be made much more challenging when factual statements about opinion are introduced.

At the top end of primary schools, and possibly with the most able children, it might be possible to explore the idea of understanding the viewpoint of people from the past. Here the research evidence is weak.

COMPARISON OF FILM CLIPS

One suggested technique from the literature, for example Cunningham (2001), is the idea of comparing two clips from films or documentaries about the past so that children can discuss the differences in interpretation. Having used this technique with trainee teachers, I think it requires careful thought: not all periods are well covered by examples on film, nor are they all easily comparable, but if good examples are found, for instance different filmed versions of Shakespeare's *Henry V*, then interesting comparisons can be made.

CONTRASTING FORMS OF ENQUIRY

Linking back to the idea of enquiry is the idea of challenging children to research different aspects, or different sides, of the same event. In many respects this is simply an expansion of the idea of comparative biographies, but of course it can be much more open-ended. It might involve researching and presenting on two sides of the same historical event (and some schools do link this outcome with drama), or it might involve several research themes (for example, the Roman questions listed towards the end of this chapter) linked to a wide range of questions linked to a history unit.

MINORITIES/CITIZENSHIP THEMES

By the end of primary school all children should be aware of the oft-neglected voices from history: minorities, women, children, social history themes in general (outlined in Chapter 2), or the vanquished as opposed to the victors. Thus, by this stage children should be ready to challenge some of the stereotypes and prejudices that have existed. The example of researching the life of Mary Seacole is just one example. There are many opportunities to explore these themes. As part of my in-school work support of using the Olympic Games as a starting point for citizenship themes, there are numerous examples of pioneering women and black competitors who challenged stereotypical thinking. Perhaps the best example from Olympic history is to challenge children to investigate the story of the Afro-American athlete Jesse Owens and the prejudice he received, not least the so-called 'snub' from Adolf Hitler. (Owens' story has become mythologised and the snub may have been targeted towards another Afro-American athlete – thus, it is a further example of historical interpretation.)

COMPARATIVE FORMS OF WRITING

Finally, there have been more advanced writing experiments, carried out by Cunningham (2001) and Guyver (2001), to get children to analyse and compare each other's accounts to understand why historians usually differ. This could be used as an end-point of a history unit and as a way of assessing both historical understanding as well as writing skills.

Arguably, it is also possible to compare texts, even within Key Stage 1. As part of a Victorian unit taught for several years in Year 2, we examined the lives of several eminent Victorians, including David Livingstone. As part of my preparation for this topic, we read Tim Jeal's well-regarded biography of Livingstone (Jeal, 1973). It has subsequently been supplanted, but at the time of teaching it was still the most authoritative source on Livingstone's life. We used short extracts to compare the reality of Livingstone's relationship with his wife and children compared to the very sanitised and simplistic Ladybird 'Adventure from History' account (written by Du Garde Peach and with beautiful illustrations by John Kenney in 1959), which suggested that the Livingstone children's time in Africa was full of happiness and 'one long picnic'. This comparison was chosen because it would be something the children could relate to as well as the fact that the truer account was also powerful and moving. My assessment of that unit of study was that most children appeared to understand, and could verbally explain, the differences between Du Guarde Peach's questionable account of Livingstone as a doting parent and the more realistic view of him as a self-absorbed and distant father who essentially abandoned his children to return to his missionary work in Africa. Short extracts from written accounts have also been used, for example contrasting eyewitness accounts of the Great Fire of London, including Samuel Pepys' diary entry, to allow children to make their own comparisons and conclusions.

There is an important teaching point to consider, especially given Pendry et al. (1997) and Husbands' (1996) sobering research findings: even if objective forms of history cannot be defended, this does not mean any account is acceptable and that a child's opinion trumps the work of experts. This is where Evans' (1997) argument that historical accounts must respect the boundaries of evidence is important. If there is no evidence for a claim, then children should be encouraged to reject it. The inclusion of historical *interpretation* should not mean that anything goes or that all accounts should carry equal weight.

HISTORICAL SIGNIFICANCE AND THE NATIONAL CURRICULUM

Nothing else demonstrates the fact that the revised National Curriculum 2014 includes a well-developed conceptual approach to the past better than the fact that the organising concept of significance, which had not featured in earlier versions of the primary National Curriculum, is now clearly identified within the general aims of historical understanding (outlined in Chapter 2). It can be argued that this addition is probably because it so obviously relates to ideas of grand narrative and the coherent chronological overview of British history. Yet it is arguably even broader than this definition in the sense that Michael Gove was also keen to promote the cultural inheritance from classical periods of history. In this sense, Gove was directly influenced by the historian and philosopher Michael Oakeshott (Oakeshott and Fuller, 1989), who promoted the importance of cultural inheritance and learning the 'best' from the past. Significance can be directly noted in this extract from the list of National Curriculum aims:

> know and understand significant aspects of the history of the wider world: the nature of ancient civilisations; the expansion and dissolution of empires; characteristic features of past non-European societies; achievements and follies of mankind. (DfE, 2013, p. 188)

THEORETICAL PERSPECTIVES

The link between 'significance' and 'interpretation' was outlined in the QCA Key Stage 3 guidance document (QCA, 2007, p. 113) in the form of changing judgements and explanations, hence the introduction of evidence-based contestability. Arguably, significance is a broader concept than this, and is essentially concerned with the developing ability of young people to understand what is worth knowing in history, and how this knowledge can inform and enrich historical understanding. Lee (1991) made a strong case for the place of knowledge-based substantive, first-order, concepts, which he argued acted as a framework for developing an understanding of significance. He associated an understanding of significance with other concepts, such as coherence, dimensionality and the ability to identify connections between different historical events. He later termed this outcome 'historical literacy' (Lee, 2011, pp. 64–9). Significance, in this account, is not simply learning knowledge for its own sake, but is the ability to synthesise content and concepts to develop understanding and to make historical connections.

Thus, although this concept is usually associated with historical learning in Key Stage 3 and above, the idea that some aspects of history are more important and worthy of study is arguably part of the overall idea of interpretation. It is because significance is essentially the ability to understand what is worth knowing in history, and how this knowledge can inform and develop historical understanding, that it should not, as Moore (1982, p. 26) argued in a much discussed example, result in trivial and questionable lines of enquiry such as 'what the Romans wore under their togas'. This is not an unimportant point: if enquiry, evidence-based research and historical interpretations are to stretch children's reasoning skills, particularly in upper Key Stage 2, and given the time constraints in terms of curriculum coverage, then it is important that their investigations are worthwhile and will result in transformative forms of knowledge and understanding.

Additionally, several academics, such as Phillips (2002) and Wrenn (2011), were influenced by Partington's (1980, pp. 112–16) schema, which listed 'importance', 'profundity', 'quantity', 'durability' and 'relevance' as a framework for planning and assessing children's understanding of historical significance. There have also been interesting and useful schemas that were developed by Robert Phillips and Christine Counsell to aid (principally secondary) practitioners in identifying the criteria for coverage and inclusion (see Table 4.1).

Table 4.1 Two schemas defining historical significance

Phillips (2002) GREAT (originally conceived to support World War I)	Counsell (2004) Five Rs
Ground-breaking	Remarkable – at the time and/or since
Remembered	Remembered – it was important at some stage in history within the collective memory of a group or groups
Effects that are far-reaching	Resulted in change – consequences for the future
Affecting the future	Resonant (ripples) – people like to make analogies with it; it is possible to connect with experiences, beliefs or situations across time and space
Terrifying	Revealing – of some other aspect of the past

Although there is not the space to consider these schemas in detail, if we return to Moore's point about triviality, consider what a worthwhile study of the Roman civilisation, such as the occupation of Britain, might include:

- Roman technology and science: practical forms of knowledge compared to the more abstract forms of Greek philosophy;
- The creation and development of the Roman army, and accounting for its unprecedented levels of success;
- Organisational developments, including the road network and settlement (potential for locality studies), sea and trade routes, and the movement of goods and people;
- Art and architectural achievements and their lasting influence on western ideas of aesthetics and beauty (one of Gove's chief concerns);
- Roman beliefs (and adaptations of local customs as well as the adoption and renaming of Greek gods);

- Eminent leaders and the hierarchical nature of Roman society;
- Food, culture and clothing (which potentially might include underwear, since archaeological finds of this nature have been found in Roman settlements);
- The role and status of women and children, including home life and education;
- Reasons for the eventual decline of the Roman Empire (including their withdrawal from the British Isles).

All these ideas can be measured against the schemas outlined above and will probably satisfy each point. All can be phrased as questions for enquiry. All will necessarily involve different accounts and interpretations or demonstrate the variety of ways in which the past can be represented. Finally, a unit of study that contains most of these ideas ought to result in worthwhile and important learning outcomes.

Hunt (2000, pp. 42–4) described the inclusion of significance as working towards an overview of the historical 'big picture', which in turn leads to an understanding of important themes and abstract, substantive concepts (see Chapter 2), such as freedom, equality and slavery. Ultimately, Hunt argued, one of the outcomes of learning history is to understand the actions and motivations of important people from the past, and the ability to make judgements about important episodes in history. Without an understanding of significance, Husbands suggested (1996, p. 133), historical 'knowledge' is reduced to quiz-level platitudes. Admittedly, much of this debate has centred on secondary-aged pupils and, as noted, this concept was previously omitted from the primary history curriculum (DfEE, 1999), but there are several strong arguments for the identification of significance as one of the key organising concepts linked to historical explanation. Given that one of the criticisms of Gove's reforms was the belief that they would result in trivial and uncritical forms of knowledge, the case for considering the role of significance would seem to be an important one.

WHAT IS MEANT BY HISTORIOGRAPHY?

'Historiography' tends to be a term that is often mentioned but infrequently explained or defined. Essentially, it means the work of historians, and how this can and should be distinguished from the past. Clearly, there is a difference between the past as it happened, even though it cannot be directly experienced, and how it has been described by historians. In other words, it is the concept of interpretation at the level of different intellectual traditions or approaches to the past, often identified by shared ideological beliefs. There are several test cases.

Marwick (1981, pp. 248–53) used the example of the English Civil War as a case study of historiography in action. Marwick termed this example a historical controversy, because the interpretations changed and developed over time and and eventually transmogrified into a heated debate along broadly conservative and Marxist lines. The contemporary, seventeenth-century interpretation was of a 'great rebellion': a lengthy process of civil discontent from the reign of Elizabeth I culminating with the autocratic rule of Charles I and increased opposition that resulted in inevitable rebellion. The contemporaneous view explained the discontent as predominately social and economic change and partly religious unrest. Nineteenth-century historians tended to take a more legalistic and liberal view of the conflict, partly based on Victorian ideas of the primacy of individual liberty and law. Thus, for Victorian historians, the 'Puritan revolution' (note – 'revolution' rather than rebellion) was a conflict fought to secure religious and political liberty. Influenced by Karl Marx, twentieth-century historians such as Laurence Stone and Christopher Hill developed an economic interpretation, namely the 'rise of the gentry', and the idea of an 'industrial' revolution underpinning support for political change. This account was challenged by conservative historians such as Hugh Trevor-Roper, who claimed that there was no such broad change or 'revolution'. To the credit of the conservatives, they backed up their claims by conducting detailed, archive-based research. At the very least, it is impossible to present the conflict as the aristocracy lined up on one side and the gentry and nascent middle classes combined on the other side. This simply is not the case, as systematic research has revealed. Indeed, at the level of a household, brothers might end up in opposite camps. Yet one of the greatest misconceptions, addressed by more recent work, is the fact that the 'revolution' was at least as Scottish as it was English, and thus the term 'English Revolution' is misleading both in its emphasis on England rather than Britain and because the term 'revolution' would not have been recognised by the participants in the conflict. This presents an important teaching point introduced by Lévi-Strauss (1963) above: first, it is important to be aware that genuine historical enquiry is highly complex and rarely results in neat and tidy outcomes; and second, that the deeper the research, the more complex and confusing the evidence becomes. One of the teaching arts is to know how to guide children's enquiry and to advise children when it is necessary for them to stop their research before it becomes counterproductive and overly complex.

In terms of English history, onc of the great historiographical traditions was what Butterfield (1957) retrospectively termed the 'Whig' interpretations of English (as opposed to British) history. By this Butterfield meant the rather optimistic and cosy view of the ineluctable rise of democracy and social cohesion in England, thus avoiding the civil wars and revolutions that arose in so many nineteenth-century states. Butterfield argued that the Whig interpretation was a form of teleological reasoning, that is, explaining the present in terms of the events in the past and not allowing that other outcomes were possible. As subsequent forms of social research have argued (for example, Vallance, 2009), England (and Britain) was never quite as far from revolution as the Whig account supposed. Compare this account to the Marxist view of the past. Here the interpretation is one of constant conflict, the domination of the ruling elite and the employment of the power of the state to thwart resistance.

A more nuanced consideration is the use of the term 'revisionism', which can occupy historians of all ideological complexions. This is essentially the idea, going back to Tosh and Lang's (2006) claim (discussed in Chapter 1), that it is the duty of historians to challenge myths and stereotypes. As an illustration, Jeal's biography on Livingstone, cited above (Jeal, 1973), is widely considered to be the first in-depth study to question the status and achievements of Livingstone and his place as one of the most famous and eminent Victorians – indeed, Britons. Jeal later researched Livingstone's contemporary, Henry Morton Stanley (Jeal, 2007), in a publication which attempted to rehabilitate Stanley's reputation. It received roughly equal amounts of praise, for the quality of the research and scholarship, and criticism of the book's overall aims and conclusions. It drew anger from African academics and commentators who viewed it as a justification of a racist individual and colonial system (not least Stanley's role in the development of Belgian colonies in the Congo). It seems fair to conclude that Jeal likes to challenge the received opinion on major historical figures. As a generalisation, most historians seem to adopt a revisionist approach to some degree. Indeed, if there is nothing new to add to the debate, then why contribute more to the literature? Most upper-junior children are capable of understanding this point; they can also understand the second, overriding consideration discussed in this chapter, that the practice of history is fundamentally about enquiry, evidence and challenging received opinion rather than passively accepting cosy stories set in the past.

CHAPTER SUMMARY

- This chapter has considered three of the most important organising (or procedural/ second-order) concepts which require considerable thought and preparation to teach thoroughly.
- The activity of being a historian is essentially based on enquiry, investigation and research. While full historical enquiry is above children's capabilities, the requirement to ask questions about the past and use historical evidence is supported by constructivist theories of learning and pioneering forms of pedagogy from the 1960s onwards.
- Enquiry remains a key element in the National Curriculum for history.
- The way in which historical understanding is contested is principally due to the nature of historical evidence and the way in which data are selected and used.

- Although highly controversial and under-researched, interpretation also remains part of the National Curriculum.
- Significance and what is important in history have now received a fuller place in the primary National Curriculum and are clearly linked with an increased emphasis on important and transformative forms of knowledge.
- All three organising concepts will promote high-level thinking skills if they are introduced thoroughly and are allowed to develop with appropriate activities and resources.
- Above all, children should understand the limits of historical knowledge, but also be able to learn to value the importance of evidence; historical accounts should value the boundaries of evidence, including children's own accounts of the past.

FURTHER READING

Collingwood, R.G. (1939) *An Autobiography*. Oxford: Oxford University Press.

For teachers whose interest has been piqued by the content of this chapter, Collingwood's autobiography is his clearest and most accessible statement on his thoughts on the philosophy of history.

Evans, R.J. (1997) *In Defence of History*. London: Granta Books.

Arguably the wisest account of the work of the academic historian based on professional reflections alongside deep scholarship concerning the main debates within the philosophy of history.

Hunt, M. (2000) Teaching Historical Significance. In J. Arthur and R. Phillips (eds), *Issues in History Teaching*. Abingdon: Routledge, pp. 39–53.

One of the few pieces published on this under-researched aspect of history pedagogy.

McAleavy, T. (2000) Teaching about Interpretations. In J. Arthur and R. Phillips (Eds.), *Issues in Teaching History*. Abingdon: Routledge, pp. 72–82.

This is similarly one of the few short articles outlining the research base and suggesting suitable teaching approaches.

CHAPTER 5

DEVELOPING CHILDREN'S HISTORICAL UNDERSTANDING

What this chapter will cover

This is another challenging chapter, and therefore some practitioners may feel that the early sections on constructivist models of learning and their overlap with idealist forms of history may be safely skipped. The chapter begins with a historical overview of research into children's historical understanding and how a more optimistic, and partially research-based, account has developed. Constructivist models of learning, principally those of Piaget, Bruner and Vygotsky, are introduced. This is followed by the theories of Collingwood and Oakeshott, and how the two quite separate schools of thought may be reconciled through more recent work on the importance of children's imagination, including visualisation. If accepted, these theories have important implications for pedagogy. Examples of how this might work in the classroom are provided, including a detailed example from Anglo-Saxon British history. The final section examines one of the most complex concepts central to historical reasoning, namely the place of causation. Examples linked to the primary curriculum are discussed.

INTRODUCTION

The nature of historical reasoning must be considered because it should underpin any notion of what good practice in primary history should look like. Early research into children's historical reasoning and understanding tended to be based on Piagetian levels, his ontogenetic stage theory of intellectual development (Piaget, 1954), and his equilibrium theory of assimilation and accommodation (Piaget, 1954, pp. 350–7). There were a small number of research projects in the 1960s which tended to support the widespread belief that investigatory forms of history teaching and learning were too challenging for most primary-aged children, and more generally to the belief, mentioned previously, that history was a 'hard' subject. However, generic challenges to Piagetian levels have subsequently been made over many years, particularly the work of Harris (2000), who argued that the greater use of play and imagination allowed young children to attain higher levels of cognitive ability than Piaget allowed. In primary history, West (1986, pp. 17–18) not only questioned the assumption that reasoning and understanding in history were necessarily harder than other disciplines, he also produced evidence from a large-scale four-year study of 7–11-year-old children that suggested that they were capable of highly plausible historical reasoning with the right levels of support and guidance. Booth (1983, 1987), influenced by Fischer's (1970, pp. xv–xvi) model of adductive reasoning, further argued that upper juniors and adolescents were capable of genuine historical thinking if the subject was adapted to include discussion and explanations of how historians construct arguments.

Despite Lee's (1998) claim that research into children's historical understanding has been limited, with much guesswork, there have also been some significant research initiatives, including Lee's own Concepts of History and Teaching Approaches (CHATA) project from the 1990s (Lee et al., 1996a, 1996b, 1997). There have been two main outcomes of recent empirical research: first, the production of several schemas that track children's understanding from early childhood to adolescence, and second, the many research projects that reported the wide span of historical understanding and ability in any average classroom. Early findings for substantial range and overlap included Thornton and Vukelich (1988) and Knight (1989a), while the CHATA project (Lee and Shemilt, 2004) reported a seven-year differential in any average classroom. If accepted, the teaching implications of these consistent findings are significant: a class of older juniors may include some who are operating at secondary levels of understanding, emphasising the importance of both differentiation and appropriate challenge. The principal aim of the CHATA project was to explore concepts of evidence and explanation in children's reasoning between the ages of 7 and 14 (Lee et al., 1996a). The impact of teaching on the acceleration of learning was also explored, and its conclusion, thus further countering earlier research, was that teaching could make a difference, particularly when linked to more explicit teaching and explanation of historical concepts such as causation and change (Lee et al., 1996b). There will be further discussion about the project's findings in Chapter 12.

CONSTRUCTIVIST ACCOUNTS OF LEARNING

In addition to the work of educationalists, it is arguably the theories of social constructivism where the greatest optimism for children's engagement with history can be found. Constructivism may admittedly be described as a 'heterogeneous body of theoretical approaches across different disciplines' (Vianna and Stetsenko, 2006, p. 81), but all approaches have a core belief in the active construction of children's understanding rather than the passive transmission of fixed knowledge into children's deficient minds. Additionally, there have been two very important constructivist pedagogical models to aid educators. The first is Bruner's concept of the 'spiral curriculum' (Bruner, 1960, pp. 52–4), which heavily influenced the History Working Group (DES, 1990). Bruner argued that the 'essential disciplinary concepts' should retain their integrity and should be introduced in honest and accessible ways to children of all ages. The second concept is Vygotsky's 'Zone of Proximal Development' (ZDP) (Vygotsky, 1978, pp. 84–91). Vygotsky argued that a skilled teacher can bridge the gap between a child's potentiality and the actual level of development. The emphasis was strongly based around the mediating role of language and active learning methods. Linked to the latter model is the Vygotskian-influenced concept of 'scaffolding', an approach that involves the modelling and demonstration of ideas and a close working relationship between teacher and learner.

Bruner argued for the central role of enquiry and discussion, and the identification of connections when children are building explanatory accounts (Bruner, 1960, pp. 21–2); indeed, discussion and dialogic talk, as a pedagogical approach, was promoted by Alexander (2004) as one of the key foundations of learning. Language has often been a barrier to children's attainment of historical understanding, partly due to the superficial ordinariness of historical terms, resulting in teachers making assumptions about pupils' understanding of historical language. The outcome is a 'gulf' between transcending the 'now' and 'then' of history and, according to Sampson et al. (1998), there seems to be a strong case for ensuring that children do understand historical terms through teacher exposition and discussion, particularly the words that overlap with common meanings.

Bruner further considered the role of intuition as a valuable intellectual tool (Bruner, 1960, pp. 64–7), and in the case of history, where the past cannot be directly experienced, this would seem to allow for more speculative forms of reasoning, including the importance of imagination and imagery. Given that history is about real people and events in identifiable locations, but separated by the unbridgeable gap of time, it might be supposed that most of historical reasoning is indeed visual in form, but it would be a mistake, as Piaget and Inhelder (1963, pp. 659–60) argued, to reduce imagery solely to visualisation. Perhaps surprisingly, few historians seem to have considered the nature of historical imagination. Stanford (1986, pp. 84–7) discussed the role of 'mental pictures' and the historian's 'picture of the past' as well as being 'eavesdroppers' (aural imagery perhaps?) into past conversations, while Bloch (1954, pp. 49–71) obliquely mentioned the role of mental imagery, but these are notable exceptions. Nevertheless, there are good prima facie reasons for thinking that historical imagery is predominately visual in form.

Egan (1997) has similarly explored the importance of imagery in developing children's understanding, and frequently used examples from history to illustrate his ideas. Influenced by both Collingwood (Egan, 1997, p. 93) and the enlightenment philosopher, Immanuel Kant (Egan, 1997, p. 123), Egan adopted the Kantian argument that true imagination goes beyond the senses, although clearly founded in sensory experience, and he further argued that visual imagery is at the heart of children's developing understanding, particularly in history (Egan, 1992, pp. 115–17). For Egan, such imagery is best developed through the power of the written word, due to the emotional power of words, the scope for originality and ownership, and for 'imagery to incorporate the world' in children's minds (Egan, 1997, p. 60). In this respect, Egan followed Piaget in rejecting teaching approaches that provide children with ready-made images, but this does beg the question as to where and how children develop their starting points for imagination and reasoning? The obvious answer is that Egan was wrong to reject the use of artefacts, illustrations, photographs and films either from the past or about the past, and that these sources are vital in the development of children's burgeoning historical understanding. It also recalls the cliché that a picture is worth a thousand words. It is not unreasonable to infer that professional historians develop their pictures of the past in very similar ways, and that imagery directs their understanding in more efficient, but possibly inchoate, ways. However, it is less certain how such imagery then translates into historical ideas.

IDEALIST ACCOUNTS OF HISTORY

A link between constructivist models of children's learning and the philosophy of history can be found in the work of Collingwood and Michael Oakeshott. Collingwood's account of enquiry and questioning, introduced in Chapter 4, was supplemented by his description of history as ultimately concerned with the recovery of thought. This approach, heavily influenced by Croce (1960), is the best-known aspect of Collingwood's philosophy and the aspect most frequently referred to by educationalists (Hughes-Warrington, 2012). In his *An Autobiography*, Collingwood (1939) described his regular walk past the Albert Memorial in Kensington Gardens and being struck by the ugliness of the monument. Considering this incongruity – in that its designers cannot have purposively intended this effect – Collingwood realised that historical questions required historical answers. He then adopted one of the central tenets of nineteenth-century historicism, the idea of understanding historical periods in their own terms, rather than judging history from a modern perspective, and borrowed from Croce the idea of studying history from 'within itself' allied to a concentration on 'thought' rather than action (Croce, 1960, pp. 117–18). In *The Idea of History* (Collingwood, 1946, p. 213), Collingwood made an important distinction between the 'inside' and 'outside' of events, the latter being the description of the less significant, physical and material aspects of history. He further stated that the historian's aim should be to 'get inside other peoples' heads, looking at their situation through their eyes and thinking for yourself the way in which they tackled it was the right way' (Collingwood, 1939, p. 58).

Only in *An Autobiography* (1939) is the historical method concisely explained. Collingwood defined it according to three propositions. The first is, as outlined above, that the pursuit of history is ultimately about the history of thought or thoughts that have taken place in the past. The second proposition is that 'historical knowledge is the re-enactment in the historian's mind of the thoughts whose history he is studying' (Collingwood, 1939, p. 112). Using the example of Nelson, Collingwood explained how the historian seeking to understand Nelson's decision making at a particular point, to an extent still debated, 'relives' exactly the same thought as Nelson, having undertaken the same mental processes, and at that point. Here Collingwood was absolutely clear: the historian 'is Nelson', thus making a historical thought both contemporary and real, if 'encapsulated' (Collingwood, 1939, pp. 112–13).

This activity is unquestionably a form of construction (or re-construction), but in order that the historian is able to analyse Nelson's thoughts at this point, there has to be a form of separation, or duality. Hence the third proposition: the 'encapsulation of a past thought in a context of present thoughts which by contradicting it, confine it to a plane different from theirs' (Collingwood, 1939, p. 114). Thus, history ultimately becomes a form of 'self-knowledge' because through re-enactment the historian retains a personal memory of the historical event under scrutiny. Throughout all his work, the importance of both enquiry and historical imagination are consistently emphasised. Collingwood also discussed at considerable length the nature of historical reasoning, which he principally defined as both a priori and inferential, based as it is on an incomplete or fragmentary evidence base. Hence the importance of creative and imaginative reasoning to interpolate or bridge the gaps between historical facts, which are also 'constructions' (Collingwood, 1946, p. 243), and sometimes to go 'beyond' the statements in the sources (Collingwood, 1946, pp. 237–41).

Collingwood's ideas on the nature and role of imagination were certainly based on those of Immanuel Kant, particularly the idea of the construction of mental images that are not directly perceived from sensory experience (Collingwood, 1946, pp. 241–2). In a seminal passage, he summarised this form of reasoning as 'a web of imaginative constructions stretched between certain fixed points', namely the facts of history (Collingwood, 1946, p. 242). This statement implies a visual element in historical knowledge and understanding; indeed, Collingwood frequently alluded to the visual nature of history, describing it as the 'historian's picture of the past'

(Collingwood, 1946, p. 243). Collingwood was also concerned to demonstrate that the historian's form of imaginative reasoning could not simply be invention, like the novelist, but had to be based on 'truth' (Collingwood, 1946, p. 246). Thus history should also be a highly self-reflective and critical form of reasoning, and always needs to be verified against historical sources. This was his chief bulwark against accusations that imaginative reasoning was 'arbitrary fancy' (Collingwood, 1946, p. 242), but unquestionably by the end of his life he shared a scepticism with Croce (1960, p. 51) about the possibility of achieving absolute historical knowledge.

There is further support for imaginative forms of historical reasoning from another philosopher of history from the idealist school, Michael Oakeshott. Oakeshott's main contribution to the philosophy of history was his definition of history as an autonomous mode of thought. Oakeshott's libertarian beliefs resulted in his rejection of the deterministic and teleological elements of historicism – in other words, the predictive elements – which he associated with Marxism. In his seminal work, *Experience and its Modes* (1933), Oakeshott negated the Baconian notion of 'objective' history, a separation between history as it happened and the mind of the historian. Instead, he argued that history was a self-contained 'world of ideas' (Oakeshott, 1933, pp. 90–2), and that facts, the basis of historical evidence, are not 'discovered' or 'recaptured', as the empiricists claimed, but instead are 'constructed' in the historian's mind, thus unifying evidence and interpretation of the evidence (Oakeshott, 1933, pp. 93–4). Hence, there cannot be any appeal to external, universal standards (Oakeshott, 1933, pp. 117 and 143).

History was also defined as a 'system of logic' (Oakeshott, 1933, p. 97), which begins with postulates, or ideas, in the historian's mind, thus rejecting any notion of a Lockean 'tabula rasa' or blank slate. The judgements that occur in historical reasoning are manifested through creative processes such as discussion and writing, and in so doing become the historian's experience (Oakeshott, 1933, pp. 98–9). 'Judgment' (sic), the outcome of history, is also based on the organising ability of the historian's mind, and the 'transformation' of evidence into knowledge (Oakeshott, 1933, pp. 95–6). He summarised thus: the creation of history is ultimately 'a world of ideas, the historian's world of ideas' (Oakeshott, 1933, p. 95), and the character of history, the judgement, should account for the relationship between events in the form of limited generalisations (Oakeshott, 1983, pp. 100–2).

HISTORY FROM THE INSIDE: DEVELOPING A THEORY OF MIND

While not directly acknowledging Collingwood's influence, Bruner similarly made a distinction between the 'inside', the 'internal' and the 'intersubjectivity' of historical knowledge (Bruner, 1996, pp. 63–5), and ultimately the development of 'metacognition' and an active engagement with the past that leads to a burgeoning 'theory of mind' (Bruner, 1996, p. 104). The influence of Vygotsky is also evident in Bruner's later publications, where he directly acknowledged the theories of Harris (2000), who in turn drew upon a wide range of influences, and especially on the role of imagination in children's cognitive development. With strongly idealist overtones, Harris described how from a very young age, and corresponding with the development of language, children can engage in coherent and causal forms of play through which they make sense of the world. Particularly important is role play – adopting different personas – which Harris concluded is not only highly imaginative, but also allows children to develop an understanding of other peoples' perspectives. He further argued that through play, children begin to see the world through the eyes of others, 'temporarily setting aside their current reality' (Harris, 2000, p. 54) and further learning to recreate emotional responses that replicate real events. Cooper (1995, pp. 20–1) argued that young children will frequently interpret historical events through spontaneous play, creating their own narrative understanding of what they have experienced, although she was doubtful that this was truly comparable with the historical imagination of professional historians.

Harris was influenced by multidimensional situation models of cognition, and he cited convincing experimental evidence that suggests that mental constructions of accounts of the past are highly imaginative, visual and narrative in form, even to the extent that volunteers' eyeballs were noted to track their reconstructions of 'the mental model of the narrative being described' (Harris, 2000, p. 192). In other words, an individual listening to an account of a story will be recreating the story in their head to the extent that the movement of their eyes mirrors the events they are imagining. This is the crux of Harris's model, and he argued that it is only possible because humans are 'capable, temporarily, of setting current reality to one side and constructing a situationist model pertaining to a different spatio-temporal locus' (Harris, 2000, p. 194), which certainly includes scenarios not directly perceived by the senses. Harris's account appears to resonate with Collingwood's 'history as re-enactment', but whether it is necessarily history from the inside is less certain. One can speculate that Harris's model may include both situations from the inside and from a protagonist's point of view, perhaps directly through their eyes, or alternatively it may be more of a third-person perspective. Two things, however, clearly stand out from Harris's work. The first is the 'theory of mind', or Collingwoodian self-knowledge, which is a necessary part of such constructions and increasingly works towards the adult world, particularly the emotional and psychological perspectives of the protagonist(s). Second is the importance of narrative as both a historical form and a model of learning. There will be a thorough discussion on the role of narrative in the following chapter.

IDEAS FOR TEACHING

As with other philosophical and psychological theories presented in this book, it may be questioned how relevant these debates are for primary practitioners. Although the idea of imaginative constructions has become Collingwood's major contribution to the philosophy of history (Van der Dussen, 1994, pp. xxiv–xxv), understandably many historians have found this method to be unnecessarily reductionist, due to his concentration on thought rather than the more accessible 'outside' events of history. A further criticism was that Collingwood restricted historical enquiry to narrow social and political elites, or that his ideas were simply impossible to achieve (Marwick, 2001, pp. 42–4). Indeed, Marwick became increasingly critical towards what he viewed as Collingwood's dated and limited views of historical enquiry. Yet they are worth recounting, not solely because Collingwood and others directly influenced educationalists and projects such as the History in Education Project (discussed in a research interview with Jon Nichols – see Sheldon, 2009c), but also because of the strong links between constructivism and the idealist view of historical reasoning. This overlap provides a powerful rationale for pedagogy; and if the foundations of teaching are not based on theories of learning, such as social constructivism, as outlined in this chapter, then how strong are the claims of teaching to be a profession?

Second, the ideas in this chapter are complex, and the academic forms of history, as stated throughout this text, are challenging; but so is the work of mathematicians or natural scientists compared to children's understanding and this is rarely presented as an argument for not carrying out mathematical investigations or, for example, carrying out scientific investigations. A final thought: if the above account is an accurate and important representation of historical reasoning, and a strong case has been made that it is, then the main consideration is how to support children's developing imaginative constructions and burgeoning historical understanding. Key questions would include how to expand and develop the range of children's bank of historical imagery, which is likely to be predominately visual for the reasons outlined above. Then to consider the forms of pedagogy that can support the process of external knowledge into imaginative, 'insider' accounts, which have admittedly been under-researched. These are likely to include opportunities for discussion and the exploration of ideas, and opportunities for drama and role play. Let us now have a look at several suggestions on teaching approaches to support historical reasoning.

EVIDENCE AND IMAGERY

John West's research (1981a, 1981b) was among the first to examine where children gain their historical imagery. He concluded that much of it came from informal, out-of-school settings such as television and children's literature. Levstik and Barton (1996), from a North American perspective, drew similar results. Due to the internet and the ability to stream video presentations, not to mention the high-quality illustrations available in most children's history texts, all children should be able to access high-quality and accurate images from the past. Yet teaching points remain: teachers should not assume that this knowledge is evenly spread, for cultural as well as economic reasons; children may still hold misconceptions that need to be explored and challenged; and teachers ought to model the interpretation of imagery and evidence (refer to Chapter 7). Good practice would clearly include providing as many examples of artefacts and illustrations as possible, including developing prominent displays, etc.

HISTORICAL ACCOUNTS TO DEVELOP IMAGINATION

A second way in which children can develop their historical imagination is to listen attentively to narrative accounts (see the next chapter for more details on the use of narrative approaches). Most primary teachers become skilled readers and storytellers. These are the situations when the ideas of Harris and multidimensional situation theory are relevant. Cooper (2007, p. 62) argued that narrative is 'crucial' for stimulating children's imagination, creating a sense of history and evocation to help them fill in the gaps of the past and engaging their interest in the subject.

VISITS AND VISITORS

In terms of gaining evidence, information and a bank of personal imagery, the use of visits and visitors linked to history units is clearly beneficial. Anyone who has experienced actors who adopt the role of figures from history while wearing facsimile costumes will understand the level of interest most children take. For example, the opportunity to understand exactly how a Roman soldier's armour and shield worked in terms of protection, and the costs in terms of weight and lost mobility, cannot easily be gained through text, illustrations or even videos. There is something about direct experience that is simply more memorable and powerful. Similarly, the opportunity to visit historic sites in support of history units is key. Naturally, this is not always possible, but all children should receive the opportunity to research the locality of the school combined with episodes from British history. Most schools will have some local links with Roman, Anglo-Saxon or Viking history, and a county-level museum.

DRAMA AND HOT-SEATING

In terms of allowing children to adopt Collingwood's idea of the 'inside' of history, or the more general cognitive development linked to a theory of mind, the obvious way is to allow children to explore historical ideas through role play, for example 'hot-seating'. A detailed example is provided in Chapter 6. However, any teacher who has attempted hot-seating or 'teacher in role' (Turner-Bisset, 2005) will know that it takes a lot of preparation to develop the character's biography and to anticipate the likely questions. For the purposes of school visits and INSET, I developed the character of a Roman legionary soldier originally from Gaul (see Chapter 6 for more details). It took a lot of research to develop and refine the character. Teaching points will therefore include allowing children time to carry out the research (enquiry and evidence), to test the plausibility of the character, and to develop worthwhile questions and further elaboration. Thus, the mid-point of a history unit will have allowed some prior knowledge to have developed, while allowing time for further development.

WRITTEN OUTCOMES

An obvious link with literacy is to plan for both chronological and factual accounts, or imaginative stories set in the past, which naturally combine historical understanding with writing and compositional skills. Both require different forms of support and draw on different aspects of historical understanding. Factual accounts may allow sequencing and ordering of information, but fictional accounts may reveal more insight and contextual understanding as well as 'insider' perspectives.

SUMMARY DEBATES

The opportunity to carry out debates, probably at the end of a unit of study, allows children a forum in which they can demonstrate their mastery of the period and events studied. Presented below is one detailed example of how 'imaginative' and 'inside' forms of historical reasoning may be approached with lower-junior-aged children (7 to 9 years). It is firmly based on the current requirements for the National Curriculum.

THE LIFE OF AN ANGLO-SAXON GIRL

Let us consider the life of an 8-year-old Anglo-Saxon girl living in an English village in the ninth century. To begin with, such an approach would have to follow initial work explaining aspects of Anglo-Saxon invasion, settlement, language and society. It might even follow work on the 'Heptarchy' (refer to Chapter 9) and the main Anglo-Saxon towns and villages, possibly linked to the locality of the school. It would also be useful for children to know that most Anglo-Saxon society was illiterate and that historians have very few documentary sources (hence terms such as the 'Dark Ages'), and therefore much of the evidence for Anglo-Saxon society has emerged through archaeology. Much of what follows should be developed through enquiry and a range of evidence, including museums and educational visits wherever possible, but the lack of information would justifiably allow children to draw upon their imaginations for some learning outcomes, while not exceeding the limits of plausibility. Using aspects of the school's locality to place this project into an authentic space as well as historical time is also recommended.

FAMILY AND HOME LIFE The first resource for any Anglo-Saxon child would be the family, and given relatively high mortality rates, this might often include extended families or step-parents. Key themes would include the lack of childhood as contemporary children would understand it (since this is a largely twentieth-century invention) and the importance of kinship and family bonds.

Other themes could include clothing (largely woollen and leather), and food, which would be dominated by cereals and vegetables and supplemented by some meat, fish and seasonal fruits. For lower juniors it may come as a surprise to find that fruits and vegetables would only have been available for some of the year. Investigating how foods were preserved would make a strong link with science.

Home would almost certainly be a wooden-framed mud hut. Little archaeology remains from many wooden buildings, but many cooking and storage utensils and metal workings have survived. These give some indications about everyday life.

HER LIKELY ACTIVITIES The importance of children as a resource for the family would be the key theme. Children would work as soon as they were able – as indeed children continue to do in developing countries and did in the UK until comparatively recently – whether tending animals, weeding and watering crops, helping with the harvest and food storage and preparation, etc. As the Sutton Hoo treasure indicates, it would be a mistake to believe that Anglo-Saxons lacked skills and knowledge. While in some respects the Anglo-Saxon times were a regression from Roman levels of organisation, skills like jewellery making and metallurgy were the equal of any earlier time.

WHAT SHE WOULD KNOW The sexual division of labour would emerge quite soon, and girls would be expected to help in the home with cooking, cleaning and clothing. An 8-year-old Anglo-Saxon girl may well have already developed essential skills, such as weaving, dyeing and making clothes. Almost certainly she would be illiterate, along with the rest of her family. Her language would include some words that would be recognised today, but it would essentially be a form of what linguists term 'West-German' languages, and now termed 'Old English'. A link with literacy could be made by studying, in introductory form, a story such as *Beowulf*.

She would probably be brought up in the Christian faith, but there was conflict between Celtic and Roman forms of Christianity, and almost certainly some forms of Anglo-Saxon polytheism, including local forms of worship (Stenton, 1971), such as Woden, spirits and belief in dragons, would have continued. Much of this may seem beyond the ability of lower juniors to understand, but there is an important teaching point about the long traditions of Christian worship in the British Isles. Depending on the locality of the school, there may be a local link with Anglo-Saxon Christianity.

VILLAGE AND TRIBAL LIFE Beyond the family would be the village community. Beyond the sense of kin and family would be the importance of the clan and tribal affiliation. Although this was not as formalised as under the later Norman Feudal system, our Anglo-Saxon girl would not grow up with a modern, liberal sense of individualism and individual rights. There would be obligations to support the local leader, essentially a system of kingships, and to share responsibilities in terms of agriculture, harvesting and protection. Thus, the village would almost certainly encompass the whole of what our Anglo-Saxon girl knew.

LOCALITY Given the exploratory nature of this example, the most open aspect would be to combine a theoretical study with a real example of an Anglo-Saxon settlement. This would depend on the locality of the school, but it would almost certainly fit into one of the teaching and learning inputs on the main Anglo-Saxon regions, the Heptarchy, and the remaining Celtic tribes in Wales, Scotland, Ireland and South-West England. Many English settlements and place names can be traced to this period.

WIDER WORLD For any Anglo-Saxon child the three main influences from the outside world would be the growing influence of Christianity, trade with Europe and (from 793 CE/AD onwards) Viking raids and settlement. Naturally the boundaries of evidence need to be respected, but research could be carried out to discover whether the locality was subject to Viking raids and settlement in the ninth century. Archaeology has suggested that trade links with Europe were previously underestimated, and this seems to hold true for most historical eras.

LEARNING OUTCOMES

Virtually all the examples suggested so far can be viewed as factual and a form of history from the 'outside', but this is probably a necessary foundation for any meaningful 'insider' accounts to emerge. Once the parameters of knowledge have been investigated and discussed, then children can be encouraged to:

- Make plans and diagrams of a likely Anglo-Saxon village;
- Make a model of an Anglo-Saxon village and museum of artefacts;

- Write an account of a day/month/year from the girl's perspective;
- Write a play/drama activity based on the girl's life;
- Take part in a themed Anglo-Saxon day;
- Make comparisons between the life of a child in Anglo-Saxon times and today (similarities and differences).

Another way to view this suggested project is to think of it as a concentric series of rings, working either from the outside inwards or, if an investigation has already been carried out, from the individual outwards, but with a key learning point being the interconnectedness between the individual and community.

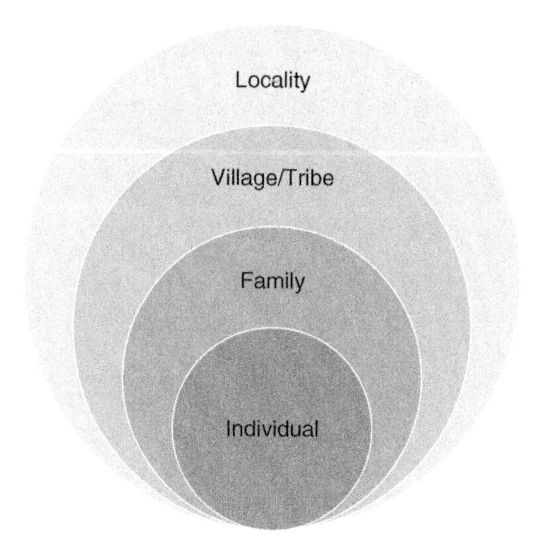

Figure 5.1 An Anglo-Saxon child's sense of place

THE CONTENTIOUS CONCEPT OF EMPATHY

There is a clear overlap between the account of history as the recovery of thought, understanding events from the inside through re-enactment, and the adoption of empathy, essentially viewing history from the perspective of the period under review, as a school-based teaching approach. Indeed, as Portal (1987) and Knight (1989b) explained, the foundations of empathetic reconstructions in classrooms drew very much from idealist approaches to history. Nevertheless, despite the strong argument for empathy based on its clear links with the philosophy of history and the use of historical imagination (Low-Beer, 1989), as a starting point for historical enquiry (May and Williams, 1987) and as a heuristic device that allowed children to engage with ideas such as causation in history (Portal, 1987; Husbands and Pendry, 2000), there was no other aspect of the 'new' approaches to history pedagogy that received so much criticism. The strongest argument was the reasonable point that it required very high levels of expert knowledge for it to become a worthwhile and genuine form of historical reasoning. It is surely significant that the concept of empathy was dropped from the moment discussions around the introduction of the National Curriculum began in the early 1990s. Nevertheless, if supported by reasonably high levels of knowledge, and in the watered-down forms described above, insider perspectives can be considered as a realistic learning outcome. They are also far more likely to engage children's interest in a period of English history that may seem very remote from children's experiences and lack the glamour of more eventful, exciting and perhaps glamorous periods, such as the Roman Empire, or the vivid contrast with more exotic units, such as the Aztec civilisation. In some respects, a case can be made that the greater the contrast, the easier it may be to enter these distinct times. With the Anglo-Saxon idea above, subtleties and nuances would provide the challenge. The activities described above would arguably move children from knowledge to burgeoning forms of historical reasoning, and so could be justified on those grounds alone. Above all, restricting children to a diet of facts in an era desperately short of information would result in a rather thin learning experience.

HISTORICAL EXPLANATION: CAUSE AND EFFECT/CAUSE AND CONSEQUENCE

As noted above, the idea of insider accounts has been linked with higher forms of historical understanding, but the principal organising concept, or pair of concepts, linked to children's engagement with historical explanation has tended to be the idea of causality in history, termed either 'cause and effect' or 'cause and consequence'. However, if the idea of insider viewpoints, historical imagination and theory of mind are considered difficult, then it needs to be stated from the outset that the idea of causality is particularly challenging for historians at any level.

In terms of the National Curriculum, the initial guidance (DES, 1990) was that as children progressed, chronological accounts, reflected in Oakeshott's ideas presented above, would include explanations of historical change, principally ideas such as cause and effect, and the identification of differences between past and present times. The Qualification and Curriculum Authority (QCA) defined the aims of these related concepts as balancing the importance of different causal elements and 'making explanatory links between causes and effects' (QCA, 2007, p. 112) based on established arguments, evidence and contrasting interpretations. In the revised National Curriculum, cause and consequence are presented as a pair of concepts linked to overall understanding and explanation:

> Understand historical concepts such as continuity and change, cause and consequence, similarity, difference and significance, and use them to make connections, draw contrasts, analyse trends, frame historically-valid questions and create their own structured accounts, including written narratives and analyses. (DfE, 2013, pp. 189–90)

However, none of the statements above comes close to accurately reflecting the controversial status of causality in the philosophy of history. In many respects, causality, accounting for reasons why historical events occurred, became one of the main preoccupations of early philosophers. A more ambitious aim, linked to the rise of history as a science of social change, was to identify testable laws of human progress. Most were doomed to failure, not least because, as Popper (1966) argued, there are no circumstances in which the laws of history could be controlled for, or tested, and therefore they could neither be proved nor falsified. Thus the 'laws' of history cannot count as laws in an accurate scientific sense. It is certainly the case that all the attempts to identify laws of historical development in the nineteenth century, which could then be used for prediction, notably those of Georg Hegel and Karl Marx, have been unsuccessful. Thus, determinist and teleological theories of historical processes, including linear or cyclical accounts of historical progress (or regression), particularly under the umbrella term of 'historicism' (Oakeshott, 1983; Evans, 1997; Elton, 2002), have been almost entirely discredited. From a liberal perspective, a powerful critique against determinist accounts was provided by Berlin (1960), who emphasised human agency and free will; and while Nagel (1960) allowed the possibility of determinism, largely on the grounds of propositional logic, his position was motivated more by a desire to prevent limits being placed on future historical developments than a belief that such laws would be identified. The elusive nature of the past, the fragmentary nature of historical evidence, the inclusion of contingency, human agency and the ability to purposefully change outcomes, explain why few contemporary historians hold such ambitious aims.

The fundamental problem, and why a full understanding of causality is probably too difficult for anyone other than academic historians, is that there are no straightforward, mono-causal explanations in history and the development of human society; and, as stated above, absolutely none that can be put to the test since there are no re-runs in history. For the sake of brevity, the point will be illustrated through the use of an extremely simplistic example. Most young people, if asked, would probably explain the cause of the World War II as the result of Germany's aggression, possibly even due to the personality and power of Adolf Hitler. While superficially this may explain quite a lot, a mono-causal explanation of this sort would therefore conclude that had Hitler not been born, the war would have been averted. One might even claim that Hitler's parents were therefore the 'cause' of a war that resulted in 60 million deaths.

Yet this 'explanation' would not account for why one unbalanced individual with oratorical gifts achieved supreme power in a modern industrial society and received support from millions of its citizens. A deeper account would have to explain the economic and political failures of the Weimar Republic, resentment over the terms of the Versailles Treaty of 1919, and the settlement that occurred after the Great War. Therefore, the tensions that existed within Europe prior to World War I would also have to be explored as part of this causal chain, and this would reveal deep-seated resistance towards Britain's dominant position in terms of Empire building and control of the seas. Furthermore, Germany's history of Prussian militarism and antisemitism both had deep roots, which Hitler to a certain extent merely exploited. A.J.P. Taylor's (1961) controversial revisionist account tried to broaden the debate to beyond Germany and Nazism, and though not widely accepted, it certainly sparked a serious debate. Consider the fact that Hitler and Germany had nothing to do with the tensions in the east and Japan's wholly separate wars with China, Britain and the USA. (Incidentally, this is a strong argument against primary schools covering aspects of World War II because of the tendency towards oversimplification.) Furthermore, even if the 'causes' of World War II were identified and agreed upon, this would not necessarily help predict future events.

These were the principal reasons why Oakeshott (1983) argued that history was ultimately a series of *contingent events* which lacked pattern and predictability rather than obeying laws of historical inevitability. Thus, the pursuit of history is simply to understand the past through the operation of reason, with no sense of trying to explain the present in terms of the past, or searching for overarching laws. Indeed, simply establishing a coherent, evidence-based account of the past is challenging enough.

Arguably, the most sophisticated and tenable viewpoint is a structuralist position, adopted by historians such as Braudel and Hobsbawm. While accepting that the identification of causal factors is very complex and virtually impossible to settle, and that the future can in no sense be determined, it would be a mistake to think that absolutely anything could have happened in the past, or that all possible future events are equally likely to happen. Braudel likened the structures that underpin history to envelopes, often geographical and tangible, that often act to resist and shape historical change, imprisoning those subjected to them (Braudel, 1980, pp. 30–2), and that these structures are more readily identified by adopting long timescales, the '*longue durée*', through which structural events might be identified. Braudel further recognised the differing ways in which change is perceived – the pace of the fast-moving micro-history of events and the intermediate-paced, cyclical forms of historical change – but argued that these were often far more transitory and ephemeral, although often more visible, and he likened them to the 'surface disturbances, crests of foam on the tides of history carrying on their strong backs' (translation and summary from Clark, 1985, p. 184). The relationship between the different elements was described as hierarchical, with the structures of the *longue durée* defining the main channels of historical change, and the 'foam' of events and personalities being correspondingly the least important, if the most superficially noticeable.

Ultimately, the Annales School was more concerned with explanation and social realism than with objectivity. To a considerable extent they were successful with this aim, and were certainly highly influential on subsequent historians, not least for the great success of their publications, such as Braudel and Reynolds' (1972) history of the Mediterranean world. A similar position, from a Structuralist-Marxist perspective, was presented by Eric Hobsbawm (1997, pp. 38–41). Hobsbawm argued that historians should aim to identify the 'mechanisms of change' in history, based on the identification of historical 'transformations' and other revolutionary episodes. Evidence of this sort can then aid the historian in assessing the 'potentiality' of future events based on soundly based historical judgements (Hobsbawm, 1997, pp. 209–20).

IMPLICATIONS FOR TEACHING: WALSH AND THE IDEA OF COLLIGATION

Having stated that causality in its fullest sense is too difficult for children to engage with at a meaningful level, in the interests of balance it is important to suggest some approaches to teaching and learning to support coverage of this concept (or pair of concepts if consequence is considered a separate element) with primary-aged children. A further consideration is that the level of research into developing children's understanding of causality is exceptionally underdeveloped. What is also evident, from reviewing the literature, is that this aspect of history has rarely been considered at all in primary schools other than overly simplistic and distorting mono-causal explanations along the lines of the 'A resulted in B models' criticised above.

Intriguingly, however, there is a possible solution that emerges from the philosophy of history. In rejecting the search for causal explanations as a practical mode of thinking (and therefore not true historical thought), Oakeshott preferred to describe the process of historical change as contingent, or conditional, in form. He argued that the practice of history is ultimately concerned with explaining what happened by concentrating on a series of events rather than attempting either 'total' or 'atomised' approaches (Oakeshott, 1983, pp. 65–6), and that the aim of history should be to identify 'significant relationships' between what he termed 'antecedal and 'subsequent' events' (Oakeshott, 1983, p. 76). In summary, Oakeshott argued for the importance of establishing a chronological relationship between significant historical events to support reasoning about the past, possibly in the form of limited generalisations (Oakeshott, 1983, pp. 100–2).

Oakeshott's ideas, which emerged in the 1930s, appear to have influenced the philosopher of history W.H. Walsh (1951), who then adopted the term 'colligation' from the nineteenth-century logician Whewell to account for one form of historical explanation. Walsh described how the first aim of the historian, when asked to provide an explanatory account, 'is to see it as part of such a process, to locate it in its context by mentioning other events with which it is bound up' (1951, pp. 24–5). Further influenced by Oakeshott, Walsh advised against overly deterministic and rule-based accounts, appearing to favour Oakeshott's idea of contingency, hence colligatory accounts of the past should be limited in scope and ambition.

Nevertheless, the idea of colligation had quite a significant impact on history educators, not least the CHATA (Concepts of History and Teaching Approaches) project, for several obvious reasons. The limitations of intellectual scope were not a barrier for those working with children in schools. The most important reason, however, was the extent of the overlap between the idea of colligation and pedagogical techniques such as narrative approaches and timelines. Historical accounts in this view are concerned with seeing the connections between a series of events and understanding how historical outcomes are bound up with a series of earlier events. For example, Rogers (1987) and Hoodless (2002) both argued that narrative accounts help children to identify and understand the causal links, and Cooper (1995) made a case for the importance of chronology in developing children's ideas of cause and consequence in history. Arguably, the greatest influence of Walsh's ideas can be found in the first, and subsequent, iterations of the National Curriculum (DES, 1991a, pp. 3–5) where 'chronology' and 'cause and consequence' were combined.

Here are some suggested teaching ideas:

- Colligation: considering the links between causality and chronology in a more considered way. For example, the timelines included in Chapter 3 would certainly help children to identify Oakeshott's concept of 'antecedal and subsequent' events within a limited range of understanding. The failure to win the Battle of Britain did not 'cause' the Luftwaffe to begin the bombing of British cities, because the Blitz was almost certainly an independent war aim, but the end of one event and the start of a second were unquestionably linked in some way.
- Links with interpretation: Given that a key theme in this book has been the qualified nature of historical knowledge, children could be

encouraged to explore the evidence explanations for events. For example, a common Key Stage 1 unit has been to cover the Great Fire of London, for which there are many contemporary versions of how the fire started. With the beginning of a fire, one might properly talk of a *cause of the fire*, although the explanation for why this event was so destructive, namely the nature of the building materials, the narrow and tightly packed streets, a hot summer and poor firefighting equipment, are arguably more structural. In other words, the source of the fire might have emerged in several places, but still yielded similar results.

- What would you have done? Returning to the theme of history from the inside, a learning outcome that involves children considering the decisions facing people from history and the options they had would be both highly creative and a good example of Collingwood's idea of historical reasoning as a form of self-knowledge.
- What happened next? The use of 'half-stories' and 'event framing' are discussed in the following chapter.
- Counterfactuals: This approach will also be considered in the following chapter, but a brief example would be to account for the demise of the Aztec civilisation after the Spanish invasion. Although the initial spread of European diseases may have been avoided had the Spanish not explored South America, it is inconceivable that European settlers would not have ended up exploring the Americas. This would also count as a good example of Braudel's metaphor of the foam and the waves. Focusing on specific explorers, decisions and events would count as the foam; the fact that Europeans would almost certainly have explored and settled in the Americas, with similar consequences, would be the structure of the waves.
- Exploring deep patterns in exploration, ideas and discovery: One of the truly fascinating aspects of history is how key philosophical, scientific and technological breakthroughs have emerged simultaneously; for example, Isaac Newton and Gottfried Leibniz independently discovering calculus in England and Germany, respectively. Once again, this might be thought of as structural: namely, that human beings faced with similar challenges produce identical solutions. One can also find similar examples in the development of the internal combustion engine, the jet engine and electronic computers. While all of these would count as historical interpretation, they would also be examples of the idea of progress and discoveries that have *caused* some changes in human society.
- Placing more emphasis on the outcomes of historical events, in other words the *consequences/effects*, not least because of their links with the procedural concept of significance (Chapter 4). This was one of Counsell's (2004) arguments in the sense that the identification of

significant events is a retrospective activity, and while all historical events have consequences, it is surely better to encourage pupils to construct their own understanding of why some historical outcomes are more visible, celebrated or debated than others.

CHAPTER SUMMARY

- Social constructivism, especially the work of Bruner, offers a more positive and workable model of how to develop children's understanding, including history.
- This chapter has provided evidence for the importance of imaginative forms of thought, including visualisation, as an important component in many forms of historical reasoning.
- 'Outside' and 'inside' accounts of history are both important, but insider forms of historical reasoning are supported by the ideas of Collingwood, Vygotsky and Harris, and they may support children's overall cognitive development, including developing their 'theory of mind'.
- Cause and effect are troubling concepts within the National Curriculum for history because they do not fully acknowledge the limitations of identifying causes of historical change, but a range of teaching approaches has been suggested, including Walsh's concept of colligation.
- This chapter supports Copeland's (1998, p. 21) claim, introduced in the Introduction, that history is the 'most overtly constructivist subject in the primary curriculum'.

FURTHER READING

Egan, K. (1992) *Imagination in Teaching and Learning*. Abingdon: Routledge.

Kieran Egan is always an engaging writer and this text summarises his arguments for the importance of imagination, including its specific importance for historical understanding.

Harris, P.L. (2000) *The Work of the Imagination*. Oxford: Blackwell

This text summarises the important research into the development of children's imaginations and the role of visualisation.

Oakeshott, M. (1983) *On History and Other Essays*. Indianapolis, IN: Liberty Press.

The main recommendation for Collingwood can be found in Chapter 4. This text is therefore the main recommendation for understanding Oakeshott's contribution to the debate on historical understanding. It is not an easy read, but it does repay careful study.

CHAPTER 6

NARRATIVE, COUNTERFACTUALISM AND CONSTRUCTIVIST LEARNING

What this chapter will cover

This chapter follows on from the themes contained in the previous chapter, including theoretical discussions illustrated with practical examples. It begins with making a case for narrative approaches to history. The limitations of narrative for academic historians are discussed, including postmodern accounts. The educational case for narrative is stronger, not least due to the inclusion of constructivist accounts, particularly the work of Bruner and a reiteration of the importance of developing children's historical imagination and ability to visualise the past. Idealist approaches to history are also discussed again, and here the focus is on developing 'insider' accounts of the past, including a theory of mind. The chapter continues with examples of narrative-based pedagogy, including drama, hot-seating, and the use of powerful stories as a stimulus for 'insider' accounts of the past. It concludes with a discussion about the controversial use of counterfactual approaches in history.

INTRODUCTION

Despite Green and Troup's (1999, p. 204) claim that narrative forms have been perceived as a defining aspect of history writing, many professionals have demonstrated a rather uneasy relationship with narrative forms, possibly fearful of postmodernist accusations that history is little more than unverifiable stories about the past. Yet the links between narrative forms and historical accounts are strong, and as Stone (1987, p. 74) stated, 'historians have always told stories', often using elegant, literary forms. Indeed, Stone made a strong case for the return of narrative form in history after unsuccessful flirtations with social science methodology (Stone, 1987, pp. 74–96). Michael Wood used his 2014 Cockcroft Rutherford Lecture at the University of Manchester to explore his belief that the enduring appeal of his long and successful television career has principally been due to his ability to engage the viewer with historical narratives. Wood commented that 'history is story and we're all story tellers. I've always loved stories and found them fascinating' (Wood, 2014, p. 18). Tosh and Lang (2006, pp. 148–9) made a similar point when they claimed that the great writers of history have generally been skilled at creating 'dramatic and vividly evocative narrative', and perhaps unsurprisingly, other successful popularist historians, such as A.J.P. Taylor (1983) and David Starkey (2005), have also described themselves as essentially storytellers using narrative forms of writing. Tosh and Lang (2006), while acknowledging the limitations and weaknesses of a narrative approach, further argued that to write good history requires high levels of imagination and empathy as well as historical skill; but perhaps understandably, many other professional historians, such as Hobsbawm (1997, p. 284), have been keener on analysis rather than description as the product of history, the latter identified as the principal weakness of many narrative accounts.

There is considerable support for narrative forms of history in the work of Collingwood and Oakeshott introduced in the preceding chapters. Oakeshott (1933, p. 107) emphasised that history was not the same as literature, although it could be narrative in form, and should always be both 'coherent' and clearly based on 'what the evidence obliges us to believe'. In his early essays, Collingwood also had something to say about the importance of narrative and understanding the 'plot' of history (Collingwood, 1925), even going so far as calling history a form of 'extemporised drama', rather than a predetermined plot, thus allowing for the identification of possible causes, albeit with the risk of oversimplification mentioned in the previous chapter, limited generalisations and the possibility of different outcomes (Collingwood, 1925, p. 36).

Hayden White's postmodernist contribution to the narrative debate has been his synthesis of a number of different conceptual frameworks, not least Collingwood's idealist philosophy, and including ideology, epistemology, ethics and literary theory into a persuasive theory based upon a 'quaternary' of key literary devices, termed 'emplotment' or 'tropes', which can be used as an analytical tool with historical literature, and which undermines any notion of objectivity in history. At the heart of White's philosophy is the belief that historians inevitably select, shape and interpret their ideas in the form of their political and philosophical belief systems, which are then manifested in the form of literary devices, represented and transformed by the device of 'emplotment' (White, 1999, pp. 7–10).

In later essays, White (1999, pp. 7–8) did not dispute the reality of the past, or the importance of historical methods and enquiry. Instead, he claimed that any sense of historical truth is inevitably distorted and influenced by both the writer and the literary style adopted – the emplotment or narrative form. Even if not constrained by narrative forms, White also argued that historians are hampered by either too much or too little evidence for the creation of an accurate representation of the past, and that nor is there any 'innocent eye' when it comes to selecting and interpreting data, since both are cognitive acts (White, 1978, pp. 51–4). It seems fair to conclude that narrative approaches remain problematic within the philosophy of history.

RESEARCH FROM EDUCATIONAL PSYCHOLOGY

Narrative modes of teaching and learning have much firmer foundations in educational psychology. Atavistic accounts of the development of human society suggest that it was based on an oral tradition of storytelling and therefore an important part of what it means to be human. Bruner (1996) included narrative in its fullest sense as part of his constructivist model of learning. Narrative forms, he argued, offered an alternative to the logico-mathematical form of reasoning and testability, through offering a 'test of truth', based on verisimilitude, internal cohesion and plausibility (Bruner, 1996, pp. 90–2). Specifically considering the case of history, Bruner further argued that history offered a 'narrative construal of reality' (Bruner, 1996, pp. 143–7), and one that imposed coherence on the past through a 'culturally shared' from of knowledge that rebutted solipsism, given the impossibility of testing historical knowledge, and is strongly reminiscent of Oakeshott's narrative account of history, which does appear to rest on shared and contingent forms of 'truth' and reinforces Evans's (1997) point about the structures of evidence.

Egan (1997) developed these themes even further with his 'recapitulation' account of cultural history and education. Accounting for the development of human understanding from mythic origins to ironic understanding, he argued that very young children should be introduced to mythic accounts that emphasise binary language structures, such as good and evil or heroes and villains, etc., and told through powerful narrative and rhythmic forms (Egan, 1997, pp. 33–70). For older primary-aged children to adolescents, the approach should be based on the romantic mode, with its emphasis on Ancient Greek models of knowledge and understanding, including stories from history, mythology, the life histories of flamboyant and successful people, and significant events (Egan, 1997, pp. 71–103). Romantic understanding was also described as essentially chronological, certainly strongly narrative and story based, and highly emotive and dramatic in style (Egan, 1997, p. 221). He frequently included examples from history to illustrate all his models, and he noted the importance and relevance of highly humanised forms of historical knowledge and understanding, which were strongly underpinned by the power of children's imagination and mental imagery. The educational implications included short bursts of intense enquiry, focused on the topics that cover the 'exotic', 'exciting', and the 'mega' in the true Greek sense of the word (Egan, 1997, pp. 217–20). If Collingwood was critical of the tendency of narrative approaches to cover the weary, foot-slogging marches (Collingwood, 1939, p. 110), in other words the 'outside' of history, then his solution to study the thought and actions of the great men, the decision makers, strongly overlaps with Egan's recapitulation model.

SCHOOL-BASED APPROACHES

Of arguably greater significance for history educators, particularly primary teachers who are not necessarily subject specialists, is the relatively recent rehabilitation of narrative as a pedagogical approach from several educational theorists, including a claim that narrative is one of the main organising concepts of history (Lang, 2003; Levstik and Barton, 2011; Counsell, 2012). Narrative approaches, recommended in early guidance for primary history (Keating and Sheldon, 2011), have also been an implicit aspect of the primary National Curriculum from the beginning. Story and narrative were recommended by Her Majesty's Inspectorate as 'central' to history teaching (DES, 1988a, p. 19), and narrative was implied in many of the Programmes of Study in the first iteration of the National Curriculum, not least those linked to the previously discussed elements of interpretation and chronology alongside coverage of myths and legends (DES, 1991a, p. 13).

Chapter 5 introduced the idea that narrative accounts can help develop children's imagination and imagery associated with the past. It has also been claimed that narrative approaches can support chronological understanding, which helps children to see the 'big picture' of history. This in turn both allows the development of an overview combined with depth, and is linked to the concept of colligation, also introduced in Chapter 5. Grant Bage has been a powerful advocate for narrative approaches to history. He argued that children have a 'natural narrative competence' (Bage, 1999, p. 23), and that part of a teacher's approach should be based on these ancient and fundamental models of learning. According to Hake and Haydn (1995), the drive to find out 'what happened next', due to the forward-looking, chronological nature of narrative, is particularly potent. Furthermore, by using story as a pedagogic approach, Farmer and Cooper (1998) argued that children will develop an increased sense of the teacher's authority, although this requires skill and preparation on behalf of teachers.

Nevertheless, history's uneasy relationship with narrative approaches, introduced at the beginning of this chapter, is not without foundation. Lang (2003) advised that since narrative is a construction, and not a given, children need careful guidance concerning the rules of evidence and plausibility. Similarly, Levstik's (1995) research conclusively demonstrated that children often accepted narrative accounts uncritically, thus requiring teacher interventions and modelling, and the careful selection of a range of texts, while Bage (1999, pp. 88–96), in the interests of balance, produced a concatenation of arguments used against narrative approaches, including the dangers of singularity, oversimplification, propaganda and the blurring of fact and fiction. These are all important reminders that there are several clearly identifiable and genuine weaknesses associated with stories that must be considered if narrative is to be used as a teaching and organising approach to the study of history.

There is also one final consideration, the thorny question of fictional stories set in the past. Understandably distrusted in some quarters, Vass (1992) was an early proponent of adapting a more relaxed approach to the use of story, based on the argument that fiction can still provide children with genuine historical insight and understanding. This theme has been adapted by Hicks and Martin (1997) for context setting, while Little et al. (2007) and Cox and Hughes (1998) have stressed the role of fiction in creating the imagery and mental pictures that could help to create an imaginative grasp of the past. Teachers do need to be careful to introduce such texts as fiction, but it might be argued that the key considerations are the age and maturity of the class. The best historical fiction does reveal certain, possibly deeper, 'truths' about the past, not least insight into the context of the era under review. The chapters outlining the National Curriculum requirements will occasionally include suggested fictional texts to support teaching and learning, but not without the importance of balancing engagement against accuracy. Of course, comparing fictional accounts against historical research would be an excellent method of addressing the concept of historical interpretation.

DRAMA AND HISTORICAL UNDERSTANDING

The use of factual stories has long been advocated by the Early Years specialists, for example Low-Beer and Blyth (1990), but more recently there has been a greater appreciation of story with older children, particularly due to the usefulness of detailed narrative as a way of introducing children to complex ideas (Husbands, 1996, pp. 49–50; Banham, 2000), while still engaging with the evidence in a critical way. The links with drama are both obvious and extensive, and there have been many convincing accounts of the successful use of historical understanding conducted through drama, including Turner-Bisset (2005, pp. 102–5), who argued that it was a method '*par excellence*' for attempting to understand history from the 'inside', firmly based on the available evidence, thus retaining accuracy and criticality. One of the most detailed and convincing accounts was a pioneering research project carried out by John Fines (1980, pp. 3–5), who was working alongside secondary history specialists in a Year 1 class. Based on a topic of 'castles', Fines acted out the role of an incompetent noble, Sir Ralph, who required help preparing his castle for a visit by the king, played by a student whom the children had not met. Fines' conclusion was that the children quickly fell into the story lines and suggested solutions to Sir Ralph's manifold problems.

There have been several drama techniques utilised in history lessons, including 'freeze-frame', 'teacher-in-role' and 'conscience alley', alongside the more typical full re-enactments (Turner-Bisset, 2005; Vass, 2005). 'Teacher in role', including 'hot-seating' (Turner-Bisset, 2005, pp. 103–10), has been widely promoted. As part of my consultancy work with primary schools, I developed the character of a Roman Legionnaire named 'Perseus' to support the 'Invaders' National Curriculum unit (DfEE, 1999, p. 106) (now part of the overall British narrative), which I adopted for a hot-seating role. I typically began in character outlining my history from being born in Gaul, modern-day France, and how I became a Roman Legionnaire after the Roman conquest and occupation of Gaul. I invented an account of my family and early life and then explained how I came to join the XIV Gemina Legion before joining Claudius's invasion of Britannia in AD/CE 43, subsequently settling down to live in Britain. I then described my many battles with Celtic tribes, including our defeat of Boudicca in AD/CE 60, and the creation of a Legionary fortress in modern-day Colchester.

One of the main themes was to explain that few soldiers would have visited Rome and that the Roman Empire was a cultural concept as much as a physical reality. The preparation required a lot of research, thus supporting the idea that imaginative accounts can and should respect the boundaries of evidence, and the account was always strictly chronological in order to retain the integrity of the narrative. The input nearly always acted as a culmination of the history unit, and so children, usually in Years 3 or 4, were often well informed and came with prepared questions. The hot-seating activity usually took between 20 and 30 minutes, but the question-and-answer session often stretched the session to 60 minutes or more, and by remaining in role, it arguably added credibility to my answers. Subsequent revisions added more detail and also a slightly provocative attitude was developed, in which the British weather, food, wine (usually a glass of water was taken so I could pretend to spit it out) and the fighting ability of the British tribes were dismissed. It was noticeable that lower Key Stage 2 children were more than willing to suspend their disbelief and were often defensive when the critiques of aspects of Britain started, particularly the fighting ability of the Celtic tribes. Follow-up letters nearly always focused on my purported dislike of British food and wine.

RESEARCH INTO ENGAGEMENT THROUGH 'POWERFUL STORIES'

The project with trainee primary teachers (Percival, 2017b), which I discuss below, began with the development of powerful stories leading up to the 2016 Olympic Games in Rio de Janeiro. This technique was principally employed in undergraduate sessions, during the second year of a three-year primary Initial Teacher Training course and assessed at undergraduate level. I also conducted several in-school sessions for qualified teachers. Over the years I have used many different examples of powerful stories from history, covering many aspects of the English National Curriculum for history. One story I have developed is based on eyewitness accounts of the Great Fire of London in 1666 (which has long been one of the recommended units for infants in the English National Curriculum); a second has been based on Howard Carter's discovery of Tutankhamun's tomb in 1922 (which dovetails with the Key Stage 2 focus on 'Ancient Civilisations').

However, to coincide with an acknowledgement that many schools spent time on cross-curricular work leading up to the London (2012) and Rio (2016) Olympics, I developed powerful stories linked to the history of the Olympic Games. A case can be made that the history of the Olympic movement (both ancient and modern) offers so many well-known examples of narrative that it is difficult to narrow them down, but to draw out broader themes, including aspects of social history and citizenship, I developed stories that alternated between Jesse Owens at the 1936 Berlin Games and Ron Clarke at the 1968 Mexico City Games. For the purposes of this text, however, we will focus on a narrative that features citizenship and equality themes (gender and sport) and the interplay of enquiry, evidence and interpretation. As a justification of my story choice, and to provide some contextual information, the history of the Olympic Games, both ancient and modern, has been taken far more seriously by academic historians, including dedicated journals. It is therefore a further example of how the dimensions of academic history have broadened, although journalists and amateur historians still provide important contributions. In addition, there are now several online databases where Olympic facts and figures can be accessed, as well as newspaper archives, and so there are opportunities for children to engage directly with the evidence.

The narrative begins with the first modern Olympic Games in Athens in 1896. It was a rather muted affair with only 12 participating nations, including Great Britain (GBR as opposed to the UK in the Olympics), 176 competitors (no female participants), and nine sports. Incidentally, Great Britain remains the only nation to have attended every modern Olympic Games. In the following Games in Paris, in 1900, 23 women competed, but were restricted to 'ladylike' events such as lawn tennis or archery. A breakthrough of a sort was achieved for the VIII Summer Games held in Amsterdam in 1928; this was the first time that women could compete in more athletic events, such as track and field (Jobling, 2006). Nevertheless, restricted to running no further than 800 metres, compared with men running up to the marathon distance, there was great controversy about the final of the women's 800-metre race. The incontrovertible facts are that 28 women entered the event, nine women completed the final (from a probable 11 starters), which was won by Lina Radke-Batschauer in a world record time, and that at least one competitor in the final failed to finish. However, what continues of be researched and debated is the extent to which the press reports reflected the actual events of the 800-metre final. Several newspapers, principally from the USA and the UK, claimed that up to five competitors failed to complete due to exhaustion, and that those who did finish were 'distressed' at the end. There are newspaper reports, accessible from the archives, that clearly state that in the opinion of the male journalists, the 800-metre race was simply too demanding for women, and that running these distances would 'prematurely age' women and would ultimately cause them 'reproductive problems' (English, 2015).

The claim that up to five women failed to finish is contradicted by the official record, and is therefore a good example of evidence limiting what can be legitimately claimed. Furthermore, the film evidence that exists does not support the second claim that most of the finishers collapsed in an exhausted state. At the very least it would seem that male journalists, allowing for the fact that some may not even have witnessed the race, made the accounts fit their preconceptions of female athleticism and proprietary. It also seems to be the case that the International Olympic Committee president, Comte de Baillet-Latour, was deeply opposed to women participating in the Olympics. Both officials and journalists conveniently overlooked the fact that men routinely collapsed from exhaustion at the end of middle-distance races. The official outcome, however, was the ban on women running further than 200 metres at the Olympics until 1960, which seems astonishingly recent. By the 1970s and 1980s, the rise in feminist theory in history and sociology resulted in several researchers tracking down the surviving competitors to get their accounts on record. Much more is now known about the events before, during and after the race, and what is clear is that any shortcomings in terms of the ability of the female competitors to complete the race were due to having been entered for a race that they had never run before and were not adequately prepared to run through specialist training.

A good story requires an ending to complete the narrative arc. The ending of this story was not the alleged failure of women to cope with running half a mile, nor the way it was reported at the time. With the benefit of almost 100 years of hindsight, it is now possible to see the events of 1928 as the *beginning* of a much longer narrative regarding the fight for women to achieve sporting equality. The narrative about the status of women's sport is now probably at the top of arc, with many more battles yet to be fought. What history can inform us about is that men of the interwar period were spectacularly wrong – and the word is used advisedly – about the physical capabilities of women. Table 6.1 compares the male victors from the Amsterdam Games with the current world records (2019) for female competitors. It demonstrates quite clearly that modern female competitors would be very competitive against male athletes from the 1928 Olympic Games.

Table 6.1 Comparison between male victors from the Amsterdam Games with current world records (2019) for female competitors

Male winners – 1928	Female World Record Holders – 2019
100m – Percy Williams (Canada) 10.8	Florence Griffiths-Joyner – 10.49
400m – Ray Barbuti (USA) 47.8	Marita Koch – 47.60
10,000m – Paavo Nurmi (Finland) 30:18.8	Almaz Ayana – 29: 17.45
Marathon – El Ouafi (France) 2:32:57	Mary Keitany – 2:14:04

As Table 6.1 further indicates, the greatest differential in favour of modern female athletes has been in the distance events, and there is convincing biomedical evidence that women's bodies are very well suited to endurance events such as long-distance running, cycling and swimming. The idea that women were not capable of running distances including and beyond 800 metres was demonstrably false.

It is also a powerful lesson in the way in which history is interpreted in different ways, and about how new evidence allows for new perspectives and greater levels of complexity. As indicated, some women did find the event challenging, but this was due to inadequate preparation rather than inherent physical limitations. Indeed, it can be argued that this account is a strong example of the claim made by a number of theorists (Husbands, 1996; Banham, 2000; Hoodless, 2004) for the efficacy of detailed narrative accounts as an effective mode for introducing young children to relatively complex ideas while still engaging with evidence in a critical way. Also, some children may begin to understand why historical events nearly always involve controversy and confusion. A slightly less optimistic tone was adopted by Lang (2003) and Levstik (1995), who argued that children require careful guidance from their teachers concerning the rules of evidence. It seems fair to conclude that narrative approaches in the form of powerful stories may help children *begin* to understand the highly complex organising concept of historical interpretation if teachers choose their stories carefully, understand the some of the complexity surrounding the narrative, and are prepared to introduce some of the contested elements.

Additionally, if teachers do know the narrative elements in all their complexity and detail, and then tell the story well, it supports children's sense of the teacher's authority, described above. As part of my research, I have certainly witnessed teachers who are skilled storytellers engage a class and hold children's attention for extended periods. Indeed, Christine Counsell (2011, pp. 110–20) also made a strong case for the use of historical narrative to engage pupil interest. She further suggested that once pupils' interest has been piqued by powerful stories, this curiosity should then be followed up with effective questioning strategies, also allowing sufficient time for pupil reflection. Therefore, in university seminars, trainee teachers are allowed time to examine some of the evidence for the range of Olympic narratives, and then are challenged to come up with a range of possible questions, lines of future enquiry, and the identification of historical elements and themes they could then use in sessions to direct pupils' follow-up work. Over the last three years, research time has been provided in sessions to enable them to carry out follow-up enquiries using internet-based sources. Perhaps the strongest argument for this approach is that the human aspects of the Olympics, including consideration of moral themes such as equality, social justice and the occasional unfairness of competition, will engage the curiosity of primary-aged pupils far more than will general overviews and accounts of the Olympic movement or specific Olympic Games.

EVENT FRAMING, COUNTERFACTUALS AND THE FURTHER ROLE OF HISTORICAL IMAGINATION

Given the power of history to explore significant and transformative events, it is perhaps not surprising that this has sometimes resulted in speculative forms of reasoning to consider how things may have occurred differently. This has now tended to be termed *counterfactualism*, that is, counter the facts of what really happened (given the limitations of historical knowledge outlined in previous chapters). Overall, historians have tended to be dismissive of this approach. E.H. Carr (1961/2001, pp. 97–8) famously stated that it amounted to little more than 'parlour games' carried out by the 'losers' of history. It is also a form of wishful thinking, as Stone argued, along the lines of 'if my granny had been born with wheels, she'd be a greyhound bus' (Stone, 1987, pp. 26–7). A more philosophical critique was provided by Oakeshott (1933, p. 128), who argued that counterfactualism was a 'practical' form of reasoning which failed to recognise the complexity and intertwined nature of the past and was therefore a 'complete rejection of history'.

However, more recently prominent conservative historians, such as Niall Ferguson (1997) and Andrew Roberts (2004), have employed counterfactual methods as a legitimate approach to academic writing, but with understandably mixed results. The central question, following the debate in the previous chapter, is that while determinist accounts may be rejected, and structuralist accounts limit the potential number of likely outcomes, history is ultimately about recovering the details of what did happen, and this is a sufficient challenge. Furthermore, producing speculative accounts of what might have happened inevitably undermines the status of history as a discipline based on agreed knowledge and methodology, since, as Hobsbawm (1997, p. 307) and Popper (1966) argued, such reasoning cannot be settled by evidence and therefore belongs to the domains of politics and ideology rather than history.

Nevertheless, whatever the limitations of counterfactualism as a form of legitimate historical reasoning, a stronger case can be made in terms of history pedagogy. For primary-aged children, who are clearly not academic historians, there must be a case for exploiting their curiosity and unchecked imagination to construct scenarios to explain how history might have turned out differently. For example, Wrenn (1998), Chapman (2003) and Woodcock (2011) have all argued, admittedly from a Key Stage 3 focus, for the use of 'thought experiments' and 'game approaches', using ideas such as 'Buckaroo' and 'Diamond 9' activities, alongside more cerebral approaches, such as identifying hierarchies of possible causes, and allied to the formal logic of necessary or sufficient causes derived from philosophers such as Evans (1997, pp. 156–8). Vass (2004) has also been an influential advocate of the use of counterfactual narrative approaches in primary schools. Vass argued that considering alternative narrative outcomes can promote children's historical reasoning and judgement by encouraging children to calculate the likelihood of a proposed outcome or event. Thus, Vass's work is also an important reminder of the many references to narrative approaches as an underpinning for developing children's understanding of historical concepts.

Fines (1980, pp. 3–5) was the pioneer of the use of the fictional 'half story' technique to stimulate discussion and create dramatic solutions to historical questions. This involved providing children with the beginning of a historical account and then allowing them to complete it by using a combination of their imagination and burgeoning personal knowledge, thus incorporating their understanding of narrative conventions, while receiving guidance from the teacher about the likelihood of the outcome occurring. Vass, Galloway and Ullathorne (2003) developed the 'half story' approach into something he termed 'event framing', where children would be introduced to the first part of a true story and then invited to outline subsequent events in a series of frames. In this case, he used the story of the government-censored Bethnal Green tube station disaster on 3 March 1943, when an air raid alarm at 8.17pm resulted in the largest British civilian loss of life in World War II, with the death of 173 people alongside 90 serious injuries. Vass introduced the first part of the story then asked the children to outline the subsequent events in six frames from immediately after the sirens sounded up to the present day. The only other information they were given was that it was officially secret until 1973. This story would have fitted strongly into the previous National Curriculum unit entitled 'Britain since the 1930s', which included a focus on the 'home front' during World War II, but in the revised Curriculum it could be incorporated into a 'Theme beyond 1066' (DfE, 2013, p. 191).

Since 2013, I have adapted event framing for both undergraduate and post-graduate primary teacher trainees, using a variety of starting points that would reflect the revised National Curriculum (Percival, 2017b). Recent sessions have included Julius Caesar's first expedition to the British Isles in BC/BCE 55. Most of the text was taken from *History Today* (Cavendish, 2005), which is a more appropriate level for adults. The students are then provided with the following account:

> Julius Caesar organised the assemblage of eighty wooden ships at Boulogne to carry two legions, the VII and the X. Along with auxiliary soldiers he commanded 12,000 men. To the north, in Ambleteuse, the cavalry and horses were to sail separately. The wait for good conditions was not long, and on the 26th of August the army set sail. In the early hours of the morning the white cliffs of Dover came into view. The Celtic warriors were visible and posed a formidable sight. Almost immediately things went badly for the Romans; there was not an obvious place to land, and the cavalry had not been able to set sail. In the afternoon the Roman fleet sailed northwards up the coast of Britain and eventually found a flat shore where they could land. They were not alone, however; the Celts had tracked their movement and had kept pace with the fleet along the shore. (Adapted from Cavendish, 2005)

The question is posed in this form: having landed around modern-day Deal in Kent (the exact location is not known), what do you think happened next? The students then use an event frame (see Table 6.2) – usually six squares, but obviously this can be adapted – to jot down ideas in written or pictorial form to describe how the historical event unfolded. There is clearly a chronological element to this activity in that the participants are required to determine an order, and imagination and speculation are involved to come up with the main ideas.

Table 6.2 Event framing template

26 August, 9 am, BC55 Near Deal, Kent		

Through my experience of using this technique with primary trainees, I have identified several key points and reflections. First, many students, even those with a degree or A-level history, struggle with some of the factual elements. This is not surprising given that history, by definition, includes everything in human civilisation over the last 10,000 years, and the completion of high-level study is no guarantee that specialist knowledge will have been acquired. For primary-aged children, it would seem to be a pointless exercise to carry out without some preparatory work. Vass's projects were generally introduced after the topic had been presented to the children. Second, the principal conclusion was that, as an approach to historical reasoning, it consistently promoted high levels of discussion and engagement as various scenarios were considered, debated and frequently rejected. As a method of stimulating historical reasoning at a high level, it has considerable merit. The final reflection, linking back to narrative theory, is that the story arc must be completed; students consistently wanted to know how close their speculations mirrored the real events. In the case of Caesar's landing, it was not a great success. Having faced several challenging skirmishes, he returned to France, and in his memoirs described the landing, and a second in BC/BCE 54, as a form of reconnaissance. It seems likely that Caesar underestimated the amount of opposition he would face. A century later, in AD/CE 43 (a fact which indicates how long the Roman Empire lasted), Claudius landed with four legions and 20,000 men and successfully established Roman fortress settlements (Salway, 1981), including Colchester, mentioned in my *Perseus* hot-seating activity.

THE OUTCOME OF HISTORY: A CONSTRUCTIVIST ACCOUNT OF HISTORICAL UNDERSTANDING

At this stage it is worth summarising the principal arguments introduced in this book to outline a constructivist account of learning history. The emphasis on Collingwood and Oakeshott has not been accidental. A strong case has been made that their idealist form of history contains similarities with constructivist accounts of children's learning. It should be stated that both Collingwood and Oakeshott were politically conservative, and it would be dangerous to assume that they would be sympathetic to progressive forms of education, but an argument can still be made. In the case of Collingwood, there is clear evidence that his account of history did influence the form of the 'new' history. As noted, following Croce (1960), Collingwood (1946) described the activity of history as ultimately a form of self-knowledge since the recovery of thought was a psychological form of understanding.

In the case of Oakeshott, who wrote extensively on education, and his renown as a political philosopher, more care should be taken when claiming support for constructivist forms of history. Politically, he was an intriguing mix of libertarianism, notably his social and economic beliefs, allied to a conservative disposition and an adherence to cultural traditions. On educational matters, Oakeshott (1972) argued for the primacy of traditional forms of knowledge, children's induction into a shared cultural inheritance, and resistance to educational reform. He was particularly scathing about educational theory, which he felt traduced the craft of teaching. Oakeshott's principal influence on politicians has been his argument for the great cultural inheritance and to focus on knowledge that had endured, hence Michael Gove's reforms, which emphasised 'powerful' and 'traditional forms of knowledge'. However, as a philosopher, Oakeshott only discussed the general aims of education rather than pedagogy, and so there is some intellectual space for manoeuvre.

Oakeshott argued that the outcome of history was 'judgment' (sic); again, a form of self-learning in the sense that this cannot simply be acquired solely through the transmission of knowledge. He wrote that the outcome of history is based on the organising ability of the historian's mind and the 'transformation' of evidence into knowledge (Oakeshott, 1933, pp. 95–6), and that the character of history, the judgement, should account for the relationship between historical events (Oakeshott, 1983, pp. 100–2). He also used the metaphor of musical echoes (1983, p. 127) carried and distorted by the wind to describe the elusive nature of historical reasoning. Oakeshott rejected materialistic metaphors, such as the jigsaw with its missing pieces, in favour of something far more imaginative and visual in form. He repeatedly used the language of imagination and constructivism in describing this process (Oakeshott, 1933, pp. 2–4; 1962, p. 161; 1983, pp. 103–4), and in some respects it does run counter to his educational beliefs. The reconciliation is probably that the importance Oakeshott places on traditional knowledge and cultural inheritance is mediated by his idealist philosophy and his contingent view of human nature. Finally, as an intellectual liberal, he accepted that learning is a mediated activity.

In terms of primary pedagogy, at the very least it would involve the ideas of Egan (1997) and Harris (2000) contained in Chapter 5, including guided discussion, opportunities for role-play, drama, storytelling and narrative accounts (Turner-Bisset, 2005, pp. 69–84), and the development of imaginative reasoning (Husbands, 1996, pp. 54–70). The second aspect would be the central place of enquiry and the importance of historical evidence, including artefacts, visits and the inclusion of historical imagery. It is therefore unsurprising that history educators who have adapted aspects of constructivism in their work have advocated some of these approaches; examples include the use of the raw materials of historical sources and the use of artefacts, discussion and drama. The use of tangible primary evidence helps to tackle one of the great challenges of historical enquiry: the lack of direct experience with the past, which arguably makes historical enquiry necessarily problematic and challenging.

The development of historical imagery, including visualisation, introduced in Chapter 5, has been under-researched by educators. Research into the development of historical imagery includes Blyth (1989, pp. 70–5) and Turner-Bisset (2005, pp. 59–69), both of whom advocated the use of pictures with young children and offered practical advice. Harnett (1993) and Lynn (1993) wrote separately about the same research project, which used images from the past as an assessment exercise with primary-aged children. They concluded that children hold rather uncritical and stereotypical views of the past. Stow and Haydn (2000) cited evidence from their own research that suggested pictures can help children to understand chronology. Of greater interest was the research carried out by Rogers (1984) based on Bruner's (1960, p. 33) 'ikonic' model of understanding. The aim was to carry out transformative, enquiry-based historical reconstructions, predominately using visual materials, with young adolescents. Despite the resistance of some pupils, Rogers concluded that the test and pupil questionnaire results revealed that this approach was both more popular and more academically successful. A further argument was that visual materials alone could result in high levels of conceptualisation, and translation from imagery to conceptual and symbolic notation, a process Bruner had doubted.

Yet the dearth of research into children's historical imagery is surprising for one very good reason: professional historians can be forgiven for assuming that their peers have well-developed imagery of the past derived from a lifetime of exposure to historical evidence, but plainly children are not born with knowledge of either history or images from the past, and therefore if they are to engage with history fully, then this imagery must come from somewhere. West (1986, p. 17) carried out a large-scale survey of children's understanding of the past and determined that 65 per cent of children's knowledge was gained out of school, with television (at 31 per cent) the single most important source, and printed material, including comics, a significant influence. Allowing some latitude regarding the precision of measurement, West's research has the ring of truth about it. If history is only a small proportion of the curriculum in the primary school, then other forms of information including imagery will be important. Therefore, an important role for educators is to ensure that children are challenged to consider the reliability of their imagery of the past.

Let us consider Collingwood's example from Chapter 5 describing the process of re-enactment. If a child was required to consider life on board a nineteenth-century gunboat, employing Collingwood's example, without a notion of what an early wooden fighting ship looked like, or an image of the clothes sailors wore, the sounds and smells of the sea, the noise and confusion of a battle, even knowledge of what gunpowder smells like, how can such an act of re-enactment be truly possible?

The Kantian notion of going beyond the senses implies that the senses have been stimulated in the first place. At the very least children should have to be exposed to sensory information that can be adapted for historical reasoning. If a child has never seen a nineteenth-century gunboat, or even an illustration of one, nor smelled the spray of the ocean or the gunpowder from a firework, etc., it is hard to imagine how far mere words will help children to produce realistic or meaningful imagery of such scenes.

Clearly there is a strong case to be made that children should be exposed to as much physical and visual evidence as possible: artefacts, pictures, photographs, films and television programmes. Better still, they should undertake historical visits and receive visitors for every historical topic studied. Few would dispute that all kinds of historical imagery are important sources of evidence about the past, but what is argued here is that genuine historical reasoning cannot happen without that imagery. Equally, since children's historical reasoning cannot in any sense be based on personal memory, it strongly suggests the importance of narrative as a model of learning and that pedagogical devices such as historical narratives, role-play and dramatic reconstructions within the classroom of historical situations are important, probably vital, stages in the development of children's imaginative reasoning about the past. Thus, the teacher's role in modelling the language of history and guiding discussion can be equally important.

CHAPTER SUMMARY

- Narrative forms of history are controversial within the philosophy of history, and postmodern theories question the validity of written forms of history, but narrative remains one of the main outcomes of historical research.
- Narrative accounts require high levels of imagination, including visualisation, and they are also linked with student engagement and enjoyment.
- Stories set in the past can help children to understand some of the complexity of historical events, thus making links with evidence and interpretation.
- Narrative accounts can be combined with drama and include 'insider' perspectives, such as hot-seating.
- Counterfactualism may be a controversial approach within history, but in adapted forms such as 'event framing', speculative forms of reasoning may help children to engage with historical events and outcomes.
- The overall theme of the book so far is that historical understanding, as the ultimate outcome of primary history pedagogy, can be thought of as a constructivist activity in which children develop their own understanding of the past.

FURTHER READING

Bage, G. (1999) *Narrative Matters: Teaching and Learning History through Story*. London: Falmer.

Although not cited much in this chapter, Bage has been one of the leading researchers and advocates of the use of narrative pedagogy in history. This is his seminal text summarising his research and key suggestions.

Bruner, J. (1996) *The Culture of Education*. Cambridge, MA: Harvard University Press.

Bruner's book is his clearest statement on the nature of children's reasoning, the importance of narrative as a mode of understanding, and the place of history.

Turner-Bisset, R. (2005) *Creative Teaching: History in the Primary Classroom*. London: David Fulton.

Again, although not widely cited, Turner-Bisset's text is one of the most thoughtful and original of the standard primary history texts, and narrative performs an important role in her case for creative approaches to primary history pedagogy.

CHAPTER 7

SOURCES OF HISTORICAL EVIDENCE

What this chapter will cover

The intention in this chapter is to outline some of the research and scholarship conducted to investigate children's use of objects, images, text and educational visits as sources of historical enquiry. The chapter includes detailed examples from my own practice covering the use of objects and paintings. This is also the chapter where more detail is provided about the place of the local study and its links with primary geography.

INTRODUCTION

The proceeding chapters have outlined and deconstructed the principal concepts and form of historical teaching and learning recommended both from research and the philosophy of history contained within the National Curriculum requirements. The aim of this chapter is to suggest the forms and sources of historical evidence that children can profitably access to gain historical knowledge and as an underpinning for investigation and enquiry. To begin with, it may be useful to make a distinction between primary and secondary forms of historical evidence:

- **Primary**: Essentially the raw materials of history, and principally the original documents, images or artefacts. Obvious examples would include census records, newspaper archives and original paintings.
- **Secondary**: Materials, principally written in form, which add at least one layer of subsequent interpretation. Obvious examples would include textbooks and the work of historians and archivists.

In practice, the distinction is not always so clear-cut, and this is one of the reasons that some educators (for example, Shemilt in interview with Sheldon; see Sheldon, 2009a) have argued against explaining this point to primary-aged children. Many ancient manuscripts have been heavily altered, filtered or censored and so have undergone at least one level of analysis or interpretation, and this is often true of official documents. Equally, secondary sources that have become part of the past can act as a form of primary evidence in the sense of historiography, including the problematic term 'historicism', as an example of how the past was formerly interpreted and understood. This may seem a complex point, but returning to the example of motion pictures, a film from the 1950s depicting ancient Rome is now evidence of how some creative people from half a century ago viewed Roman civilisation. Similarly, historical research from the nineteenth century can act as primary evidence for the attitudes of that era as well as providing a secondary source of information in terms of the history content. In short, the distinction is not always easy to maintain, and it probably is not something that primary teachers should be overly concerned about. There is also the question of facsimile artefacts and documents. Since commercial organisations have often produced copies of original Roman and Egyptian objects, for example – and publishers have also reproduced images and texts from the past – arguably, teachers should simply make full use of these resources whenever they are available. The list included in this chapter includes the most suitable forms of evidence that children can both access and understand.

ARTEFACTS AND BUILDINGS

It is perhaps unsurprising that most of the research into children's use of historical evidence has centred on historical artefacts, which can be defined as objects created by people. The reasons are clear enough: objects are tangible and can be scrutinised – and handled, shared and discussed. There is also the question of availability: many schools have built up collections of artefacts over several decades. Local Authorities often maintained collections of artefacts linked to popular history topics that could be borrowed by schools. A strongly related point is the ongoing use of museum support services (Harrison and Woff, 2004; Markland, 2010) both as a source of artefacts and as centres of expertise, principally the availability of museum education officers who are often former teachers. Acquiring interesting and relevant objects can be challenging, and although it can never be an adequate replacement for the tangibility of objects, organisations such as the British Museum have started the process of providing high-quality panoramic images of key objects. Hence a virtual examination of historical objects, using image rotation and zooming in, can now be carried out (www.britishmuseum.org/

research/collection_online/search.aspx). The museum also allows downloads for non-commercial use.

In terms of projects and research, pioneering work with artefacts was carried out by Bamford (1970, pp. 205–14) and West (1978). Bamford was one of the first researchers to develop techniques that utilised deduction and inferential reasoning, based on activities such as the 'mystery wallet'. The wallet has often been extended to the idea of a small suitcase of objects, for example the Nuffield Primary History Project (Fines and Nichol, 1997), and the concept of children acting as a 'history detective'. An example of this approach is included later in this chapter.

Further ideas for practice have been provided by Wright (1996) and Turner-Bisset (2005), who both outlined useful advice and guidance for developing children's close observation skills and their application of prior knowledge to make more informed statements about objects. Other widely recognised aspects of good practice, for example Verrier (2007), include the creation of interactive class museums, often involving play areas.

Let us explore an example of how observational skills and the application of reasoning, described by Turner-Bisset (2005), work in practice. Almost all of my consultancy and teacher education work starts with an object for discussion. Often, I begin with a late Victorian-era lantern. I sometimes set the scene by including a poem, such as 'The Highwayman' by Alfred Noyes, or an excerpt from Dickens, to create the atmosphere of a dark and stormy night in late Victorian Britain. I am mindful that not everyone has necessarily experienced dark, poorly lit conditions, but it is important as a starting point to the observations and analysis – in other words, posing the question of why would someone require a lamp?

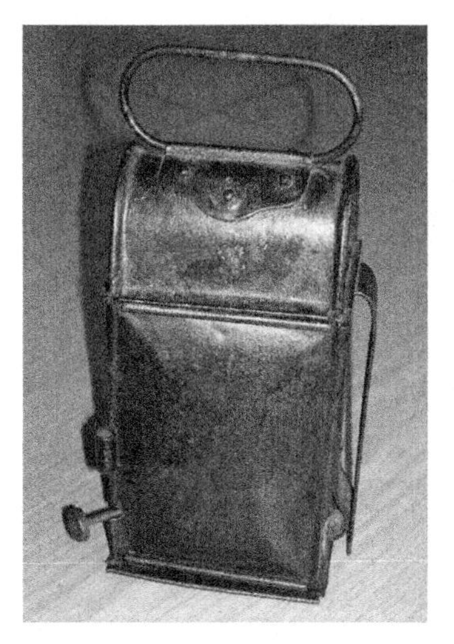
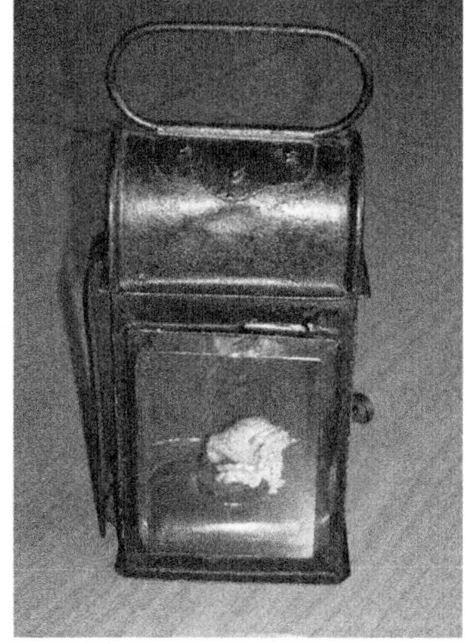

Figure 7.1 Victorian oil lamp

I then rotate the lamp, asking people to contribute any comments they wish to make based on a reasonably close observation. The usual responses begin with these observations and statements:

- It is made of metal and glass;
- It has a handle;
- It contains a wick;
- It has clip on the side;
- It has small round holes at the bottom of each side.

The distinction between knowledge (information one has picked up through life in all sorts of ways) and deductive reasoning ('top-down', logical forms of thinking that result in a series of agreed statements) is not always so clear-cut. While the presence of the handle on the top may be evidence of prior knowledge, understanding that this implies that the lamp is designed to be carried may also be based on personal experience rather than deduction. Nevertheless, after a short observation and discussion several statements can be made with confidence:

- The lamp is comparatively small and its handle indicates that it is designed to be carried.
- We know it is a lamp due to its design – a flame from a wick produces light (and heat) and the light shines through the transparent glass front.
- It is made from common materials such as metal, glass and cloth.

Figure 7.2 Rear of lamp with open back

At this stage, and before I send it around for closer observation and handling, I open out the back (see Figure 7.2), which allows a closer examination of the internal design and the opportunity for more inferential forms of reasoning. For our purposes, inference may be defined as a form of reasoning based on logical principles and involving a certain amount of speculative thinking to produce hypotheses and statements linked to probability (that is, a likelihood of it being true). It is because of the lack of the direct relationship with the past – for example, we cannot go back in time to see the object being made, sold or used – that historical evidence frequently requires inferential forms of reasoning. Furthermore, the lamp provides an opportunity to look at the (literal) gaps in the evidence base, for example missing parts, or to see whether an object is one part of a larger object. In the case of the lamp, by opening the back panel one can view the reservoir that contained a fuel of some sort (so what is this likely to have been?) and to speculate on the strips that are visible on the inside of the panel. Given its position, it is likely to have been adhesive strips that held a reflective surface; indeed, one would expect to find a mirror at the back of modern lamps and torches. Older children normally reach this conclusion with the help of directed comments and opportunities to test out ideas and think, but it often does take time and therefore an important teaching point is to plan guiding questions (for example, what would you find behind the bulb of a torch?). At this point I usually broaden the scope of inferential reasoning by getting children, or trainee teachers, to think about the likely use of purpose of the lamp. These are the points that seem reasonable to make:

- It is crudely made and non-decorative, so it is likely to be associated with outdoor work and employment rather than use in the home – a corollary is that a domestic lamp is likely to have been more decorative.
- Furthermore, a domestic lamp would almost certainly not have a directed and reflected beam.
- It is probably made of tin, or a mouldable alloy, that can easily be worked and shaped. The magnet test would indicate the presence of ferrous metals, which would narrow down some of the possibilities as well as providing another link with science and materials.
- The fact that it has a clip as well as a handle suggests that it was also designed to be both a carriage lamp and a hand-held torch – both uses are linked to work associated with either the night-time or in dark conditions.
- Despite the frequent suggestion of use in a (coal) mine, this is unlikely due to the danger of combustion.

The next stage is to consider how the artefact might act as a starting point for enquiry. This is often the most challenging aspect of all, since there is no obvious reason, other than most children's natural curiosity, for wanting to find out more. My suggestion is that this is the part of planning that teachers need to consider most carefully in the sense of how a line of enquiry might support general learning aims linked to history units. This is less of a consideration for Key Stage 1 colleagues since the learning outcomes for this stage are much broader, but given that the Key Stage 2 topics no longer include the Victorians of Britain since 1930, the opportunities for artefact use need to be carefully considered. This is also probably the point at which to mention the possibility of using facsimile objects, which have been produced for ancient history topics, rather than solely relying on original artefacts.

Having modelled the process with one object, and from experience this can take up to 20 minutes with an enthusiastic class, it is then possible to give pairs, or small groups of children, an object for them to carry out their own interrogation. Rosie Turner-Bisset (2005) produced an interesting idea which she termed the 'Consequences Game', presented in Table 7.1, in which the process of reasoning can be charted. It has been adapted by adding (in brackets) the forms of reasoning covered in each section.

Table 7.1 The Consequences Game (adapted from Turner-Bisset, 2005, p. 36)

The Consequences Game				
Name of object (if known)	**What I definitely know (knowledge, deduction)**	**What I think I know/ hypothesise (inference, speculation)**	**What I need to find out (investigation, enquiry)**	**Where would I find the information? (Sources of historical evidence)**
Object 1 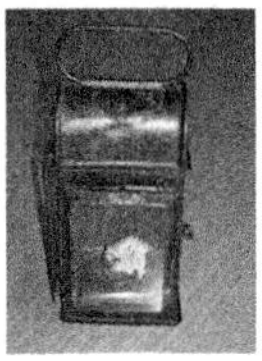	A lamp! Used for providing light in dark places; Made from metal, glass and fabric; Used a flame to produce light; Had a directional beam; Designed to be carried.	Probably linked to work; Could be clipped to an object; Probably quite cheap to make and buy; Probably had a mirror on the back. (This emphasises how inferential reasoning can be linked to probability models.)	What sort of jobs used a hand-held lamp? How bright was the light? How long would it burn? Was it dangerous due to flammable fuel? What type of metal is it made from? (Emphasises links with science.)	Can we visit a museum of industry and work? Are there websites devoted to lamps and Victorian era artefacts? Are there reference books produced by collectors?
Object 2				
Object 3				

Buildings may be superficially considered as a separate category of historical evidence, but in a definitional sense both objects and buildings are human-created artefacts that survive in the present. Thus, the approach in terms of evidence and enquiry, using the same techniques outlined above, can be applied. Nevertheless, there are important differences in terms of opportunities for access and the technical language of design, construction and materials. The obvious way for children to gain access to historical buildings is through school visits, and links with the local study (see below), and supported by careful observations, photographs or drawing activities. Virtually all town centres will have been remodelled in some way, and the trace evidence is often there when one takes the time to look closely.

IMAGES: PAINTINGS, PHOTOGRAPHS AND OTHER IMAGES

According to Hawkes (1996), objects have advantages over illustrations because of their multi-sensory nature, but visual sources of evidence are important and accessible too. West (1978, 1981a, 1981b) used photographs and paintings for most of his research, and he similarly argued that children require careful modelling and teacher instruction for them to extract the maximum amount of information from visual images. West emphasised the careful use of analytical language, particularly for the higher levels of criticality and skill in interpretation, themes later taken up by Harnett (1998), who argued that images are crucial to children's burgeoning concepts of comparison and change. Echoing West's work, Turner-Bisset produced a list of general stages to help children decode images, including scanning, observing, continuous questioning, and finally attempting to 'enter' into the scene.

Replicating the example of the artefact above, I shall attempt to model how I approach the analysis of paintings through a similar activity. The first point to make is that the internet and computer technology have transformed what can be accessed in the classroom. In pre-internet times, teachers would have been restricted to reproductions of paintings in large books, poster reproductions, or even slide copies which could be bought from galleries and shown to a class via a slide projector. Indeed, I personally collected slide reproductions when I visited galleries, and although projecting them on a wall or screen was cumbersome, it did produce a powerful experience. However, thanks to the internet and projects such as the Google 'Art and Culture' project (https://artsandculture.google.com/), it is now possible to project exceptionally high-quality scans in a classroom. The background to this project is that the Google Corporation, ostensibly as an act of philanthropy, asked the major art galleries throughout the world to submit one painting in high resolution. This has now expanded to include many more paintings and, more recently, artefacts. Not all paintings and objects are available in extremely high definition, but the painting I predominately use for both INSET and university sessions – 'The Ambassadors' (1533) by Hans Holbein the Younger, from the National Gallery in London – is scanned to such a high resolution that it is possible to 'zoom in' until individual brush strokes can be observed. It is difficult to overstate just how powerful this tool is, so I would encourage you to follow this link and explore the image before reading on: https://artsandculture.google.com/asset/the-ambassadors/bQEWbLB26MG1LA.

In addition to the decidedly international Google 'Art and Culture' project, there are national and local initiatives to support children's access to art. The National Gallery launched the 'Take One Picture' initiative (www.nationalgallery.org.uk/take-one-picture), which was designed to get children into galleries. After a general tour, they would study one painting in considerable detail, under the direction of museum staff, and then carry out several weeks of cross-curricular work, including history based on resources provided by the gallery. At the local level, museums such as the

Figure 7.3 Hans Holbein the Younger. Jean de Dinteville and Georges de Selve ('The Ambassadors') © The National Gallery, London

Ashmolean in Oxford have adopted their own schemes. In the case of the Ashmolean, the project is called 'Take One' (www.ashmolean.org/take-one) and it similarly offers expert education staff and online resources to aid planning and follow-up work.

Naturally, the opportunity to visit a gallery and to observe a painting first-hand is inevitably more transformative than an online experience, and teachers could always create their own project based on a local gallery. There is, almost always, a history focus, because of the age of the paintings, but as with objects, the links with National Curriculum history units are now harder to make. That stated, a 'Theme beyond 1066' could easily be planned around art and culture or exploration and trade in Tudor times. Indeed, there are few better ways in which this National Curriculum theme might be utilised.

'The Ambassadors' is a justifiably famous painting, one of the undoubted jewels within the National Gallery collection. In size and execution, it cannot fail to impress. It contains so much detail, and so many themes, including several allegories, that it is impossible to cover them all in this brief section. Nevertheless, if you have access to the 'Art and Culture' project and have examined the image, the following lines of enquiry can be investigated:

- While the provenance of the painting is established, the life of Holbein the Younger could be investigated. It also offers an opportunity to research the broader theme on the great flowering of Tudor arts and culture. Unquestionably, the Tudor times represent one of the greatest periods in English (British) history, with creative geniuses in science, music, art and literature.
- The identity of the two ambassadors (on the left, Jean de Dinteville, French ambassador to England in 1533, and on the right, Georges de Selve, Bishop of Lavaur) (www.nationalgallery.org.uk/paintings/hans-holbein-the-younger-the-ambassadors) is generally accepted, but there are counter-claims, so this would be a worthwhile opportunity to cover this aspect of evidence and interpretation.
- Investigating the symbolic aspects, why are the ambassadors painted in front of so many objects? To begin with, what are the objects? What are they meant to represent? Naturally, most upper-junior children can understand that the painting is a form of symbolic representation in which they are demonstrating their worldliness and learning, hence the early globe, the navigational tools, the lute, open music book, and fine clothes. All these can be investigated through further research. In this sense, the purpose of the painting is not so different from the world of Instagram and v-blogging.
- The more allegorical aspects are probably beyond the understanding of most primary-aged children. For example, the broken lute string is thought by some scholars to represent the religious divisions of the time. However, the elongated, anamorphic skull, once it has been

pointed out, fascinates everyone. It is an excellent example of the importance of historical interpretation because its purpose is still debated, but it is generally agreed that Holbein was using a common Tudor motif, the skull, to remind even the wealthiest and most powerful people that they would still face their day of judgement. Holbein was probably also showing off his technical skill because the anamorphic stretching of the skull remains an astonishing accomplishment.

Paintings do offer advantages over photographs in at least two ways. First, even though photography is older than is commonly realised, with photographs dating back to around the 1820s, they clearly do not go back as far in time as human art, which is approximately 30,000 years before the present. Second, art has undergone at least one layer of interpretation through the process of creation and the decision over the subject matter and themes, and therefore there is usually more to observe and discuss. That stated, of course photographs are an excellent and accessible form of historical evidence and should be used whenever possible.

A MOMENT IN TIME

Beyond the obvious development of getting children to ask questions of an image, for example writing around a reproduction of an image (a common activity in geography too), or comparing contrasting images, it is possible to engage children with higher levels of thinking. The Nuffield project (Fines and Nichol, 1997, pp. 128–9) suggested an approach they termed 'entering a picture', which I have entitled 'A moment in time' in my university sessions. The central concepts covered in this activity are essentially related to imagination, empathy and interpretation. It is the idea of the viewer trying to understand the perspective of the person or people within the image.

In the painting in Figure 7.4, 'Work', by one of the celebrated Pre-Raphaelite artists Ford Maddox-Brown from the mid-Victorian era, we can observe several different and subtle (and not so subtle) points Maddox-Brown was trying to make. In essence, the painting is allegorical in purpose and meant to represent work in all its forms during the middle of the nineteenth century. Maddox-Brown was also making a statement about changing Victorian society, including growing urbanisation – the men are laying one of the essential drains that improved sanitation in London and other cities. In other words, it is a 'state of the nation' piece. It would be very difficult to summarise all the references Maddox-Brown was making (guidance for teachers is provided by the Manchester City Art Gallery: http://manchesterartgallery.org/fmb/fmb_2015.html), but most children understand the contrast between the muscular and dynamic 'navvies' in the centre of the painting contrasted with the intellectual middle-class observers to the right, and also the wealthy women of leisure walking

Figure 7.4 'Work' by Ford Maddox-Brown (1852–63) © Manchester Art Gallery, UK/Bridgeman Images

to the left, and the 'idle' unemployed people on the embankment. The responsibilities of the workers are represented by the young girl, presumably a daughter, who is looking after other children, possibly her siblings. The significance of the black armband on the baby in the centre is that their mother has recently died.

Children can be encouraged to 'enter' the painting (or photograph) to consider what came before or after the image, thus creating a narrative account. Alternatively, they can be encouraged to enter one character's world and to develop some form of life story, including hopes and ambitions. For example, with children, I have tended to focus on one of the two middle-class men on the right of the painting. These are some of the questions that have emerged, based on one of these two figures:

- How did the man become wealthy?
- Does he have a job? (The figures are based on real people, Victorian intellectuals carrying out their own necessary and important work, including commenting on social change.)
- Does he have a wife and family? If so, what sort of lives did middle-class woman and children have?
- What sort of house does a wealthy man live in? (The location of the painting – the Mount, Heath Street, Hampstead – can be researched and shown on Google Maps, including evidence of large Victorian houses which still exist.)

- Is the man jealous of the workers? (Possibly for their strength and vitality.)
- Is the man lazy?
- Does he think he is better or more important than the workers?
- Does he feel sorrow or pity towards the young girl looking after the children and baby?

Following the character study and emergence of questions, children can then present their findings in several ways. They can write a character sketch, outlining the life history of their character (real or imaginary). It can be presented as a report rather than prose, and of course it can result in a drama outcome. Equally, the questions can act as a starting point. Many children are likely to be shocked to discover that there was no system of financial support for families other than that provided by charity, usually administered at the local level by churches. Naturally, similar questions can be asked of other figures in the painting, and it would be possible to split the class into teams looking at all the different Victorian characters and social classes represented in this painting. Once again, paintings offer more scope in this respect because of their representative and allegorical origins; it would be virtually impossible to find a photograph from the 1860s which contained so many themes.

VISITS AND VISITORS (ORAL HISTORY)

According to Blyth (1989) and Bage (1999), oral history was taken more seriously by educators once it started to be taken more seriously by professional historians. Certainly, as Redfern (1998) argued, pioneering oral history work has encouraged many primary schools to invite visitors in to supplement other forms of information, and to consider memory as a form of evidence. However, Vass (1993) and Loader (1993) identified the importance of preparing children by critically evaluating the usefulness of children's questions, and then rehearsing interview techniques to ensure that potentially worthwhile evidence and historical insight will not be lost. The timing of visitors is important too, with early visits unlikely to be fully exploited due to the children's lack of knowledge when preparing questions, while the end of a unit of work will result in a lack of time to carry out follow-up research and activities.

DOCUMENTS AND ARCHIVES

Given that this book began with a definition of history as an archive-based discipline, there is a general agreement that text-based historical sources pose significant challenges for primary-aged children, particularly those below upper Key Stage 2 (Cooper, 1995, p. 99). Understandably, therefore, written sources have proved less popular with teachers. Nevertheless, educators have taken up the challenge. Bamford (1970) and West (1978) were early pioneers in the use of written sources of evidence, with admittedly variable results. West's four-year study with 7–11-year old children did at least demonstrate that older primary-aged children could carry out meaningful forms of deductive reasoning and questioning strategies when introduced to written forms of evidence. Low-Beer and Blyth (1990) argued that written evidence is more successfully introduced as a whole-class activity, with the teacher modelling their interpretation and decoding, rather than as independent work.

Another strategy has been to use more accessible forms of evidence, and with younger children a certain amount of creativity can be adopted in their selection. Cooper (1995, p. 104), Low-Beer and Blyth (1990) and Blyth and Hughes (1997) have all produced extensive lists of possible sources, including street signs, advertising logos and children's own historical documents, such as birth-cards, alongside the more traditional sources, such as school log books and Parish, church and census records. Other suggestions have included newspapers (Adams, 1998), advertisements (Blyth and Hughes, 1997) and political cartoons (Card, 2010) as more accessible sources of historical evidence for twentieth-century history themes. Maps are another source of historical evidence, although less frequently cited by primary educators. Blyth (1989) discussed a case study of a project on Chester, based on map work, that she claimed produced a powerful sense of historical evocation and stimulus for further lines of enquiry.

Examples of the successful use of written evidence include Smith and Holden's (1994) work. They used discussion and group work to allow mutual peer support, and they also used teacher intervention to scaffold children's thinking. More recently, Nichol (2010) has refined analytical approaches in the classroom to include techniques such as 'codebreaker'. This approach helps children to categorise the content into categories such as form, voice and context, and it aims to skilfully link information and historical interpretation.

Fines and Nichol's (1997) long-term Nuffield History Project between 1991 and 1999 led to successful work outcomes and useful guidance for teachers, which was further adapted by Turner-Bisset (2005, p. 48). A summary of the key recommendations is summarised below:

WHOLE-CLASS WORK

- Read the whole document with children following the text;
- Whole-class modelling and teaching of the interpretive process.

INDIVIDUAL WORK

- Encourage rapid text scanning to facilitate an initial overall understanding;

- Ask for repeated scanning of text to deepen understanding;
- Provide differentiated/graded texts to match reading and cognition;
- Ask children to pick out key words and phrases;
- Ask children for a summary of the text under review;
- Praise and reward children at every stage.

(Adapted from Fines and Nichol, 1997, p. 83; Turner-Bisset, 2005, p. 48)

BECOMING A HISTORY DETECTIVE

The idea of using a suitcase as a starting point for an investigation featuring several objects, images and text has a long provenance; an early idea was to use an old chest as part of an introduction to evidence, and it was subsequently promoted by the Nuffield History Project (Fines and Nichol, 1997, pp. 154–5) as part of a chapter centred on children acting as 'history detectives' analysing historical evidence. In many respects the suggestions for using questioning and reasoning overlap with the discussion on artefacts, written sources and images, but there are important differences. First, the concepts of detection and reasoning are amplified when they are linked to one person or family, and when based on several forms of evidence rather than a solitary object or image. Second, the potential for independent work in pairs or small groups is also greater given the clearer rationale along these lines: 'Here is a suitcase. Like real detectives, can you find out something about the owner of the suitcase based on the objects and evidence contained within it?' (Figure 7.5). Most children will be motivated when faced with this sort of challenge. Indeed, this is exactly what the Nuffield History Project reported, but it would be unwise to think that this will be true for all children.

Over the years, as part of my university and consultancy work, I have developed such an activity with primary trainees and teachers. Based on genuine objects and archives that are associated with my maternal grandfather, although I rarely reveal this to the participants, I ask them to reconstruct the life of the mystery person and to identify key facts based on deductive and inferential forms of reasoning.

The evidence varies from year to year, and understandably I tend to withhold the most personal and valuable items, but it usually includes:

- Photocopies of birth, marriage and death certificates;
- Birth certificates for two children;
- A railway map from the 1930s;
- A souvenir brochure from the opening of the Altrincham to Manchester electric railway in 1931;
- A Stanley Gibbons colour chart to classify postage stamps;
- Cigarette cards;
- A souvenir collection of pre-decimal coins;

Figure 7.5 Mystery person activity

- A set of unpacked World War II medals which indicate that the owner fought in Normandy in 1944–1945;
- A *Smiths Astral* retirement watch from 1969, indicating that the owner retired from British Railways after 43 years' service;
- Several instruction books for learning Welsh and French;
- A passport stamp for entering the Pyrenean Principality of Andorra;
- Photographic travel diaries, including a trip to the Pyrenees in 1951 to visit Andorra.

During this activity I usually expect student teachers to have worked out a reasonably accurate timeline, and that the owner of the objects lived in the Manchester area. The evidence of his marriage and children is not always fully understood, despite the official documents, and although most work out that my grandfather was a smoker, worked on the railways, fought in World War II and was interested in travel, languages and collecting things, it is very rare that a team of students will infer that my grandfather collected stamps from Andorra.

My further experience of using this activity over many years is that most trainee teachers understand the relevance of their task, and most enjoy it. However, a sizeable minority do not seem to engage with the task and are reluctant participants. My other main reflection is that teachers have found it a challenging activity to complete, albeit they are not given much time in university sessions or INSET. What seems obvious to an insider – that is, the life of my own grandfather – is not obvious to someone presented with decontextualised evidence. There is an important teaching point here: it suggests that to use this activity successfully with children, a considerable amount of preparation time and teacher modelling of the evidence is required, and possibly more than the Nuffield authors admitted. Once again, the challenge of constructing history from evidence should not be underestimated.

Before any objection is made about the appropriateness of some of the evidence, I should state that I designed the task for adults, and of course I would not suggest using and presenting death certificates even with upper Key Stage 2 children. However, the evidence and context can be adapted for children throughout the primary school. Some practitioners have used a random series of objects to allow children to use their imagination as much as the interrogation of evidence in the creation of an imaginary historical character. Equally, the objects could be based on a literary figure, thus developing links with English. Here the emphasis would be on 'character' rather than evidence, but the principles of imagination and reasoning are reasonably similar. It would also be possible to model some of the initial reasoning and evidence, and then use teams of children to look at different aspects of the person's life. It should also be reiterated that the links with the revised curriculum are harder to make in Key Stage 2 and so links with a local history project or literacy work may be the main rationale for inclusion. I would argue that the suitcase activity can be justified on the grounds that it develops children's overall cognition and reasoning skills rather than solely relating to the history curriculum.

FIELD WORK AND THE 'LOCAL STUDY' UNIT

One way in which the discussion of historical sources of evidence can be pulled together is to consider the place of educational visits, out-of-school learning and the importance of the 'locality' or 'local study' as a way of immersing children in evidence and enquiry. Arguably, the *local study* is one of the most significant aspects of primary history – indeed, the whole of the humanities – because of its potential for evidence-based investigations in a context that is both accessible and understandable to children of all ages, as well as its potential to combine a number of subjects in a justifiable and workable way.

The local study is now a firmly established part of the primary curriculum, enshrined as it is as one of the history study units, and a rich source of accessible and understandable historical evidence and impetus for further enquiry (Griffin and Eddershaw, 1996; Dixon and Hales, 2014). However, initially it was a radical departure for educators and schools to explore the immediate locality of the school as a source of historical enquiry and evidence, and partly a reflection of the burgeoning rise in status of local history in universities. It is therefore another strong example of school-based history reflecting some of the disciplinary changes taking place within university departments.

In terms of National Curriculum coverage, in the first iteration (DES, 1991b, p. 36) the local area was meant to be studied as part of geography in both Key Stages, with Key Stage 2-level working including the possibility of carrying out high levels of economic and communication analysis (such as transport, land use and buildings) alongside map work. For history, there was less emphasis, but the unit 'based on local history' was one of the supplementary study units (DES, 1991a, p. 31). It recommended themes such as education and religion, and was aimed to support learning in other British units, such as examples of Roman settlements or industrial change. Two things can be stated from these beginnings: the slightly greater prominence of local studies in geography, although naturally schools tended to combine both subjects in one Key Stage 2 topic, and the identification of themes that could support broader historical knowledge. The revised National Curriculum (DfE, 1995, p. 76) retained 'Local History' as one of the Key Stage 2 study units. In the National Curriculum 2000 (DfEE, 1999, pp. 104–5), there were elements of local history in Key Stage 1, and the requirement to carry out a 'Local History Study' unit in Key Stage 2 with the inclusion of nationally significant events and individuals where appropriate. Place studies, including the locality of the school, were increasingly emphasised in geography too.

As stated in Chapter 2, despite fears that the local study would be lost in the revised National Curriculum for Key Stage 2, it has been retained for both geography and history. The Key Stage 2 section entitled *A Local Study Unit* (DfE, 2013, p. 191) contains many of the elements included in the previous iterations. It suggests that children carry out:

> A depth study linked to one of the British areas of study listed above;
>
> A study over time tracing how several aspects of national history are reflected in the locality (this can go beyond 1066);
>
> A study of an aspect of history or a site dating from a period beyond 1066 that is significant in the locality.

The scope is wide, but with greater links to the overall narrative of British history, and of course it is not realistic to expect that children cover all these dimensions.

The key opportunities for history include coverage of many of the elements outlined in this chapter. There is the possibility of visiting locally interesting buildings, museums and places of worship and involving people from the community around the school. It is also a clear opportunity to look at historical documents that junior-aged children should be able to access without too much support, such as significant buildings, school logbooks, church records and historical maps, etc. The latter is an example of the clear overlap with geography in that mapping skills and geographical processes, such as patterns of settlement, economic activity and transport links, are also a clear form of historical evidence and reasoning.

I have occasionally heard complaints from primary practitioners that the locality of their school is uninteresting and not worthy of an in-depth study. Of course, not all localities are equal in terms of the length of settlement and links with important events or interesting residents. Equally, it can also be the case that not enough research has been conducted to find the engaging and important themes. For example, the Cheshire village I grew up in can superficially appear to be an unpromising series of farms, without even an obvious village centre or green, one public house on the outskirts, and latterly not even a shop; but deeper research reveals several important historical and geographical themes, presented here in roughly time order:

- Evidence of fossilised sandstone containing ripples, which can be found in several locations, demonstrating that Cheshire was once part of a seabed (hence the salt deposits which remains an important Cheshire industry);
- Two large granite boulders, technically termed 'glacial erratics', placed outside the village church, which act as a physical reminder that the village was at the edge of the last ice sheet to cover northern England circa 11,500 years ago;
- The location of a Roman road linking Chester and Manchester;
- Archaeological evidence of Saxon settlement and burials;
- A small mention in the Norman Doomsday book;
- The remains of a huge oak tree which was reputed to be roughly 1,000 years old;
- Two feudal families who had large houses and estates, and with similar names, although only very distantly related;
- An extant sixteenth-century chapel;
- A late nineteenth-century neo-Tudor church constructed after the previous building was destroyed by fire;
- A state primary school which can trace its origins as a 'British' school (i.e., Church of England organised and managed) from at least 1833 (thus right at the beginning of state-funded education in England and Wales), which later became a Voluntary Controlled (C of E) elementary school in the late Victorian period after the 1870 Forster Act;
- The building of a large army camp in the 1940s, traces of which can still be found, and on the very outskirts of the village the vestiges of a 1940s airfield which was used for pilot training;
- The sale of estate lands for the construction of a modern commuter village in the 1960s;

- The creation of a 'County' primary school when a new school building was opened in 1967;
- Conversion of farmland into a golf course in the 1990s;
- Industries such as dairy farming, tree plantations, market gardening and a locally well-known garden centre;
- At the northern edge of the village, the location of the M56 motorway was constructed between 1972 and 1975, with the constructors, McGregor, using the old brick yard as their main base for surveyors and managers, etc.;
- Several famous residents, including Robert Moffat (who worked as a gardener in one of the estates), Sir Garfield Sobers and many other sporting and television celebrities;
- The village is part of the proposed location of the northern part of HS2 – thus having a connection to a nationally important transport and environmental debate.

This appears to be an impressive list of events and connections, and I would argue that the most obvious key themes would be 'change and continuity' (including an environmental focus), and 'communication/transport links' (including extensive map work reflecting the position of the village near two major cities). This example also demonstrates how the locality of the school will almost certainly reflect some of the key themes of the overview of British history. In this example, there are clear links with the end of glaciation, Roman conquest, and later Saxon invasion and settlement.

SECONDARY SOURCES

It may be the case that historians create knowledge, and to some extent, like science, educators would prefer children to develop their own historical knowledge, but it would arguably be naïve and errant to suppose that there is no place for secondary sources of historical information. It is also arguable that children now have access to more and better forms of publications than at any time previously. Older texts, such as the 1950s and 1960s Ladybird publications, still have their place, not least for the wonderful illustrations. As discussed in Chapter 4 on interpretation, they can also be useful as examples of how the received view of the past has changed, by contrasting the very British view of the world with more nuanced accounts.

As Scanlon and Buckingham (2002) indicated, more recently there has been a trend in children's history publishing to focus on entertainment as well as sophisticated educational themes. Scanlon (2011) further argued that part of the success of the more contemporary success of children's literature has been the exploitation of horror and humour, which has unquestionably been popular with children. The best contemporary example is the success of Terry Deary's *Horrible Histories* series, which has been published since 1993 and achieved wide acclaim and millions of sales (Preston, 2013). Although the illustrations in Deary's series, and the comparable Tony Robinson's children's history series (Standford, 2012), are relatively crude line drawings, since 2001 *Horrible Histories* has been filmed by the BBC with high production values and almost consistent repeats on the CBBC channel. The very high standard of illustrations and photographs in publications such as the Dorling Kindersley 'Eyewitness' series (Scanlon and Buckingham, 2002, p. 145) has also been acknowledged.

One new source for historical knowledge and imagery that is just beginning to be considered is the place of the internet and the ability for many primary-aged children to conduct their own historical enquiries, including access to an almost incalculable amount of historical information, incorporating images, photographs and film. However, while there are accurate and worthy sites, including the art galleries and museums already cited, and publicly funded bodies such as the BBC, whose websites for both schools and history form part of the requirements of their charter (as outlined in Chapter 3), there is the danger of the unregulated blogosphere. The fact that internet search engines' algorithms are more attuned to high-volume traffic and popularity rather than reliability is also a very real problem. Google, Yahoo and Bing are just as likely to direct children to a lone blogger regurgitating content from other bloggers as to a reliable source, such as the British Museum. This can be thought of as a teaching opportunity by encouraging children to reflect on understanding the origins and intentions of internet-based sources.

CHAPTER SUMMARY

- The distinction between primary and secondary sources should be understood, but it is not a significant consideration.
- The most accessible forms of historical evidence can be found with historical artefacts, including buildings, and paintings and other historical imagery.
- Although these are more accessible, they still need to be carefully introduced and modelled through close observations and the application of reasoning.
- The use of historical texts (archives) is more problematic and needs careful consideration and very clear modelling if used.
- Evidence should always be linked to enquiry and the interrogation of evidence to answer questions. Employing terms such as 'history detective' is a useful reminder that enquiry should attempt to answer questions about the past.
- The use of high-resolution scans of paintings and objects should be exploited to help bring historical evidence that was previously inaccessible into the classroom.
- The greatest opportunity for the application of enquiry and evidence, not to mention clear links with geography and active forms of learning, is through the local study.

FURTHER READING

Blyth, J. and Hughes, P. (1997) *Using Written Sources in Primary History*. London: Hodder & Stoughton.

Although now quite dated, there has not been a better or more thorough book highlighting the opportunities and challenges of working with original sources with primary-aged children.

Dixon, L. and Hales, A. (2014) *Bringing History Alive through Local People and Places: A Guide for Primary School Teachers*. Abingdon: Routledge.

Similarly, this text is the most comprehensive account of the use of the locality of the school to support primary history research and understanding.

Fines, J. and Nichol, J. (eds) (1997) *Teaching Primary History – Nuffield Primary History Project*. Oxford: Heinemann Educational.

Although now over 20 years old and dated in some respects, this text is based on an extensive research project and contains several key ideas and teaching approaches which have profoundly influenced primary pedagogy.

CHAPTER 8

KEY STAGE 1 HISTORY

What this chapter will cover

The aim of this chapter is to summarise the very earliest requirements for the study of history in the Early Years Curriculum. The Key Stage 1 curriculum is introduced in a progressive and systematic way from Year 1 onwards, beginning with thematic topics that contain historical elements, planning around a story with historical links, and on to the more detailed and systematic approaches based on key people and events from the past. Reasonably detailed examples are provided. The importance of enquiry, historical evidence and historical forms of reasoning are reiterated.

INTRODUCTION

For many Early Years and Key Stage 1 practitioners, it may be argued that the theoretical and philosophical sections of this book have little relevance. However, one the fascinating aspects of the National Curriculum was the aforementioned influence of Jerome Bruner, notably his concept of the spiral curriculum (Bruner, 1960, p. 52), in which he argued that the core structural and disciplinary concepts associated with each curriculum subject (he cited history relatively frequently in this respect) should be introduced to children at the start of their formal education and then returned to at increasingly sophisticated levels throughout their education. Chapter 2 introduced the argument that Bruner's influence can be found in diagrams of curriculum spirals in the working documents as well as in the identification of 'Statements of Attainment' for each subject. They then followed Black's 10-point National Curriculum levels schema (Sheldon, 2011, p. 6), through which children were assessed against the same elements from Key Stages 1 to 4. Bruner's famous and contentious claim was that 'the foundation of any subject can be taught to anybody at any age in some form' (1960, p. 12). If accepted, this suggests that the most capable teachers ought to be working in the Early Years because they have the intellectual and pedagogical challenge of making concepts understandable to the youngest children. What is indisputable, whether due to the influence of Bruner or not, is that the key concepts and skills of history are virtually identical in both Key Stages, and this is still reflected in the revised curriculum.

It may also be argued (as outlined in Chapter 2) that since the Key Stage 1 curriculum has changed very little, a fresh perspective is not really required. Nevertheless, despite the minimal changes in the revised National Curriculum 2014 it will still be new to many Key Stage 1 practitioners, and thus requires a detailed introduction with examples. It will also be useful for lower Key Stage 2 teachers to have some idea of previous coverage. Furthermore, many professionals will move between the two Key Stages and so the idea of a specialist infant teacher is arguably less prevalent than it used to be.

THE EARLY YEARS FOUNDATION CURRICULUM

For the sake of completion, a short introduction to historical elements in the most recent iteration of the Early Years Foundation (EFYS) curriculum (DfE, 2017) is required to provide a context of what follows in Key Stage 1. This is essentially taken from the area of study entitled *Knowledge and Understanding of the World* (DfE, 2017, p. 12) and can be approximately summarised under the following three points:

- Look closely at similarities, differences, patterns and change;
- Find out about the past and present events in their own lives, and those of their families and other people they know;
- Begin to know about their own cultures and beliefs and those of other people.

The suggestion of looking for similarities, differences and patterns might be conducted through the main ideas outlined in Chapters 3 and 7 of this book, such as an examination of historical artefacts or images, ideally through objects that very young children can relate to, such as clothes and household objects. Comparing old and modern objects is an obvious activity.

Similarly, the opportunity to carry out an enquiry into their own lives, and those of their families, would allow parents, grandparents and the wider family to discuss significant events and to establish some of the language of time. As stated in Chapter 3 on chronology, one of the key learning goals is to establish the language of time, including the oft-confused prepositions. However, these are very embryonic and early stages of understanding the concept of time and antecedent events, let alone historical time, and practitioners should be realistic about what can be achieved.

KEY STAGE 1 CURRICULUM

Chapter 2 introduced the revised curriculum for Key Stage 1, presented here in Table 8.1. The addition of numbers is to create a useful checklist for teachers, which can aid planning and assessment.

Table 8.1 Key Stage 1 core curriculum (DfE, 2013, p. 189)

1	Awareness of the past
2	People and events placed in a chronological framework
3	Ask and answer questions
4	Understand how we find out about the past and the different ways it is represented
5	Know key features of historical events
6	Changes in living memory
7	Events beyond living memory that are significant nationally or globally
8	The lives of significant individuals in the past (nationally and internationally)
9	Significant events and people in their locality

As in the case of the Foundation Stage, a starting point is to recap the content from the earlier chapters, namely the historical evidence and activities based on the following list, which will account for most of the content of the first four strands of Key Stage 1 history:

- Developing personal timelines;
- Accessing and using historical artefacts;
- The use of paintings and photographs;
- Oral history through visits and visitors;
- Opportunities to visit and examine historical buildings;
- Developing historical imagination through images, stories and drama or role-play activities.

SUGGESTED RECEPTION/YEAR 1 APPROACHES

To enable Year 1 children to address changes in living memory and the preceding strands, practitioners have often taught history through self-contained topics or units, such as the 'castles' example presented in

Chapter 6, which can often introduce cross-curricular themes linked to literacy, geography, art and design, and drama, etc. A key theme, associated with Piagetian notions of 'concrete operational' modes of understanding, is the importance of relating history to children's personal experience, such as the local study discussed in Chapter 7, and accessible forms of evidence, such as artefacts, family history and oral accounts. In terms of the content, while no list should be thought of as definitive, the list provided below is indicative of the most commonly found approaches. They have been placed in a roughly ascending order of challenge, and each unit is briefly described.

OURSELVES

This has often been introduced to 'rising fives' in Reception classrooms. It is usually cross-curricular, including PSHE themes, and allows young children to reflect on their place in the world, and specifically family, friends and the locality where they live (Low-Beer and Blyth, 1990, pp. 18–20). It would naturally lend itself to family trees, personal timelines and sequencing the principal events in a child's life, thus helping young children to place events into temporal order. Family photographs, favourite objects and oral accounts would be the main forms of historical evidence.

GRANDPARENTS

Some primary schools have also adopted a topic on grandparents, sometimes under the catchier title of 'When Granny Was a Girl'. Despite the lack of a clear provenance of its origin, Lomas et al. (1996, p. 81) suggested 'Grannies and Grandads' (sic), and the topic has also featured in the Scottish Curriculum and is supported by BBC Scotland for Schools. There have also been several commercial schemes in which a general approach to covering the past is conducted through a focus on a grandmother (or grandfather for that matter). Not only does this provide a meaningful context that virtually all children can understand, but it allows them to carry out some preparatory research, compose questions and then invite grandparents in for discussions and opportunities to ask questions.

A simple analysis suggests that over several years the content of this unit will inevitably become a shifting target. All my grandparents lived through World War I and could remember transformative events throughout the twentieth century, but children born after 2010 may have grandparents who were born in the 1960s and 1970s. Therefore, the study unit may include far more contemporary themes, such as changing working patterns, the growth of technology, or music and fashion. All is the stuff of history and we must endeavour to remind ourselves that for young children the past is necessarily a foreign place, however familiar it may appear to adults. A second consideration is that almost invariably a

Key Stage 1 classroom will involve grandparents who were born or live abroad and so there will also be geographical and citizenship themes to consider.

HOMES (INCLUDING CLOTHES)

All children can relate to the concept of a home, although of course personal experience will vary quite widely (Lomas et al., 1996). Although this topic can also cover contemporary objects and items found in a typical home, there will be many opportunities to compare and contrast homes from the past, thus covering element 6 of the National Curriculum, including items on the kitchen such as utensils, clothes, washing and cleaning, heating, furniture and transport links, etc. Some of the investigations could involve local museums, which often feature changing domestic conditions around design and function or displays of costumes. It may also include inviting visitors to the classroom to talk about homes in the past. Secondary sources of information, such as educational videos or internet sites, are useful for children to see images from homes and of clothes in the past. Some schools, such as the first primary school I taught in in Oxfordshire, may have collections of artefacts, such as a set of cleaning materials, including a wash tub, glass washboard, dolly (look it up), wooden pegs and early irons.

This is clearly an accessible topic and one that can be easily planned for and resourced.

TOYS AND GAMES (CHILDHOOD IN THE PAST)

An equally accessible and very popular topic is to carry out an investigation into toys from the past (Lomas et al., 1996). Most adults retain a few favourite toys from their childhood, and so this unit can introduce the idea of special objects and the symbolic quality they may embody. It is generally not too difficult to collect many toys by involving parents and the local community. Similarly, county museums often have collections of toys and there are several dedicated toy museums throughout England and Wales. An obvious follow-up to visiting a toy collection is to create a toy museum, including labelling, as a classroom display (Fines and Nichol, 1997, pp. 148–9).

Following on from the key ideas in Chapter 7, this will be an opportunity to model close observations, focusing on changing design, materials, technology (for example, electric motors in place of clockwork) and function. Research can be carried out to create timelines demonstrating how certain toys, such as trainsets or dolls, have changed over time. Children can even speculate, using historical imagination, what children of the future may play with. There is also the opportunity to involve geography and to compare popular British toys with toys from the wider world.

CHILDREN AT SCHOOL

The inclusion of the history of schools is another obvious Key Stage 1 topic due to the combination of personal knowledge and relevance. In Year 1, the nature and purpose of school is something all children can reflect on, while the evidence is also close to hand (Blyth, 1988, pp. 33–5). Many primary schools can trace their origins back to the nineteenth century; 'British' and 'National' Schools were founded as far back as 1833, while 'Board' schools were founded after 1870. In rural areas the original Victorian building often exists as part of the fabric of the school, and where new schools were built, the original Victorian building often remains as a community centre. The existence of old school buildings is less certain in urban areas, and those that remain have often been converted into houses, but the majority of primary schools have a reasonably extensive history of some kind; and if not, the topic can be made more generic to include an overview of elementary and primary schools in England and Wales.

Similarly, in terms of documentation, state schools were required to keep logbooks until the 1980s. While many of these are now held by county libraries in their archives, some schools may still hold them.

A school history topic allows for visits to one of the many education centres where Victorian or Edwardian era lessons are led by actors and children can go into role as pupils from the era. The drama approaches are more suited to a Year 2 class, however, so this needs to be considered when planning a curriculum overview.

PLANNING AROUND A STORY

Another successful and well-tested approach is to plan history around a story that has some aspect of its content or setting linked to the past. Margaret Wright (1996) provided an example of how a story like Jane Hissey's *Old Bear* (1986) can act as a starting point for a historical study with younger children, and specifically from Year 1, while specifically addressing historical elements such as developing an awareness of the past, understanding how the past can be represented, and as a starting point for enquiry.

The schema presented in Figure 8.1 is adapted from Wright's work (1996, p. 22). The planning overview can be summarised under five main headings: reasoning, chronology, enquiry, extension, and communication and interpretation. There are further opportunities to work with artefacts, carry out sequencing activities and create a class timeline, and to engage in historical reasoning by challenging children to re-tell the story from Old Bear's point of view. *Old Bear* may be an excellent example, but there are many other picture books or traditional tales that are equally suitable. Furthermore, the skilled Key Stage 1 practitioner will know how to extract the most relevant elements of history, and other National Curriculum subjects, while ignoring the parts that do not easily fit into the narrative frame of a picture book; less coverage, in greater depth, should always be preferable to a blunderbuss approach.

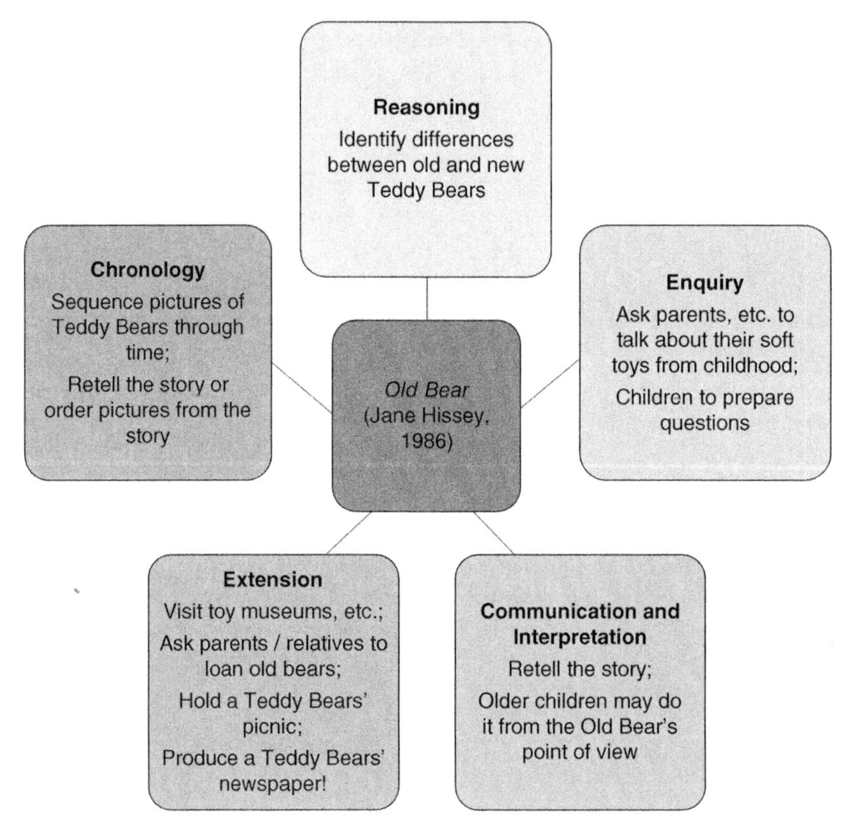

Figure 8.1 Planning based on *Old Bear* (Hissey, 1986) (adapted from Margaret Wright's example: 1996, p. 22)

SUGGESTED YEAR 2 APPROACHES: SIGNIFICANT INDIVIDUALS

Colleagues who have taught in Year 2 will attest to the exponential growth in children's independence and cognitive skills during the year. This suggests that there can be a substantial increase in outcomes and expectations, and opportunities to cover the remaining elements of the Key Stage 1 National Curriculum for history. The requirement to study 'significant individuals' is contained in the following extract from the National Curriculum 2014 document:

> The lives of significant individuals in the past who have contributed to national and international achievements. Some should be used to compare aspects of life in different periods [for example, Elizabeth

> I and Queen Victoria, Christopher Columbus and Neil Armstrong, William Caxton and Tim Berners-Lee, Pieter Bruegel the Elder and L.S. Lowry, Rosa Parks and Emily Davison, Mary Seacole and/or Florence Nightingale and Edith Cavell]. (DfE, 2013, p. 189)

The suggestion for studying the life of Mary Seacole in depth, and then comparing her life with her contemporary, Florence Nightingale, provides an opportunity to focus on previously hidden elements of black history while promoting the women's history. It also provides an opportunity for children to focus on comparative biographies and a higher level of analysis. The suggested list of eminent people is only indicative, and there is nothing to prevent practitioners from making their own choice of a significant person who has, in some way, contributed to national and world history. The subtext in the National Curriculum list, namely the promotion of women and campaigners, in addition to the previously included suggestions for explorers, inventors and engineers (DfEE, 1999, p. 104), is indicative of the revised intentions for this element of history.

The suggestion here for retaining the previous focus on Florence Nightingale (outlined in Chapters 2 and 4) is to carry out the comparative biographies suggested above, which not only allows for enquiry, investigation, evidence and written outcomes, but also permits the aforementioned aspects of citizenship, principally women's history, hidden history, eminent black Britons, and overall inclusivity. It can also be an opportunity for children to consider the role of historical interpretation.

During training sessions, I usually introduce the activity with the following provocative statement:

> Florence Nightingale is principally famous for taking a team of nurses to the Crimean War and consequently is one of the most famous Britons ever, and certainly one of the most eminent British women. Mary Seacole, by comparison, was hardly known, yet she also carried out nursing in the Crimea. A key question is why Florence continues to be so well remembered and celebrated while Mary was barely known outside narrow academic fields until, apparently, she was placed into school history?

To adapt this critical and questioning approach for Year 2 children, I would further suggest two principal foci:

- The opportunity to challenge and counter myths associated with both women;
- The opportunity to phrase enquiry around a challenging question rather than an unfocused 'finding out'; specifically, 'Did Florence deserve the level of fame she has maintained for over 100 years?' and 'Was Mary's story, which is far less known and therefore an example of hidden history, principally due to discrimination?'

To illustrate of how this might be framed in terms of children's research and work outcomes, including class displays, an example is provided in Table 8.2.

Table 8.2 Contrasting the lives of Florence Nightingale and Mary Seacole

Florence Nightingale (1820–1910)	Mary Seacole (1805–1881)
Early life and family	**Early life and family**
Florence and her sister Parthenope were born in Italy during their parents' two-year 'grand tour' honeymoon; Florence was named after the city of her birth, Firenze. The Nightingales were a wealthy and influential family, essentially aristocratic, rather than upper middle-class, and well-connected. Intellectually gifted, Florence received a rigorous home education from her father; upper-class girls generally did not attend school and were not allowed to attend university. Florence had a very deep Christian faith and she decided to dedicate her life to a career helping less fortunate people rather than marriage, but this was against her family's wishes, which caused considerable conflict within the whole family. Having decided to become a nurse, she undertook some hospital training in England and Germany in 1851. Florence began to study mathematics, which again was not usual for a young woman of her class, and she demonstrated considerable aptitude, particularly with statistics.	Mary (Grant) Seacole had a fascinating life story. She was born in Kingston, Jamaica in 1805 to a 'free' (i.e., not a slave) mother of African origin and a Scottish army officer father. Today she would call herself 'mixed race', but the contemporary terms which she referred to are 'creole' and 'mulattoe', both of which are considered offensive in modern society. As a mixed-race child, she would not have associated herself with slaves. Although many Jamaicans considered themselves English or British, generally whites were fearful of free black or mixed-race people because of the fear of rebellion and so there were restrictions on what she could own and do. Mary's mother ran a hotel, or boarding house, and worked as a 'doctress' or unofficial clinician. Mary followed both vocations. Mary demonstrated an early commitment to travel and adventure. She spent time in Panama, Nicaragua and England. She married an Englishman, Edwin Seacole, but was widowed after eight years.
Main claim to fame	**Main claim to fame**
The complex Crimean War (in modern-day Turkey), 1853–1856, in which Great Britain largely got involved to protect her eastern Empire, was going badly and exposed weaknesses in Britain's organisation of the army. Partly due to family connections, Sidney Herbert, the minister for war, invited Florence to act as 'Superintendent' for an initial team of 38 nurses sent out to the military hospital in Scutari in November 1854.	Mary had grown up with the British army in Jamaica, and when news of the Crimean War reached her, she wanted to support British troops. Her work as a doctress had provided her with an extensive knowledge of tropical diseases and her treatments would have been as effective as official medicine in the mid-nineteenth century. Additionally, she was an experienced and skilled minor surgeon.

Florence Nightingale (1820–1910)	Mary Seacole (1805–1881)
It has been argued by several historians that the critical British press were looking for a positive story, and Florence's organisational ability and drive allowed the creation of the 'Lady with the Lamp' myth, a term coined by the poet Longfellow, during her time in the Crimea. Her fame had aspects of modern celebrity, including merchandise, songs and music hall sketches. Less certain is the impact Florence and her nurses made, but she was unquestionably a tireless and able administrator and recognised the improvements that needed to be enacted. On her return to England she worked hard to campaign for important reforms, provided data for a Government Commission into Army welfare, published two important pamphlets, was consulted about the design of hospitals, and founded the first 'School for Nurses' in 1860 using money raised from public donations. In short, she was an effective campaigner and administrator and can claim a very important role in the elevation of nursing as a recognised profession.	Mary arrived in England in autumn 1854 and hoped to join the second batch of nurses sent out in December. Mary's account is that she was ignored and rejected by Sidney Herbert's wife, Elizabeth. Mary then resolved to pay her own way to the Crimea. Once she arrived, she set up a 'British Hotel' boarding house near the battlefields at Balaclava, where she worked as a 'suter' (semi-official supplier of food and drink due to the fact that the army did not always organise these things) and a nurse. Mary's chief claim to fame is that she worked directly on the battlefields, unlike Florence, who almost exclusively stayed in the hospitals at Scutari, and she was very highly regarded in this respect. Fundamentally, she was a business-woman, but her effectiveness as a nurse was appreciated at the time. On her return to England she was feted as a hero and received many glowing testimonials and four official awards. She mixed with royalty, and although she lost money and went through bankruptcy, there were public campaigns to raise money for her and she died a relatively wealthy woman.
Amazing facts Florence may or may not have 'invented' the pie chart, but she certainly was one of the first writers to use it to present complex statistics in a visual way. The diagram below demonstrates the proportion of the causes of military deaths. She was the first British Woman to receive the Order of Merit in 1907. Florence appeared on the back of the £10 note between 1975 and 1984. There is considerable speculation about Florence's long periods of bedbound ill health. At the very least, whether caused by a bacterial infection, a form of ME, or a mental breakdown (Small, 1998), her time in the Crimea permanently and adversely affected her health, although she lived to be 90 years old.	**Amazing facts** Mary Seacole wrote a best-selling autobiography in 1857, and although several commentators argued that she could not have written it unaided, the modern view is that it has few signs of editing. Mary received glowing testimonials from leading doctors such as Sir John Hall, several army officers and journalists such as Sir William Russell. Mary was also acquainted with members of the Royal family. Mary received a posthumous Jamaican Order of Merit in 1990. In recent decades Mary has had several statues and hospital and university wings named after her.

(Continued)

Table 8.2 (Continued)

Florence Nightingale (1820–1910)	Mary Seacole (1805–1881)
In later life Florence improved her relationship with her sister Parthenope, and often stayed with her sister at Upton House near Buckingham, where there is a permanent museum dedicated to her.	She topped the 'Great Black Britons' poll (www.100greatblackbritons.com/results.htm)
Challenging myths	**Challenging myths**
'The Lady with the Lamp'. Quite recent research, for example Bostridge's (2008) access to new information, has led modern historians to play down her effectiveness as a nurse. While it is true that she did walk the wards at night with a lamp, she was more a determined and talented administrator than a skilled nurse. A modern question has centred on whether Florence accepted the late nineteenth-century account of '*germ theory*' to explain disease, which we now know to be true. The balance of opinion is that she did not, but she did eventually understand the importance of cleanliness and uncontaminated water. A related question is whether her methods '*transformed the hospitals in the Crimea*'. This is also hotly debated, not least because many of her nurses, who were few in number, were unsuitable or untrained, and initially they were prevented from participating directly on the wards. It is probably more accurate to claim that Florence recognised the problems that army hospitals faced and had radical ideas for reform on her return from the Crimea.	*Mary was rejected by Florence Nightingale.* The relatively short answer is that Florence did not reject Mary because it was not really Florence's decision over the choice of nurses, many of whom were unsuitable anyway; and, more importantly, because by the time Mary applied for a position with the second group of nurses, Florence was already in the Crimea. After the Crimean War, Bostridge (2008) provided considerable evidence that Florence was sympathetic about Mary's financial difficulties, but equally she disapproved of the availability of alcohol in Mary's hotels. *Mary faded from history until she was added to the National Curriculum.* This is not wholly true. Although her fame faded quickly, especially compared to Florence, there were periodic attempts to celebrate her life. In 1954 the Jamaican Nurses' Association renamed their Kingston headquarters 'Mary Seacole House' during the centenary of the Crimean War; in the UK, the Jamaican Nurses' Association led a successful campaign to re-consecrate Mary's grave in London in 1973; and from the early 1980s there were several calls for more information about Mary's life, which resulted in the re-publication of her autobiography in 1984. Since then the interest in Mary, and forms of public recognition, have grown exponentially and only partially due to her place in school history, which began around 1999 with the Curriculum 2000 (DfEE, 1999, p. 107). It is probably truer to state that her place in the National Curriculum was a response to a growing sense of her importance and interest in her life.

Florence Nightingale (1820–1910)	Mary Seacole (1805–1881)
Did Florence deserve her fame?	**Was Mary discriminated against?**
At the end of Chapter 6, a claim was made that ultimately the principal outcome of history is informed opinion or judgement. This is my view. Overall, I think that Florence demands our continued respect. Although she was from a privileged background, which did confer advantages, equally she faced tremendous barriers because of her gender and the rigidity of social conventions. Although Florence's initial fame may have been a misrepresentation, arguably a form of propaganda, and her team of nurses may not have been as effective in the Crimea as initially claimed, as the principal founder of nursing as a modern profession and a tireless campaigner with impressive intellectual gifts, she deserves her place in British and World history.	The broad question of whether Mary experienced prejudice because of her mixed race is complex. On the one hand, she unquestionably faced racial discrimination, notably from Elizabeth Herbert. On the other hand, as Alexander and Dewjee (1984) argued in their introduction to Seacole's autobiography, Mary herself held prejudicial views about certain 'races'. She appeared to accept several racial stereotypes; for example, explaining her drive and energy as a consequence of her 'Scotch blood'. She also held very strong pro-British and pro-military views. Thus, there is a danger that she could be presented in a way that she would not have recognised or approved of. To add to the complexity, a more nuanced and balanced approach ought to include the level of public support that Mary also received following her return to England. It can be stated with security that in her later life, after the Crimean War, Mary received considerable praise and recognition. She received approbation in the press, several benefit events were organised to raise more for her following her bankruptcy, and she enjoyed public fame in the form of songs and poems. There were also official forms of recognition, for example she was awarded the Crimean Medal. Thus, the temptation to claim that she was ignored because of racial prejudice should be resisted, but it is hard to explain why her story largely disappeared for over a century.
Sources of evidence	**Sources of evidence**
Barnham, K. (2002) Bostridge, M. (2008) Small, H. (1998)	Anionwu, E. (2005) Seacole M and Salih S. (2005)

Having provided an overview of both Mary and Florence, a few further statements need to be made. Even with comparatively limited levels of research, it is possible to detect the personal characteristics they shared alongside the circumstances that differentiated them. Both demonstrated considerable drive and determination: for Mary, it was her physical energy and taste for travel and adventure that is remarkable; for Florence, it was her willingness to challenge social conventions and male authority. Both demonstrated sharp intellects and original minds, and in Florence's case her education was partially developed through family connections. One can only speculate how much more they could have achieved had they been allowed to enter leading medical schools and trained to be doctors and clinical researchers. Equally, despite their drive and intellectual radicalism, both had aspects of social conservatism.

It may be argued that this is far too complex for Year 2 children. However, it can be counter-argued that if taught well and if children are allowed to explore the key themes with sufficient time and suitable resources, the majority of 7-year-old children are capable of understanding the key events, personalities and evidence contained in this brief overview, including the important citizenship and moral themes around discrimination on the grounds of gender and race. As noted previously, these latter considerations have been bolstered by the suggested list of famous people, so there is a sense that sensitive aspects of history should be not be avoided.

Historical accuracy is essential, however, and interpretation and representations should respect the boundaries of evidence. In 2010, the BBC series *Horrible Histories* featured a sketch in which a public relations man, Cliff Whitely (a pun on white lie), is visited by Florence Nightingale and Mary Seacole. One of the virtues of *Horrible Histories* is the fact that it challenges myths and focuses on reinterpretations in humorous ways, but on this occasion, it unquestionably went too far. The sketch claimed wrongly that Nightingale had personally rejected Seacole, but the more damaging accusation, which resulted in an upheld complaint to the BBC Trust (Furness, 2014), suggested that Florence had principally rejected Mary on the grounds of her nationality and race.

As a final point, it is possible to expand the content of more recent British history by extending the study of Mary and Florence into a broader topic on the Victorians. As a former history coordinator who taught in Year 2 for three consecutive years, this was my solution for enabling full coverage of the alternative Key Stage 2 topics, *Victorian Britain* or *Britain since the 1930s*. Arguably, this is even more relevant given the newer focus on early British history, since its adoption allows schools to legitimately cover more aspects of more recent British history.

As a Year 2 topic, other key people and events can be covered, including:

- Queen Victoria and her family;
- Charles Dickens and the great Victorian novel;
- Dr Barnardo and the citizenship theme of poor and destitute children;
- Dr Livingston and the theme of Victorian exploration and 'discovery';

- The Great Exhibition, themed around trade and Empire, incorporating aspects of geography;
- The growth of railways and transport;
- Key Victorian inventions – leading to a timeline activity.

The argument against such an approach is that it takes up too much curriculum time, but my solution was to extend it over the whole spring term and to incorporate several cross-curricular links, particularly with literacy.

YEAR 2 HISTORY: SIGNIFICANT EVENTS

The Key Stage 1 curriculum also requires children to study at least one historical event from British and world history in a comparably detailed form. The wording of this requirement has changed little, and the current wording is suitably open, requiring children to study:

> Events beyond living memory that are significant nationally or globally [for example, the Great Fire of London, the first aeroplane flight or events commemorated through festivals or anniversaries]. (DfE, 2013, p. 189)

As with the case of Florence Nightingale, many schools have chosen to study the Great Fire of London because it was included in a QCA example plan. So, presented here are three alternatives which offer opportunities for detailed enquiry and opportunities for cross-curricular work.

FIRST AEROPLANE FLIGHT: THE WRIGHT BROTHERS

Unlike most crucial technological inventions, there is limited dispute around the provenance of the first powered flight. It can be stated, therefore, with some confidence that the first aeroplane flight took place in Kitty Hawk, North Carolina, on the 17 of December 1903 (Hellemans and Bunch, 1988). Nevertheless, one interesting theme to explore is the fact that few inventions stand apart from previous innovations and developments. Powered flight had been the goal of many inventors over several centuries, not least Leonardo da Vinci, and glider technology had reached a sophisticated stage by the end of the nineteenth century. Thus, the principles of wing technology were understood, but what was lacking was a method of producing a light but powerful engine. Steam engines were too heavy and required large quantities of fuel and water, which reduced their power to weight ratio (a sophisticated concept for Key Stage 1). The invention of the internal combustion engine in Europe at the end of the nineteenth century provided the perfect power source.

The Wright brothers, Orville and Wilbur, had a background in bicycle making, and their key skills were the ability to build a strong and light airframe and the ingenuity to create a small, light gasoline engine of their own design. In conclusion, like many key inventors, they were essentially adapting other people's ideas in a new and practical way. The result was the first aeroplane.

Key themes to explore and learning outcomes could include:

- Research into glider technology and key pioneers, such as Sir George Cayley and Otto Lilienthal;
- Early balloonists, such as the Montgolfier brothers;
- Early pioneers of flight, such as Bleriot (France), Alcock and Brown (UK) and Amelia Earhart (USA);
- Aeroplanes at war;
- The invention of the jet engine;
- The first supersonic flight;
- The jet age and the revolution in passenger transportation;
- The space race, resulting in the first Moon landing an astonishingly short 66 years after the first powered flight;
- A class timeline showing the development of flight in the twentieth century;
- Predictions for future developments in air travel.

THE GUNPOWDER PLOT

Although the Gunpowder Plot is not named in the current National Curriculum, it was one of the main suggestions for Key Stage 1 study in previous iterations, and it has been chosen here because it also fits into the general themes of 'festivals and anniversaries', and it highlights some of the potential hazards as well as benefits of historical study.

To begin with, the enduring appeal of this episode from British history is its engrossing narrative. It contains several important and identifiable elements, such as secret 'plotters' (note the parallels with modern-day conspiracy theories), dungeons, gunpowder, and a midnight check which revealed the plot hours before King James was due to open Parliament. Thus, it has all the essential ingredients needed for a gripping tale. The fact that it is so often told from the protagonists' point of view, an approach occasionally adopted by blockbuster movies, has arguably resulted in considerable moral fluidity.

There is also the figure of Guy Fawkes himself and his continuing hold over our collective imagination. In truth, little is really known about his life other than he was born in York, became a fervent Catholic in his teens, fought as a mercenary in Europe and so had genuine military expertise, and was committed to the plot, even though he was not the principal plotter. It was his misfortune to have been found in the cellar, but it ensured his enduring fame. Those teachers fortunate enough to work near Oxfordshire could arrange a visit to the Ashmolean museum, where the alleged lamp Guy Fawkes was holding at the time of his capture is on display.

In terms of enquiry and interpretation, the key opportunity would be to study the whole group and to understand who the main plotters were, namely Robert Catesby and Thomas Wintour. A second line of enquiry could be to study the considerable range of opinion about whether the explosion would have succeeded in killing King James and destroying Parliament. Consideration of how English and British history would have been if the plot had succeeded – an example of counterfactualism – would be challenging for undergraduates and far beyond the capabilities of young children, but it would be worth exploring the idea that British history would have been different in some way.

The issues surrounding this event from British history is that the gripping narrative can obscure the important, but complex, themes. How far would Key Stage 1 practitioners wish to explore the issue of religious intolerance? Or a monarch who wished to remove the influence of Parliament? Both are important themes with contemporary parallels, but neither can be explained easily to young children. *Horrible Histories* has emphasised the violence and cruelty of the past in a humorous way, but great care must be taken in reviewing the content with young children. In this case, children may ask what 'hanging, drawing and quartering' involved. Teachers must consider the extent to which they are willing to cover an event from history accurately and honestly, and that if the content is inappropriate for a young class, then it is surely better to seek better examples.

THE HISTORY OF CHRISTMAS (LOMAS ET AL., 1996)

The study of Christmas as a cross-curricular topic, incorporating religious education (RE), geography and history, can be adapted to include enquiry and examples of historical interpretation, although great care must be taken not to destroy the magic of Christmas. An enquiry into the history and traditions of Christmas will inform children that nearly all our modern practices can be traced to specific points from the past; that they are drawn from across the world; and finally, that they do not all have Christian roots. Examples would include the following.

The midwinter feast has two points of origin. First, the Catholic Church, which grew out of the Roman Empire after Constantine the Great's conversion to Christianity, adapted the Roman festival of 'Saturnalia', which was held in honour of the Roman god Saturn and usually took place between 17 and 23 December. This was an example of one of the many occasions when the Roman Catholic Church transmogrified an earlier celebration or feast into a Christian festival. Modern calculations place

Jesus's birth sometime in the New Year and so the date of Christmas has little to do with the historical Jesus's actual birth.

The second point of origin is that northern Europeans, termed 'pagan' by Christians, celebrated the winter solstice, which usually occurs on 21 December, through the festival of Yule. Yule was associated with the Viking god Odin and the rebirth of the sun; this is because the days begin to lengthen again after the solstice. Thus, the origins of Yule logs, wreaths, and traditions such as bringing evergreens (holly and mistletoe) into the home have absolutely no connection with Christianity, but were similarly adopted and assimilated by the early Roman church.

The Christmas tree is also a north European tradition and it is often claimed that it became popular in Britain due to our predominately German Royal family during the eighteenth and nineteenth centuries; the practice was certainly well established by the late Victorian period.

The Christmas card was very much a Victorian invention and a by-product of increasingly cheap and productive printing processes alongside an efficient postal system. Key Victorians, especially the writer Charles Dickens, should take much of the credit for creating our imagery of Christmas, involving Christmas trees, gifts, decorations, carol singing, the eating of a large bird – although this would have been a goose before the introduction of the north-American turkey, the importance of it being a family time at home and, finally, the image of the white Christmas. In many ways, this was Dickens' personal conception of the festival, and it may be concluded that in several respects our modern interpretation of Christmas is principally a Victorian invention interspliced with much earlier, non-Christian festivals.

An equally interesting, but potentially dangerous, theme would be to examine the variations in the legend and figure of Father Christmas, Santa Claus, Kris Kringle or St Nicholas. The modern myth that the iconography of Santa Claus is based on Coca-Cola advertising is not true, although there is a strong link with nineteenth-century America. This is a good example of historical enquiry challenging mythology. In short, Father Christmas is unquestionably based on the genuine historical figure of St Nicholas from the fourth century, but he has undergone many transformations and such class discussions may provoke awkward questions!

Equally, if we study traditions in other Christian countries, it is perhaps surprising how variable Christmas traditions can be, with many alternatives in terms of present giving and the main feast days. This would include the place of Epiphany on 6 January, which is widely celebrated in the Orthodox Christian church, including several East European countries, and in Catholic countries such as Portugal and Spain. In Orthodox Ethiopia, Christmas is celebrated on 7 January. Wassailing, an Anglo-Saxon tradition is still carried out in some parts of the United Kingdom, such as Oxford. It is often associated with Twelfth Night and fertility practices looking ahead to the New Year. In Scotland, the Hogmanay celebration for New Year is considered at least as important as Christmas. It is therefore worth investigating with children the claims that some branches of Christianity, principally Calvinists and Presbyterians, believe that celebrations are simply the wrong way to celebrate Christ's birth on the holiest of days. England went through a similar process during the Puritan period in the mid-seventeenth century.

CHAPTER SUMMARY

- The nature and concepts of history are the same throughout all the Key Stages, so the challenge is to make complex historical concepts and knowledge accessible and understandable for young children.
- The two to three years in Key Stage 1 should be planned to enable progression, and I have suggested ideas for how this might be approached.
- It is important to adopt a questioning and quizzical enquiry-based approach in which evidence and ideas about the past can be challenged and interrogated.
- Narrative has a crucial role as a mode of historical engagement and as a way of provoking curiosity about the past.
- Detailed case studies of significant people and events, used comparatively if possible, can stretch the range of ability in Year 2.
- Moral and citizenship themes can be included wherever possible to match the National Curriculum guidelines.
- The curriculum content should be considered carefully to ensure its appropriateness.

FURTHER READING

This list reflects the paucity of texts dedicated to Key Stage 1 history or the wider humanities. Most of these texts are long out of print, but copies can be found from the usual internet-based retailers, including portals for second-hand books.

Blyth, J. (1988) *History 5 to 9*. London: Hodder & Stoughton.

One of the first, and best, texts dedicated for Key Stage 1 practitioners.

Cooper, H. (1995) *History in the Early Years*. Abingdon: Routledge.

In several respects this is Hilary Cooper's finest book, largely because it is the most research-based and includes extended discussions.

Wright, M. (1996) *The Really Practical Guide to Primary History*. Cheltenham: Stanley Thornes.

This is very much a practitioner-based text with little evidence from research, but as a practical guide it is invaluable and full of sensible and workable ideas for teachers.

CHAPTER 9

KEY STAGE 2 HISTORY (PART 1)

What this chapter will cover

This chapter may be the most relevant in the book for practitioners working in Key Stage 2. It reviews the requirements for covering the British history overview from the end of the Ice Age to the death of Edward the Confessor in 1066. However, it is only meant to provide ideas for future research rather than include all the information a teacher will require. Similarly, suggestions for a half-termly plan are outlines rather than detailed examples. A key suggestion is that these elements are truncated and incorporated into Years 5 and 6 because of the complexity of the material and the timescales involved.

INTRODUCTION

There are at least three key points to consider before studying the first of two chapters describing the required elements to be taught in Key Stage 2, and the final consideration has profound implications for school-level planning. The first is to state that in this first chapter, the content under review is the requirement to cover the overview of British history from the end of the last Ice Age through to 1066 – approximately 11,000 years of continuous history. As was explained in the introductory chapters, while elements of this overview were present in earlier iterations of the National Curriculum (specifically, the 'Invaders' topic), the scope is now much wider, incorporating elements of early history and archaeology, and it is meant to be taught chronologically.

The second consideration is that not all state-funded primary schools will necessarily include this revised element. Free schools and academies are able to create their own curriculum and thus may decide to produce their own history curriculum. Despite the pronouncement from Ofsted

Chief Inspector Amanda Spielman that inspections from 2019 will assess coverage of the whole curriculum (Ofsted, 2019), there is still no great incentive for maintained schools to promote the teaching of and learning in the humanity subjects. Nevertheless, Michael Gove's controversial decision about the content of National Curriculum history – including the secondary sector too, given that the chronological overview extends into Key Stage 3 – is that this model was at least partially influenced by the private sector. This consideration has at least two further implications. The first is that this chapter may be useful for colleagues working in private schools. The second, and arguably more important, point is that given the new curriculum is deliberately trimmed down, and regardless of whether free schools and academies follow the proposed units or develop their own, many non-specialist primary teachers will require an analysis of the elements of history, and suggestions for curriculum management, planning and assessment. Furthermore, if they do produce their own scheme of work, as with the independent schools, they are likely to focus on British history.

The third consideration in this chapter is to include a review of school-level subject planning. Although the intention is to cover around 11,000 years of British history in chronological order, the wording of the trimmed down National Curriculum does not actually prescribe the Key Stage 2 years in which each element shold be included. The breakdown into four main periods (which is reflected in the structure of this chapter) understandably seems to suggest natural divisions between Years 3 and 6, but this is not actually stated. Although the structure of this chapter necessarily follows the outline included in the National Curriculum, it is advisable that subject leaders and school leaders consider very carefully the suggestion throughout this chapter that the overview of British history can be incorporated solely into Years 5 and 6, and in a truncated and condensed form possibly only in Year 6.

The reason for this suggestion is not so surprising or radical. Chapter 3 outlined some of the alternative models that could have been considered in developing the National Curriculum (DfE, 2013), but since this did not happen, one way in which the challenges identified in earlier chapters, and the extensive research from educational psychology into children's understanding of chronology (also described earlier in the book) would be to compress the four elements of the British history overview into the final two years of Key Stage 2. The more complex language and chronological elements included in the ancient history overview can then be presented to older children, creating greater opportunities for coherent and synoptic learning to take place. Curriculum coordinators and school leaders are advised to read the sections on early British history and then to consider whether this material really can be covered in enough detail and in an intellectually honest and rigorous way with children in Years 3 and 4.

The structure of this chapter will be to explore each of the four main periods, as identified by the National Curriculum document (DfE, 2013, pp. 189–91). Each section will comprise a summary of content and provide key ideas for teaching approaches, links with other National Curriculum subjects, an overview of coverage, and examples of educational visits. The proposal is for schools to design a framework that will allow for a half-termly teaching project (6–8 weeks) each academic year, thus allowing double coverage in Years 5 and 6 to fit in with previous suggestions for curriculum mapping.

This chapter aims to provide a basic outline of key information and sources. It is because most teachers will not have been taught ancient British history that there is a correspondingly longer discussion outlining the key knowledge needed here than in the remaining periods in this element of the National Curriculum. Likewise, I have offered more suggestions for further study in this section too. Nevertheless, in a relatively short chapter which aims to cover 11,000 years of British history, the overview can only provide a rough guide. Therefore, the book aims to concentrate on the elements of self-study that are required in order to teach successfully, rather than to provide a comprehensive account.

ANCIENT BRITISH HISTORY - YEAR 3 (ALTERNATIVELY YEAR 5)

NATIONAL CURRICULUM EXTRACT - CHANGES IN BRITAIN FROM THE STONE AGE TO THE IRON AGE

Examples could include:

- Late Neolithic hunter-gatherers and early farmers (for example, Skara Brae)
- Bronze Age religion, technology and travel (for example, Stonehenge)
- Iron Age hill forts: tribal kingdoms, farming, art and culture. (DfE, 2013, p. 190)

WHAT TEACHERS OUGHT TO KNOW: 'BIG PICTURE' THINKING

According to geologists, the planet Earth was formed approximately 4.54 billion years ago, or 4,540,000,000 to give a true sense of scale. During this period the Earth has experienced fluctuations in average temperature, including five major ice ages. The most recent, entitled the Quaternary, began around 2 million years ago, a recent event in geological terms. Technically, the world is currently experiencing an interglacial period, the Holocene epoch, and so, irrespective of human influence, at some point in the relatively near future, air temperatures will drop again, and the ice sheets will expand.

The relevance of this geological and scientific information is that the movements of ice sheets have a very direct relationship with the beginning of British history. Around 11,500 years ago (9500 BC/BCE), a mere blink of time compared with the history of our planet, when the Holocene epoch began, the northern hemisphere ice sheets retreated from the European landmass and sea levels began to rise. The extent of the ice sheets in the last cold spell reached as far as south Wales, covering most of Ireland and the Midlands of England. Ice sheets last covered southern England during the coldest period, the glacial Maximum, approximately 22,000 years ago.

Table 9.1 The grey rectangles indicate the five main glacial periods in the history of the Earth, 4,600 million years ago to the present (scale: millions of years)

Hadean	Archean	Proterozoic	Phanerozic
		■	■ ▮ ■ ▮
4,600	3,800	2,500	542

There are several open-access interactive maps, and one of the most recent has been produced by the University of Sheffield (www.sheffield.ac.uk/news/nr/britice-interactive-ice-sheet-map-1.784388). This mapping tool allow users to understand the impact of the last ice sheet at the local level – it is ideal for studying the locality of a primary school.

An obvious starting point is to consider what the emerging British Isles would have looked like in the immediate post-glacial landscape. This would be an ideal activity for children, utilising both their burgeoning knowledge of early history and their powerful imaginations. The floodwaters would have created a landscape of rivers and lakes, many of which still exist in largely unchanged form. The impact of warming had several other important outcomes, including the rapid expansion of deciduous forests throughout most of the fertile lowlands, particularly in what we now call southern England. The fauna and flora from this time, even though these topics clearly encroach into science, are a vital aspect of studying this period. Many, but not all, of the birds and mammals that we associate with the British Isles would have been present (Mahoo and Yalden, 2000). For example, animals would include wild pigs, sheep, cattle and horses, roe deer throughout the forests and glades (much as they are now spreading throughout the south and Midlands of England) and red deer in the highlands. Carnivores such as foxes, badgers, wild cats and otters were present, all of which still can be found in varying numbers, but also more impressive predators, such as wolves, bears and lynxes (Briggs, 2018). There would be some surprising omissions too: most people are familiar with the story of the introduction of the grey squirrel around 100 years ago, but equally there would be no rabbits, pheasants or fallow deer in this early British landscape. As a teaching point, it would also be necessary to explain that the exotic fauna that we often associate with the Stone Age, such as woolly mammoths, woolly rhinoceroses, cave lions, etc., would have disappeared along with the ice.

What we are interested in for the context of National Curriculum history is the creation of modern Britain. Most plants and trees from that time can still be found, although the landscape would have looked nothing like the managed British countryside with which modern Britons are familiar. There have been many introductions too, for example several non-native trees and shrubs, such as rhododendron, sweet chestnut trees and sycamores. Arguably, the best idea of what the early Holocene epoch would have looked like is to study one of the few original lowland forests that we have left (for example, the New Forest in Hampshire). Almost every square metre of land in modern Britain has been managed, altered or adapted by humans in some way or form.

The second main consideration is to account for changes due to rising sea levels. During the immediate Holocene epoch, there remained a crucially important land bridge between Britain and the rest of Europe. Of course, the most important consequence of this line of communication for our purposes is that it allowed the spread of modern humans, *Homo sapiens*, into these lands. Indeed, one of the fascinating aspects of early British history was the fertile and populated land bridge, Doggerland, which is now covered by the North Sea (Crane, 2012, pp. 5–8). It was not simply that modern humans walked across it to access the nascent British Isles; it was also the centre of early settlement and therefore had great importance. Doggerland was eventually captured by rising sea levels, but an increasingly accepted theory is that the final loss of the land bridge was due to a violent and cataclysmic event, something that has even been described as a 6-metre-high 'tsunami' (Lane, 2011; Hill et al., 2014; Rincon, 2014) approximately 8,200 years ago (6200 BC/BCE). Not only was this an important and transformative event, it also marked the point in time when we can legitimately discuss the British Isles as a distinct geological and geographical set of islands.

The Island story also truly begins with the first Britons, so who were these people? They were unquestionably modern humans, but not necessarily our direct ancestors. In definitional terms, they were Stone Age people from the early to late Mesolithic periods who largely existed as nomadic hunting-and-gathering forms of society. Archaeology and palaeontology are now accessing new forms of data which are revealing novel and sometimes startling findings. Indeed, recent DNA analysis carried out on the oldest complete skeleton found in Britain – the so-called 'Cheddar man', which was discovered in 1903 in Somerset, and the remains of which have been dated to 7100 BC/BCE – has revealed that he shared about 10 per cent of his genes with modern Britons (McKie, 2018; Rincon, 2018a, 2018b). However, the research finding that has been widely publicised was the fact that his skin was dark brown, almost black, in colour and he had blue eyes. The significance of this evidence is that it shows that the light skin we associate with north Europeans is a relatively recent development and a response to requiring more vitamin D from weaker sunlight.

Nor should this unbroken inheritance be accepted uncritically. The Cheddar man shared genes with human remains found all over Europe, including in Spain, Luxemburg and Hungary. Landmark research into DNA samples from 400 ancient humans found throughout Europe, and published in the highly prestigious scientific journal *Nature* (Olalde et al., 2018), has recently suggested that around 4,500 years ago (2500 BC/BCE) the Neolithic Britons, who were responsible for Stonehenge, were almost completely replaced by later arrivals, the 'Beaker people', who developed pottery and have left more archaeological evidence. This was an unexpected finding, which is principally why it generated so much publicity. If accepted, it means that most of the ancestry of modern Britons is far more recent than was previously supposed.

As Brace et al. (2019) in their continuing work on DNA analysis have summarised, essentially there were three main influxes. The first group, the hunter-gathers, arrived after the retreat of the ice sheets and most remains have been found in the west of the British Isles. They were replaced by the second migration to the British Isles, the Neolithic farmers. These immigrants were part of a mass exodus of people from Anatolia, in modern Turkey, in 6000 BC/BCE. They arrived in the British Isles around 4000 BC/BCE, and they brought with them the skills and knowledge of farming. Agriculture is unquestionably the single most important human discovery because a food surplus allowed the development of human culture, and in the British Isles its introduction is linked with deforestation. There is a reason for the fact that most of the modern British Isles is covered in fields and hedgerows rather than forests interspersed with clearings and glades, and that process began around 5,000 years ago. The replacement of hunting and gathering with farming was a long and evolving process (indeed, the shaping of our landscape continues). The third influx, the Bell-Beaker people from mainland Europe, arrived around 2450 BC/BCE and almost entirely replaced the Neolithic farmers. The implication from this very recent research is that the British Isles experienced two extreme cultural and genetic shifts in the space of approximately 2000 years.

The influx of the Beaker people and the development of pottery occurred also around the time that a second pan-European development started to shape modern Britain, namely the beginning of metallurgy. The extraction of ore and the development of metal tools is unarguably one of the truly defining moments in human history. The 'Bronze Age' in the British Isles began around 4,500 years ago (2500 BC/BCE) and required highly sophisticated technology, for example, the use of bellows to generate the heat needed to separate metals from ore, in addition to the knowledge needed to mix copper and tin to produce the more serviceable alloy of bronze. Around the same time, the noble precious metals, such as gold and silver, were mined to produce jewellery. This is significant not only because of the archaeological finds that had been made, but because it signifies other things: the development of what we now term 'culture' and the evidence of an agricultural surplus which allowed some people to develop specialist skills and crafts.

The Ancient British focus then concludes with the arrival of the Celtic tribes circa 3,200–2,800 years ago (1200 BC/BCE to 800 BC/BCE). It was once believed that this was more of a cultural transfer rather than a mass migration from the Celtic heartlands of central Europe, but as Harvard Professor David Reich has explained (cited in Rincon, 2018b), the recent DNA analysis outlined above is shifting opinion towards direct human migration as the principal agent for change. Historians and archaeologists know much more about the Celts. First, the Celtic period is also known as the 'Iron Age' due to the discovery and use of more robust and stronger ferrous metals. Quite simply, there have been many more archaeological finds and human burials discovered from this era. Second, and arguably more importantly, these tribes were the people with whom the Romans traded and whom they subsequently attacked when they invaded the British Isles. We therefore have several Roman accounts of the Celtic tribes they encountered. There were around two dozen main tribes. Some, like the Iceni in modern-day East Anglia or the Regni in Sussex, are probably the best known because of their greater involvement in Roman affairs, but by the first century BC/BCE the Celtic tribes had covered most of the British Isles before the Roman invasion. There would also have been a continuation of earlier British tribes, such as the Picts and Scots, in the outer reaches of the British Isles.

The survival of written accounts from the Roman period explains why this endpoint is therefore also the true start of British history. Additionally, the name 'Britain' is the one given to us by the Romans (it is shared with Brittany in northern France). This brief account thus ends 2,000 years ago, at roughly year 1 BC/BCE, with a coastline of over 4,000 islands we would recognise today and a name that resonates 2,000 years later. It is also tempting to draw out the rather obvious citizenship themes. As this chapter will demonstrate further, not only is there a very clear geological link between the British Isles and mainland Europe, but the archaeological evidence is starting to be discovered 100 metres below the surface of the North Sea. Any account of early British people is the story of successive waves of immigration, and is far more recent than is commonly realised.

IDEAS FOR A HALF-TERMLY PLAN

Given the complexity of this period of British history, it is understandable that historians and educators have expressed grave doubts about its suitability for lower-junior children, the youngest of whom in Year 3 may have just celebrated their seventh birthday. By definition, at least a quarter or a fifth of children will be below average in mathematics and therefore may not be confident with numbers over 100, let alone discussions accounting for tens of thousands up to billions of years. There is a similar issue regarding reading skills. Hence, this is a timely reminder that schools can make the decision to cover this element in the upper-junior years.

That stated, what might a half-termly plan on Ancient British history look like? It is probably a reasonable assumption to plan for six to eight main teaching inputs, or mini-topics, to ensure reasonable coverage. Already several cross-curricular links have been mentioned, and extra time might be found by combining the topic with geography, possibly science, and almost certainly aspects of literacy linked to reading for understanding and written outcomes. The addition of these elements would provide some extra teaching and learning time. Beyond these considerations, the following list is reasonably comprehensive and intellectually rigorous.

- An initial session on the Ice Ages and the point when the British Isles became cut off from the mainland of Europe (links with geography): The 'Island story' needs a punchy start, and an introduction that mentions ice sheets, scary beasts, a land bridge to Europe and a cataclysmic ending involving a tsunami would provide exactly that.
- A study of the fauna and flora of British Isles 10,000 years ago: Not only would this naturally include several aspects of science, including habitats, it could also include a mathematical sorting exercise, possibly a Venn or Carroll diagram classifying the losses, gains and areas of overlap. Arguably, the greatest opportunity would be for children to exercise their imaginations, based on some previous study, trying to picture the British Isles just after the ice sheets had left.
- Early settlers and Stone Age culture: Some of the key discoveries from archaeology could be introduced, especially if this topic begins in Year 5. This could include a focus on Skara Brae. Since this is one of the few specific references within the National Curriculum, it would seem sensible to include an input on key archaeological remains.
- Similarly, no account of the Mesolithic and Neolithic periods would be complete without a study on Stonehenge. Two points need to be made. First, Stonehenge is subject to high levels of ongoing research, and therefore it deserves reasonably detailed and thorough levels of preparatory reading to ensure a teacher presentation is accurate and up to date. Second, the visibility and fame of Stonehenge sometimes obscures the fact that ancient stones, including other circles, can be found throughout the British Isles. In Oxfordshire, teachers could be directed to the Rollright Stones near Chipping Norton. While not worthy of a whole day's trip, a morning visit to a genuine Ancient

British monument would add a certain verisimilitude for primary-aged children.

- This unit ought to include an account of the influx of new immigrants, including the Beaker people. Key themes would include deforestation and the beginning of farming and settlement. Although it would be challenging to cover this theme in the detail it arguably deserves, the introduction of metallurgy leading to the Bronze Age should be included. Links could be made to art and design technology, and ideas could include children making models of Stonehenge and their own clay pots, etc. Although not specifically relevant to British history, not least because very few examples have been discovered in the British Isles and those that have been found technically date from the last cold spell in the current Ice Age, many children are captivated by the accounts of cave paintings and this could inspire an art-based aspect within this unit of study.
- The final section would account for the migration of Celtic tribes from mid-Europe. This Iron Age topic might include more artwork with a focus on enduring Celtic designs, including jewellery. A study of the main Celtic tribes, including hill forts, could be held back until the start of the Roman period.
- In addition, a class timeline accounting for around 10,000 years of history should be developed. Whether it is introduced in Year 3 or Year 5 (for all the reasons outlined in Chapter 3), teachers would have to discuss and explain the terminology of time. The inclusion of a story, for example Clive King's *Stig of the Dump* (1963), may stimulate many children's interest in and understanding of an elusive aspect of British history.

THE ROMAN OCCUPATION OF THE BRITISH ISLES – YEAR 4 (ALTERNATIVELY YEAR 5)

NATIONAL CURRICULUM EXTRACT – THE ROMAN EMPIRE AND ITS IMPACT ON BRITAIN

Examples could include:

- Julius Caesar's attempted invasion in 55–54 BC
- The Roman Empire by AD 42 and the power of its army
- The successful invasion by Claudius and conquest, including Hadrian's Wall
- British resistance, for example, Boudicca
- 'Romanisation' of Britain: sites such as Caerwent and the impact of technology, culture and beliefs, including early Christianity examples (non-statutory). (DfE, 2013, p. 190)

WHAT TEACHERS OUGHT TO KNOW

Unlike previous versions of the National Curriculum, where Roman history was contained within the 'Invaders' topic, the National Curriculum 2014 study unit is now meant to be broader than just the Roman occupation of the British Isles. Therefore, some knowledge about the Roman civilisation and empire will add authority when teaching. That stated, time to cover the primary curriculum is always at a premium, so the balance of teaching and learning should favour the Roman invasion and occupation of the British Isles.

The legend of the origins of Rome begins with the first king, Romulus circa 750 BC/BCE (2,750 years ago). By 509 BC/BCE Rome had become a republic ruled by a senate (consider how resonant these political terms have become). A period of rapid expansion followed as the rest of modern-day Italy came under its sway (it is worth noting that the many small city states did not become modern-day Italy until political unification under Garibaldi in the nineteenth century), and then other European territories, before Roman power expanded even further into modern-day Asia and North Africa. Naturally, this involved considerable military and organisational skills, and so one of the key aspects of studying the Roman civilisation is to understand and appreciate their very practical ways of behaving and thinking. It is often claimed that the Romans plagiarised many aspects of Greek culture and civilisation, and indeed it is true that they adopted Greek ideas about architecture, religion, philosophy and literature, not least appropriating and renaming the principle Greek gods (which is taught in Year 3 in the proposed schema), but they added levels of organisation, ruthlessness and a sense of common purpose that the Greek states arguably lacked.

The story of the Roman civilisation continues with the collapse of the senate and ruling oligarchy and creation of the first Emperor Augustus in 27 BC/BCE. Emperors – some much more renowned, famous or infamous than others – subsequently ruled for over 400 years. At the height of the empire, around 200 AD/CE, it incorporated the whole of continental Europe, the British Isles, Egypt and modern-day Lebanon and Syria. The Romans created settlements, roads, buildings and a language, which have endured to the present.

The Roman invasion of the British Isles has also undergone something of a reinterpretation. The older view was that the occupation of these islands was something at the very edges of empire and had limited value and importance, but there is now a tendency for historians to view the British Isles as more strategic and important, not least for the raw materials it could provide, and with a greater movement of people and goods than was previously recognised. The story of the conquest also begins with unquestionably the most famous Roman leader of all, Julius Caesar. In 55 BC/BCE, after conquering Gaul (contemporary France), Caesar was looking for more glory. He thought he had found an opportunity to restore king Cunobelin of the Catuellauni (located in the modern-day East Midlands) to his throne. Caesar thus invaded with just two legions and faced far more opposition than he anticipated. He subsequently rationalised this expedition as a reconnaissance mission, but in contemporary terms we would probably view his account as political 'spin'. A year later, in 54 BC/BCE, Caesar returned with more purpose and with five legions, but he was not particularly successful, and he departed, complaining that there was little of value in Britain.

To give some idea of the enduring nature of the Roman civilisation, almost a century went by, to 43 AD/CE, before the emperor Claudius, with a similar agenda for personal glory, invaded the British Isles with four legions, but with a much firmer resolve. It is almost certain that Claudius's army landed near Richborough in present-day Kent, and they quickly adopted their successful empire-building tactics of dividing and conquering. On this occasion the Romans ostensibly invaded Britain in support of a disposed king named Verica, with the aim of returning him to the throne of the Atrebatic kingdom. Thus, the Romans were aided by the tribes they were apparently helping. A truthful account must therefore include more than simplistic notions of Romans versus all the Celtic tribes; history is rarely so simple. It also took about 50 years for the whole of England, Wales and the lowlands of Scotland to be conquered by Rome, while the Highlands were simply too troublesome. So, too, was the island of modern-day Ireland. Naturally, the successful invasion of the first four legions was very significant. An early task was to establish three legionary fortresses at Carleon (south Wales), Chester and York, alongside connecting roads. Almost immediately several other fortresses were built, for example in Colchester, Lincoln, Wroxeter and Exeter. The first three were maintained until the end of Roman occupation because of their strategic importance. Other settlements were also developed, not least London. An examination of the main Roman towns and roads demonstrates just how pervasive their influence has been in terms of determining the network of settlement and arterial connections in contemporary Britain.

A few final points ought to be made. The first is that the Roman occupation of the British Isles lasted for approximately three and a half centuries. This is a long time, not a simple event, and it would be like contemporary Britons contemplating the duration of time all the way back to the English Civil war, or the reign of Henry VIII if we consider Caesar's invasions. Second, the extent of Roman occupation ultimately provided these islands with the first sense of unity and Britishness, and has resulted in a local connection virtually wherever there is a primary school. Third, and being mindful of the impossibility of covering in this chapter all the knowledge that is required to teach well, this brief overview will end with a final event which demonstrates the importance of Britain's role in the empire. In AD/CE 305, during a period when the Roman Empire was in danger of fragmenting, Constantine visited Britain with his father, the emperor Constantius, who died in York in 306 AD/CE. It is reported that the soldiers in Britain immediately proclaimed Constantine as their new emperor. This event can rightly be described as one of the turning points in World history because 'Constantine the Great' not only reunited the empire for one final period of glory, but around 312 AD/CE he converted to Christianity and thus began the process through which the Roman Empire, and then the western world, became Christian. This seismic event had its foundations in York.

IDEAS FOR A HALF-TERMLY PLAN

An indicative list of teaching ideas linked to interpretation and significance was suggested in Chapter 4, ideas for narrative and event framing based on Caesar's early invasion were presented in Chapter 6, and so to supplement those suggestions, here is a proposed schema for a second half-termly plan. This could be combined with a study of the development of Rome as an example of an early civilisation. However, in Chapter 10 teachers are advised against making this decision, with the further suggestion that they select from Ancient Egypt, Iraq (Sumer) or China for increased breadth.

Therefore, the study unit ought to begin with an outline of Roman history and the development of their Empire. This could be subdivided into three main teaching inputs:

- Origins and empire: The legends and history of the origins of the Roman Empire, the extent of its reach by AD 42, and an opportunity to cover valuable mapping skills.
- Military might: An analysis of the power of its army, including training, equipment and tactics, and to answer the question of why the Roman armies were so successful.
- Culture and beliefs: A focus on the wider aspects of Roman civilisation, including the powerful legacy of classical architecture, political ideas, family, children, home life, etc., and an examination of Roman gods and spiritual beliefs.

From roughly week 4, the focus should then shift to the Romans in Britain, including the following topics:

- Invasion: The Roman concept of Britain, and Caesar's early curiosity, ambition and two limited invasions. The successful invasion by Claudius and the conquest in AD/CE 43 onwards. The establishment of military fortresses and a network of roads which can be plotted against modern roads.
- Evidence: The start of British history in a strict definitional sense. This might include the very recent discovery of the Bloomberg tablets in Roman London from roughly AD/CE 50 onwards (Smith, 2016) and

the insights that early texts have provided about (rather mundane) life in Roman Britain. Other suggestions would be a hot-seating activity described in Chapter 6, for example the life of a Roman Soldier in Britain. Recent archaeological evidence and DNA analysis have largely confirmed the belief that Roman soldiers and auxiliaries in Britain were drawn from all over the empire, including Africa.

- Resistance and co-existence: Recent work by archaeologists such as Eleanor Barraclough, presented in a BBC series on Celtic tribes (*In Search of the Celts*, 2018), has discussed how interconnected the two cultures were. Yet there were episodes of resistance, not least Boudicca's revolt around AD/CE 60.
- Roman Britain: A clear directive from the National Curriculum 2014 is to study the 'Romanisation' of Britain, including evidence from archaeological sites such as Caerwent. There could also be a focus on the growth of Roman towns, possibly a case study such as Chester where the streets and walls follow the pattern of the original Roman fortress and an amphitheatre has been found (half-excavated). Another essential aspect was the technology and ideas behind their systematic road building. And no Roman topic could possibly leave out Hadrian's Wall.
- In Chapter 2, it was suggested that the religious dimension of history has often been under-explored by primary schools. Therefore, an account of Constantine the Great would not only be a powerful ending to the Roman Empire in the British Isles, but it could also include the origins of Christianity in Europe. Another aspect to widen the focus outwards again would be to briefly account for the relatively sharp decline of the Roman Empire and the final directive to leave Britain.
- An ongoing activity ought to be a 450-year timeline, from the time of Caesar's first invasion to the Roman abandonment of Britain. Ideally, this should be placed into the context of at least 2,000 years of British history. Large map work can demonstrate the extent of Roman settlement alongside the Celtic kingdoms.

ANGLO-SAXON INVASION AND SETTLEMENT – YEAR 5 (ALTERNATIVELY YEAR 6)

NATIONAL CURRICULUM EXTRACT – BRITAIN'S SETTLEMENT BY ANGLO-SAXONS AND SCOTS

Examples could include:

- Roman withdrawal from Britain in c. AD 410 and the fall of the western Roman Empire

- Scots invasions from Ireland to north Britain (now Scotland)
- Anglo-Saxon invasions, settlements and kingdoms: place names and village life
- Anglo-Saxon art and culture
- Christian conversion – Canterbury, Iona and Lindisfarne. (DfE, 2013, p. 190)

WHAT TEACHERS OUGHT TO KNOW

Whether this study unit begins in Year 5 or Year 6, there is likely to be a gap between the previous study of Roman Britain, and therefore, as the National Curriculum 2014 suggests, this topic ought to begin with the edict from the Roman Emperor Honorius that no more reinforcements would be sent to defend the Romans in Britain. The two main immediate threats for Romano-Britons at the start of the fifth century AD/CE were from the Scotti tribes from modern-day Ireland and the Picts from modern-day Scotland. This information is important not only from the point of view of understanding what was happening at the edges of the Roman Empire, for similar threats from north European tribes were occurring in continental Europe, but also for the burgeoning identity of Scotland and Ireland. This unit introduces the concept of England as a significant part of Britain. There is also the elusive concept of Romano-Britons. As the hot-seating example was partially designed to demonstrate, for many Roman soldiers, administrators and traders the concept of belonging to Rome did not necessarily mean that they were from modern-day Italy or had even visited Rome. Additionally, after 350 years of continuous occupation, historians and archaeologists are still researching and debating the extent to which Romano-Britons and Celts had intermingled, married and worked together. Like virtually all empires, there would have been a blurring of identity at the edges and the creation of something uniquely British forged in the particular and unique circumstances of the British Isles. At the very least, it simply is not the case that all Romano-Britons suddenly departed.

There was also a third threat. From northern Europe an influx of immigrants arrived and started to settle in the north and east. These were the north European tribes named the Angles, Saxons and Jutes from modern-day Germany and Denmark. These immigrants were termed 'Saxons' by the Celts, and while the concept of the Anglo-Saxon kingdom came later, the settlers referred to themselves as 'Angli' (naturally, from these origins emerges the concept of England).

The Anglo-Saxon period has often been referred to, rather negatively, as the Dark Ages. The idea behind this concept was the lack of historical evidence and the fact that so many of the technological advances of the Roman period were lost. This was true throughout Europe where 'barbarians' replaced the Romans, but there has been an increasing tendency for historians to recognise the achievements of the post-Roman period. Some things unquestionably did regress: Roman roads were not maintained; some settlements were abandoned and declined; the stone from Roman walls and buildings was often recycled, which is why only the foundations were left to be covered and then rediscovered by archaeologists; and the British Isles returned to a more pluralistic and tribal existence. However, there were continuities too. The conversion of the Roman Empire to Christianity continued after the arrival of St Augustine's papal mission. Writing was maintained too, although only by a limited number of scribes and initially in the Roman language or Latin rather than the vernacular languages of the Celts and Anglo-Saxons. Thus, historians do have some important sources, mostly from ecclesiastical scribes such as the Venerable Bede (eighth century AD/CE). And, as treasure hordes such as Sutton Hoo have also powerfully demonstrated, the Anglo-Saxon civilisation, and indeed the Celtic tribes, included people with tremendous skill and ingenuity.

Bede's invaluable account provides much of what historians know about the early Anglo-Saxon period, and so it is worth recounting in a little detail. It is important to note that he was utilising information from oral traditions rather than textual sources, and he would have viewed himself as a theologian rather than a historian. Bede noted the essential continuity between the Roman church and the Anglo-Saxon church, which was important to him because he considered this direct link a form of authority and religious purity. For example, he recorded that Gregory the Great (who was Pope between 590 and 604 AD/CE) sent a missionary named Augustine to Britain in 595 AD/CE. Augustine received land from the leader of the Kent tribe, Aethelberht (whose wife Bertha had already converted to Christianity), to found an abbey in 598 AD/CE. Consequently, Canterbury became the centre of the English church – a position it retains – and from these foundations Christianity eventually spread throughout the British Isles (we cannot really refer to England just yet). It is also an excellent example of powerful knowledge. It explains how deep the foundations of Christianity are in the British Isles (for example, St Patrick's work in Ireland) and why Canterbury is still the centre of the English church.

From Bede's texts, historians also have some idea of the location of the main Anglo-Saxon kingdoms. The previous iterations of the National Curriculum recommended studying the 'Heptarchy', or seven major kingdoms, and this is arguably still an essential element of this period of British history. They were East Anglia, Mercia, Northumbria, including sub-kingdoms Bernicia and Deira, Wessex, Essex, Kent and Sussex.

There are several important points to consider, however. First, Bede was probably simplifying a much more complex reality, and from a post hoc perspective. This list does not include several tribes, still ethnically Celtic in composition, who existed in the periphery of the British Isles, namely in Wales, Scotland and Ireland. Thus, the burgeoning sense of Englishness must be contrasted with Britishness – a theme that resonates today. Finally, a list will not mean much to upper-junior-aged children unless it is combined with extensive map work to understand where these kingdoms existed and where we can still find place names and identity which have existed to the present. The fact that several contemporary English counties, villages and towns have their origins in these early Anglo-Saxon kingdoms is important and powerful knowledge.

Aspects of Anglo-Saxon culture and society should be included. In 1938, archaeological work began on a series of strange mounds in a field in Deben, Suffolk. These were known to be sixth- and seventh-century burial sites which had previously been disturbed by grave robbers. The initial work began with a privately funded dig organised by the landowner, but the findings were so significant – unquestionably the greatest set of Anglo-Saxon objects and treasures ever discovered – that the British government became involved and the research soon became nationally important. The excavation revealed a ship burial – an important individual buried in a wooden boat surrounded by his possessions, and even his horse. The main objects can now be found in a prominent display in the British Museum and more recently a study centre has been opened at the location in Deben. The Sutton Hoo discoveries included a highly decorative and intricate helmet, a shield and swords, and similarly skilfully made and decorative clasps, buckles and bracelets. It is considered to be one of most important archaeological discoveries in British, and even in northern European, history, and parallels between the objects found and elements of the legend of Beowulf have also been made. Important archaeological discoveries from the Anglo-Saxon period continue to be made, such as the Stafford hoard unearthed in 2009; and as the British Library exhibition in 2018 demonstrated, the Dark Ages are continually being reassessed and re-evaluated.

The emerging concept of England is important too, but also complex because it occurs at a time when the Anglo-Saxon kingdoms were united against the Viking settlements. Therefore, this unit of study necessarily overlaps with a study of the Vikings, a fact that is acknowledged in the National Curriculum. To create a memorable ending, it is advisable to study the figure of Alfred 'the Great' (849–899 AD/CE). Alfred was the son of the West Saxon king, Aethelwulf, and was born in Wantage in contemporary Oxfordshire. Sources document that he was physically frail and sickly. One of the trends in history has been the often-controversial attempt to provide modern medical analysis on historical figures, and in Alfred's case it has been speculated that he may have suffered from Crohn's disease. Alfred possessed important intellectual and leadership qualities. His fame principally rests on the fact that he organised the kingdom of Wessex to successfully resist the Viking advance, most notably in the decisive victory at the battle of Edington in 878 AD/CE. This victory resulted in a peace treaty, the treaty of Edmore, between the

Anglo-Saxons and Vikings, and the conversion to Christianity of several important Viking leaders. Apart from his considerable achievements, one of the reasons that Alfred became such an important figure in English history is the fact that he ordered the writing of the Anglo-Saxon Chronicles, one of very few source materials for historians during this period. It is also fitting to note that Alfred had a personal belief in the importance of education, including the restoration of monasteries and the promotion of spoken and written forms of English.

IDEAS FOR A HALF-TERMLY PLAN

In Chapter 2 it was noted that most trainee teachers can collectively recall the main elements of primary history since the beginning of the National Curriculum. Nevertheless, from the former 'Invaders' topic, it has been the case that the Roman and Vikings elements are far more frequently and easily recalled compared with the Anglo-Saxon period. The reasons for this ought to be considered since they offer clues about the challenges of teaching this part of British history. To begin with there is a lack of clear imagery and notable events compared with the other periods. There is no Caesar, Roman army or world famous wall to provoke interest, nor is there the ostensible violence, glamour and pantheon of enduring gods, myths and legends that spring to mind when the Vikings are considered. Arguably, this is the problem with the Anglo-Saxon period: their invasion and settlement were much less dramatic, and their culture and iconography are much more subtle and confusing. These are important teaching points to consider before one can plan this study unit. I am also advocating something of an overlap between the Anglo-Saxon and Viking periods rather than following a strictly chronological approach.

- Starting point: A recap of the Roman withdrawal from Britain in AD/CE 410 and the fall of the Western Roman Empire.
- Invasion: The key event is that the Angles, Saxons and Jutes invaded the British Isles, and so the most important initial teaching input is to consider the various threats to Romano-Britain, including the Scots and Picts invading from Ireland and Scotland. Then the boats slowly but surely bring visitors from northern Europe. This requires extensive mapping exercises and possibly links with a European theme in geography (or links to the Vikings study).
- Landscape: As discussed in the Ancient British section, time ought to be spent thinking about what the British Isles would have looked like. There would be many Roman legionary fortresses and towns, and an established network of roads. There would be extensive agriculture at this point, not least fruits, vines, cereal crops and vegetables. However, much of Britain would have remained heavily wooded

and many of the Roman settlements would be starting to decline. The children could visualise the wooden boats arriving on the coast of eastern Britain bringing families looking for a new home in this sparsely populated land.

- Settlement: It is important for children to realise that invasion was not a simple event, but a long-term process leading to settlements and the formation of kingdoms, particularly in the south and east of modern England. Children could investigate the Heptarchy, key settlements and place-names, and aspects of village life. Once again, this would involve a focus on large-scale mapping exercises.
- Anglo-Saxon art and culture: The principal focus points here are the archaeological discoveries, notably Sutton Hoo, and what these tell us about Anglo-Saxon society, skills and values. There could be a focus on literature, including an examination of *Beowulf*, which has become better known due to the successful animated film in 2007.
- Christian conversion: As noted in the brief historical overview, although the Roman Empire converted to Christianity, the key events of Britain's conversion to Christianity occurred during the Anglo-Saxon period. A study ought to include important sites, such as Canterbury, Iona and Lindisfarne, as suggested in the National Curriculum.
- Home life: It is because this unit of study is more elusive, and therefore challenging, that one way to engage interest would be to make cross-curricular links with technology and art, by looking at fabrics, food, domestic arrangements and farming, including things like food tasting, etc.
- History from the inside: As a continuation of the social history theme, Chapter 5 introduced the idea of trying to imagine the worldview of an Anglo-Saxon girl. This would be a challenging activity, as it would require extensive knowledge, and therefore should ideally be conducted at the end of the unit, but it would be a way of extending and challenging children's historical reasoning and trying to bring this more elusive aspect of British history into focus.
- Timeline: The key teaching and learning point would be to emphasise how long this period was compared with more glamorous and renowned periods of British history. Given the fact that there is no neat separation from the Viking period, Anglo-Saxon Britain can be stated to have existed from AD/CE 410 to 1066 – six centuries of history.
- The concept of England, but also Ireland and Scotland: Englishness will be discussed in the following section, because by the tenth century it is possible to talk of England, land of the Angles. Equally, Englishness contrasts with the Celtic settlements and the concept of the burgeoning Celtic nations.

VIKING INVASION AND SETTLEMENT AND THE STRUGGLE FOR THE KINGDOM OF ENGLAND – YEAR 6

NATIONAL CURRICULUM EXTRACT – THE VIKING AND ANGLO-SAXON STRUGGLE FOR THE KINGDOM OF ENGLAND TO THE TIME OF EDWARD THE CONFESSOR

Examples (which are non-statutory) could include:

- Viking raids and invasion
- Resistance by Alfred the Great and Athelstan, first king of England
- Further Viking invasions and Danegeld
- Anglo-Saxon laws and justice
- Edward the Confessor and his death in 1066. (DfE, 2013 p. 191)

WHAT TEACHERS OUGHT TO KNOW

The first consideration before one begins the process of planning and teaching this study unit is that there are few neat and tidy aspects to the Viking era in the British Isles, and considerable overlap with the Anglo-Saxon period. While there may be a relatively straightforward start of Viking invasion, the end point, leading to the Norman invasion, is particularly complex.

The Viking homelands, as most people are aware, were in modern-day Scandinavia, principally Denmark and Norway. In these lands the Viking tribes developed several impressive achievements, not least advanced metallurgy. For example, the quality of their steel rivalled anything produced elsewhere in Europe and was probably only bettered by steel from China. They developed a rich system of belief, which still resonates. When children watch Hollywood-produced films such as *Thor* (2011) and others in the *Avenger* series, two of the main protagonists, Thor and Loki, are directly taken from Norse mythology. There is clearly something deeply appealing and enduring about Viking mythology. 'Northerness' was additionally a key theme for nineteenth-century composers such as Wagner and twentieth-century writers. When C.S. Lewis and J.R.R. Tolkien studied, and subsequently taught, at the University of Oxford, their most famous stories, such as the Narnia series and *The Hobbit* (1937) and *The Lion, the Witch and Wardrobe* (1950), were directly influenced by Germanic and Viking mythology.

The Viking tribes also developed a written form of language, the runes, and in addition were successful and skilled boat makers, sailors, explorers and traders. They developed connections with places as far apart as Moscow, Paris, modern-day Turkey and almost certainly North America. They also explored and settled on the islands of Iceland and

Greenland. Therefore, the significance of the Viking raids and settlement in the British Isles ought to be placed against this background of culture, exploration and adventure. In short, the British aspect is just one, admittedly significant, part of an ambitiously outward-looking and vibrant culture.

One aspect of Viking exploration has been to answer the question of their motivation to travel. In brief, whether overpopulation, limited arable land and a challenging climate acted as 'push' factors, or whether the 'pull' factors of adventure and easy pickings were more important, has been debated by historians and geographers. Like most debates concerning historical interpretation, the truth is probably somewhere in the middle. However, it does illustrate one important teaching point, and that is to challenge some of the crude myths surrounding the Vikings and hopefully replace them with something more nuanced and accurate. Given that this will be the final point of the primary British history unit of study, it provides an opportunity to scrutinise the evidence, to challenge myths and to address the role of interpretation in history (as outlined in Chapters 4 and 5). Indeed, a case can be made that in contrast to the Anglo-Saxon period, which often lacks a clear sense of identity, key events and figures, the much more striking and 'glamorous' Viking era demands greater rigour and contextualisation to create something more accurate and truly historical. In this sense, the film industry merely reinforces the half-truths and mythology.

The Vikings join the British narrative in 793 AD/CE when Vikings raided a monastery in Lindisfarne on the north-east coast of England. This was recorded by the monk Alcuin of York in a letter he wrote to Higbald, the bishop of Lindisfarne. This may not have been the first raid, but it is the first one where there is documentary evidence. Over the subsequent decades several more raids were carried out, but there were probably many more than historians have records for simply because of the destruction and later abandonment of several monasteries. There are similar records of attacks in Ireland, but none in Scotland, although they must have occurred.

The initial raids for plunder were then followed by a period of invasion and settlement, mostly in northern England, including parts of the west coast such as the Wirral, and throughout Scotland and Ireland too. By 955 AD/CE, documents such as the Anglo-Saxon Chronicles outlined a time of peace, when King Edgar (959–975 AD/CE) noted the multi-ethnic groups in the land and described a law for Englishmen, Danes and Britons (the latter being the remaining Celtic and earlier tribes, mostly at the periphery of the British Isles). Certainly, by the middle point of the tenth century, we can now legitimately discuss the concept of England and Englishness. Many historians consider Alfred's son, Edward the Elder (899–924 AD/CE) who extended the Anglo-Saxon kingdom, to be the first English king, and if not Edward, then certainly his son Aethelstan (894–939 AD/CE). Of course, Englishness would partly have emerged as a contrast to the identity of Danes and Britons. This is also a good example of the complexity of this period as various cultures, identities and kingdoms co-existed.

By this point, we can also discuss the concept of the Danelaw, the areas of the country where the Viking settlers were in control (their laws held sway), and this is where historical maps are invaluable. Viking settlers were still connected through taxation with the Viking homelands in Scandinavia. Some of the money was also raised through bribes, or the Danegeld, which were payments of tribute to maintain the peace. The account of Alfred and his battles with the Vikings also included periods where the Vikings were paid not to attack. Thus, in many respects it was an uneasy peace. It was also an increasingly complex time in that several Viking leaders converted to Christianity, notably Harold Bluetooth, and the two north-European cultures overlapped and merged to a considerable degree. Britain, and particularly England, was also wealthy by this point, which is one of the reasons why the control of England was so contested.

A decisive moment occurred in 1013 AD/CE when Harold Bluetooth's son, Swein Forkbeard, decided to invade and conquer England, although this was only fully achieved through his son, Cnut (Canute). At this time it would be fair to state that England, though not Britain, was predominately under direct Viking, or Danish, control, but the Anglo-Saxons still had a presence and identity, particularly in the burgeoning Christian Church. To provide an illustration of the complexity by this point, king Cnut married Emma, the widow of the Anglo-Saxon king Aethelred, and they had a son together, Harthacnut. However, Harthacnut was subsequently succeeded by Emma and Aethelred's son, who became one of the most famous English monarchs, Edward II the Confessor (1042–1066 AD/CE). When Edward II died childless in January 1066, his mother's great nephew, William of Normandy, felt that he had a strong claim to the throne; but so too did the Anglo-Saxon nobleman Harold Godwinson, who also had some Danish blood. An important point to note is that the Norman ruling elite were themselves Viking settlers in northern France ('Norman' is a corruption of Norseman), and so although they had adopted the French language and culture, ethnically they were also Scandinavians.

Most people are aware of the single most famous date in English (British) history, 14 October 1066, when William of Normandy decisively beat Harold's army on the Sussex Downs, not least because Harold's army had previously fought and won a battle in Fulford, near York, against Harold Hardrada from Norway, who also desired the English throne.

The outcome of the Battle of Hastings is too well known to deserve discussion, and in theory is the starting point for history in Key Stage 3, but it was a truly decisive point in English and British history. However, as the above account hopefully demonstrates, to present the Battle of Hastings as a war between two nations is reductionist and simply wrong. Essentially, it was an internecine conflict among a largely Viking aristocracy to gain the wealth of England, and William's reign brought decisive changes in the organisation and culture of England and Britain. If it can be claimed that the Romans provided these islands with a collective sense of Britishness, then William forged a unifying political system and a sense of Englishness, tinged with French language and culture, from the disparate groups of Angles, Saxons, Jutes, Danes and Norwegians who had invaded and settled for over 600 years.

IDEAS FOR A HALF-TERMLY PLAN

We will now look at some ideas for a half-termly plan.

- Origins: Ideally, this ought to be linked to a geography topic, and the National Curriculum requirement to study an area of Europe is the obvious choice. Map work ought to include the extent of Viking trade and exploration, including North America and Asia as well as Europe. Some accounts of Viking culture in the Scandinavian homelands should be included. An obvious aspect of culture and technology would be Viking skills at boat building and metallurgy, not least since this demonstrates some of the technological advances that they held over other European cultures.
- Viking raids and invasion: This could begin with Alcuin's account, and recap some aspects of the growing Christian Church and wealth in Britain. This should include maps to demonstrate the route across the North Sea, the fear that Viking raids provoked, and questions about interpretation since we only have the Anglo-Saxon version of events. Although it may seem as if raids can only be viewed in one way, the push or pull debate could be mentioned. As a form of history from the inside, Year 6 children could be asked to produce accounts, possibly linked to drama activities, to demonstrate both viewpoints of the raids.
- Viking settlement and the Danelaw: The process of gradual settlement and conflict with the Anglo-Saxon kingdoms obviously needs to be included. The concept of the Danelew can only really be understood by carrying out more mapping activities, and possibly a specific focus on a key town such as York (Yorvik).
- Anglo-Saxon resistance: If this is not covered in the previous study unit, then the National Curriculum suggestion to study Alfred the Great, Edward the Elder and Athelstan – first kings of England – is necessary. Even if covered during the Anglo-Saxon focus, it would then require a recap, possibly in greater detail.
- Edward the Confessor and his death in 1066: The complex events leading up to the Battle of Hastings would be the end of the chronology, and hopefully this would convey the sense of increased unity between Anglo-Saxons and Vikings.

- Viking culture and technology: The important elements have been outlined above: the technical skills of boat building, navigation and exploration; the written langue of the Runes; the advances in technology linked to metallurgy and the excellence of Viking metalwork and design. It might also include aspects of social life in Scandinavia, including farming, fishing, home life and the fact that women had considerable status and legal rights.
- Viking culture, beliefs and legacy: The enduring mythology from Viking times is an obvious study theme and it could be explored in terms of explaining its continuing influence and popularity. What is it about Valhalla and the tales of the Viking gods, trolls, goblins and elves that makes it so enduring? This should be a genuinely open form of enquiry.
- Challenging myths (interpretation): The end of the primary years is the most obvious place to include the most challenging of historical concepts, such as evidence and interpretation. Some simple myths can be easily debunked – Vikings almost certainly did not have horns on their helmets. This was a nineteenth-century invention linked to Wagner's operas, although possibly influenced by one Celtic-era ceremonial helmet – the Waterloo helmet, which is part of the British Museum's online collection – which was found in the river Thames and that did have short horns. However, in recent decades there have been attempts at a more nuanced appreciation of the Viking culture that does not rest solely upon their prowess at fighting. The information in this short chapter should provide ideas for a more balanced view, but it would almost certainly be a mistake to ignore the violence at the heart of Viking society.

OPPORTUNITIES FOR FIELD WORK AND EDUCATIONAL VISITS

Chapter 7 outlined the current (and previous) requirements to study a locality near the school, and to look for themes and connections with the overview of British history presented in this chapter, as well as themes beyond 1066. It is inconceivable that an English or Welsh primary school will not have some links with the content listed in this chapter. Just as pertinently, almost all primary schools will have some opportunity to visit sites of national or international importance. Schools near the coast of southern England should be able to visit one of the invasion points in Kent or Sussex. Schools in the south may also be able to visit sites such as Stonehenge. Schools in Wales could visit Carleon or other Roman sites, not to mention the links with Celtic tribes. Teachers in counties such as Oxfordshire have an array of riches to visit, not least the work carried out at Dorchester Abbey, to support the teaching of the Roman and Anglo-Saxon periods in schools. For those in the north, the focus will probably be on the Romans or Vikings and there are several important locations that could be visited, not least Chester and York. The main point is that there will be an opportunity to make some of this content come alive wherever one teaches.

CHAPTER SUMMARY

- This chapter began with a suggestion that the complexity of dates, themes and content contained in the chronological overview of British history is sufficiently demanding to make it inappropriate for lower juniors and that it would be more successfully taught with older children.
- Given that the amount of content, if taught with intellectual honesty and integrity, would be too much for a single year group, a further suggestion has been to cover these units in Years 5 and 6.
- The chapter has summarised the main content that teachers should be reasonably confident to deliver, although the intention has been to guide further study (including providing suggested sources) rather than to cover all the information teachers will require.
- Similarly, examples of planning and content ideas for half-termly plans were suggested, and ideas for cross-curricular links where appropriate have been supplied.

USEFUL ONLINE RESOURCES

Most people need little introduction to the availability of internet-based sources, but it is important that such sources are reliable and accurate. The following list of BBC sites are taken from their 'Schools' and 'History' portals. Some have now been archived:

www.bbc.com/bitesize/subjects/zcw76sg (active in 2019)
www.bbc.co.uk/history/ancient/british_prehistory/overview_british_prehistory_01.shtml (2011 – archived) by Dr Francis Pryor
www.bbc.co.uk/history/ancient/british_prehistory/ (2011, archived) by Julian Richards
www.bbc.co.uk/history/british/timeline/neolithic_timeline_noflash.shtml (2011, archived) timeline of early British history from the BBC history department.

Other useful sites include the Historical Association (which requires an individual or school subscription to gain access to all their resources. The HA was partially created to support the teaching of history in schools. Similarly, most publicly funded museums have professional educators whose role it is to support teaching and learning. English Heritage is another publicly funded body that provides educational resources.

English Heritage offer several online and downloadable resources to support the teaching and learning of the Ancient, Roman, Anglo-Saxon and Viking periods:

www.history.org.uk/primary/categories/203
www.britishmuseum.org/learning/schools_and_teachers/resources/all_resources/resource_prehistoric_britain.aspx
www.english-heritage.org.uk/

FURTHER READING

Haigh, C. (1985) *The Cambridge Historical Encyclopaedia of Great Britain and Ireland*. Cambridge: Cambridge University Press.

More extensive and detailed than the Oxford University Press equivalent, this book provides an excellent introduction to British history and also contains a considerable number of historical maps.

Hall, S. (2001) *The Penguin Atlas of British and Irish History*. London: Penguin.

As the title suggests, this is a highly visual text, and the use of extensive historical maps is helpful in gaining an overview of the ebb and flow of early British history from the first permanent settlers onwards, not least the overlap between the successive waves of immigration. For example, it is helpful at explaining the co-existence of Anglo-Saxon and Viking settlements.

Morgan, K.O. (1988) *The Oxford History of Britain*. Oxford: Oxford University Press.

One of the many virtues of this book is the fact that each chapter is written by an established expert in a very readable style. Sales were such that it is easy to find a second-hand copy at a very reasonable price. The limitations include the lack of recent research and the fact that it essentially begins with the Roman occupation.

Salway, P. (1993) *The Oxford Illustrated History of Roman Britain*. Oxford: Oxford University Press.

This is also a highly accessible text which also benefits from many illustrations to guide the non-specialist reader.

Schama, S. (2000) *A History of Britain. Volume 1: At the Edge of the World? 3000 BC–AD 1603*. London: BBC Books.

It is a little disconcerting to realise how long ago Schama's groundbreaking BBC television series was. This is the first of three accompanying texts, but the content of the first volume is the most relevant for the primary curriculum.

CHAPTER 10

KEY STAGE 2 HISTORY (PART 2)

What this chapter will cover

This chapter continues with the remaining requirements for Key Stage 2 and therefore will be of equal interest for practitioners. In line with Chapter 9, it contains a brief introduction to the subject knowledge required to teach authoritatively and suggestions for planning a half-termly unit of study. However, a key difference in this chapter is an introduction to the range of possible topics that can be chosen within each unit, apart from Ancient Greece, and the contextual information which is useful to consider when making these decisions. Due to recommendations outlined in Chapter 9 to place the British history chronology in Years 5 and 6, a comparable case will be made for placing the remaining units in Years 3 and 4. The chapter ends with a discussion of school-level planning and how links with other subjects, notably geography and religious education (RE), can be promoted.

INTRODUCTION

The aim of this chapter is to consider the remaining statutory requirements for Key Stage 2 history. It is important to consider the fact that Michael Gove's original aim was to replace the European and World history units with a solely British focus, but following a period of further consultation, the final version of the National Curriculum 2014 ultimately contained more European, Ancient and World history topics (DfE, 2013). Naturally this has added to the burden of curriculum coverage. In the case of Ancient Greece, coverage is a requirement, but for the remaining elements, unlike the chronology of British history, there are alternate suggestions for study and therefore schools are required to decide the specific content. It was further noted in the Introduction that the high level of continuity between the National Curriculum 2014 and previous iterations will probably result in schools deciding to continue with the World and European study units that have previously been planned, taught and resourced. It should also be recalled that the local history element, 'A Local Study Unit' (DfE, 2013, p. 191), has previously been discussed in Chapter 7.

It is likely, but not so far acknowledged, that the addition of a 'Theme in British history beyond 1066' as one of the additional study requirements was essentially an 'escape clause' to reflect the fact that schools had often developed resources and expertise when covering one of the previous British history topics and were likely to carry on teaching the Key Stage 2 history study units that they feel most comfortable with. That stated, its closest analogue is with the first National Curriculum and the requirement to include a thematic unit from a suggested list (DES, 1991a, p. 30). It should also be noted that schools ought to be imaginative and courageous when approaching this element and that teachers do not have to be beholden to the perennially popular twentieth-century world wars, Tudor or Victorian topics, etc., which often lack criticality and adequate coverage.

For the sake of clarity, these are the remaining National Curriculum requirements:

- The achievements of the earliest civilisations – an overview of where and when the first civilisations appeared and an in-depth study of one of the following: Ancient Sumer; The Indus Valley; Ancient Egypt; The Shang Dynasty of Ancient China;
- Ancient Greece – a study of Greek life and achievements and their influence on the western world;
- A non-European society that provides contrasts with British history – one study chosen from: early Islamic civilisation, including a study of Baghdad c. AD 900; Mayan civilisation c. AD 900; Benin (West Africa) c. AD 900–1300;
- A study of an aspect or theme in British history that extends pupils' chronological knowledge beyond 1066 (DfE, 2013, pp. 191–2).

The overarching aim will be the same as the previous chapter: essentially to provide an overview concerning the general considerations, an introduction to and summary of important contextual knowledge required to teach authoritatively, a brief overview of the essential subject knowledge teachers ought to research as part of their preparation, followed by a suggested list of key teaching and learning ideas for a half-termly plan. Additionally, in this chapter there will be more emphasis on making links with other subjects. Given the extra teaching requirements for Key Stage 2 history, it would be prudent, if not essential, to combine history with National Curriculum geography study units, and possibly RE, art, design technology and science, to double or triple count teaching time and therefore provide a feasible solution to an overcrowded curriculum.

There are also three more considerations that deserve a brief introduction. Each section will include a short discussion about what to consider when making the choice over content. One suggested topic for each study unit will be introduced and discussed as an example, apart from the obvious exception of the Ancient Greece study unit. Thus, the 'Non-European' focus will examine the *Mayan Civilisation*; the example of an 'Early Civilisation' will introduce the *Ancient Sumer*; and the 'Theme in British history' will cover several suggestions, although the example under review will be the 'First Railways'. Although the Mayan civilisation has always been a study option, a rationale for these choices is that they are unlikely to have been previously taught in most primary schools, and therefore there is the opportunity to provoke more thought about how these elements might be covered.

At the school level, a similar decision must be made about a planning overview for each year group. This chapter will therefore conclude with two suggested school-level approaches for a single-form entry school. This chapter will continue with the case for introducing the British chronological overview in Years 5 and 6, and so here the suggestion will be to introduce the European and World elements in Years 3 and 4. However, a planning overview with British history beginning in Year 3 will also be discussed. Finally, the chapter will re-introduce the dimensions of history, and the fact that the National Curriculum recommends a range of sub-themes linked to the dimensions of history, including political, cultural and aesthetic, economic and technological – the so-called PESRC formula (introduced in Chapter 2), which now includes military history in the National Curriculum 2014.

Most of the text is a summary of my personal teaching and lecture notes, but with some key sources identified and, as in the case of the Ancient British history section, some peer-reviewed journal articles have been cited. It would be unrealistic to expect busy teachers to access academic sources, and prohibitively expensive too unless one has a university library subscription. The intention is to provoke curiosity and to guide teachers where scholarship and research are helpful. In common with the British history elements, the BBC History and Education web pages contain useful information and planning ideas, and there are other reliable sites such as the British Library and Historical Association, etc., which also provide information and planning ideas for teachers.

ANCIENT GREECE (CIRCA 3000 BC/BCE TO 300 BC/BCE) – YEAR 3

GENERAL CONSIDERATIONS

This section will make a case for placing the Ancient Greek topic in Year 3. First, the Ancient Greek topic is the only non-British study unit that has been a compulsory presence in every iteration of the National Curriculum, and therefore schools have had a quarter of a century to build up resources and expertise delivering this topic. Second, it is possible to teach this unit well with very little reference to chronology, thereby avoiding the challenges associated with complex and distant periods of time – although the concepts of BC/BCE would have to be discussed in some form. Third, the topic contains several powerful cross-curricular links and interactive teaching approaches which make it more accessible for younger children. Finally, it contains useful prior knowledge before introducing the Ancient and Roman periods of British history that were previously recommended to start in upper Key Stage 2.

WHAT TEACHERS OUGHT TO KNOW

The story of Ancient Greece begins approximately 9,000 years ago (7000 BC/BCE) in Neolithic times as part of the pan-European exodus discussed in Chapter 9. One of the current claims is that this migration was at least partially coastal (Brace et al., 2019), and an examination of a map of Greece will indicate how dominated it is by the sea. It is a complex pattern of islands and archipelagos jutting into the Mediterranean and Aegean seas, and, rather like the history of Britain, Greek history and culture has been shaped by its relationship with the sea.

According to Burn (1990), Greece experienced several waves of immigration and went through the typical pattern of agriculture, pottery making and metal working. This was followed by the first significant pan-Greek culture, the Minoans, from about 2900 BC/BCE. In many respects, the Minoan culture acted as the template for later myths and legends, and produced high-quality jewellery and art. This was the first distinctive Greek society and arguably the point at which to start the topic. Greek identity was further developed by the development of a distinctive Greek language, but not yet writing, around 2500 BC/BCE and the start of the Greek Bronze Age. One important aspect of Greek history to understand, and there are parallels with Germany and Italy, is that a unifying language and culture did not signify a modern unified state. One of the key elements of Greek history is to understand the development of small, city states, and the encroachment of Greek language and culture into the surrounding land and islands, such as Crete. Indeed, the 'heroic' age is associated with expansion and colonisation. Equally, art, particularly sculpture, continued to develop alongside the development of writing circa 1000 BC/BCE, and the first true histories were written. Writing directly led to one of the most enduring Greek developments: the writing of poetry and drama, notably by authors such as Homer, Aeschylus and Sophocles, who produced texts that have endured over 3,000 years.

Burn (1990) argued that the 'great years' era (c. 450 BC/BCE) was the high point of Greek culture. This era included the development of key ideas in philosophy, which have proved to be equally enduring. For Pedley (1993), it was also the pinnacle, or the 'golden years' period, for Athenian and Greek architecture as buildings such as the Parthenon were constructed, and there were equally impressive developments in pottery and sculpture. A key element was the creation and expansion of democracy, the rule of the people, or the *demos*, and military campaigns such as the Persian wars. However, Greek unity and the dominance of Athenian culture were not to last. The 10-year Peloponnesian war (really two wars) led to the rise of Sparta and Thebes. Texts such as Burn (1990) attest to the strangeness of Spartan life and community. Originally wealthy and opulent, it became authoritarian and militaristic, including the severe military and athletic training of boys, while girls were similarly tested to become the worthy mothers of soldiers. Its culture included an eschewing of luxury, preferring ascetic fashions in food and clothing.

A little after this time, roughly 400 BC/BCE, Greek philosophy reached its zenith with key thinkers such as Socrates, Plato and Aristotle. Again, the Greek legacy is remarkably powerful and enduring: in England, to study the 'classics' in the elite universities is still regarded as one of the pinnacles of intellectual and cultural achievement, and the Socratic ideal of testing ideas through discussion has endured as a form of pedagogy, not least in the tutorial system that continues in the medieval universities of Oxford and Cambridge.

The final notable period was the rise of the Macedonians, first through Philip II and then his son, Alexander the Great, circa 350 BC/BCE. This was a time of great conquest and influence before the Roman Empire began to encroach on and supplant the Greeks. Historians date the end of the Ancient Greek civilisation at roughly the third century AD/CE, but the Macedonian period would provide a memorable and suitable ending.

IDEAS FOR A HALF-TERMLY PLAN

Given the legacy of the Ancient Greeks, and it is truly astonishing to realise just how many words, concepts and ideas have endured through to the present, it is difficult to channel them into something workable and appropriate for Year 3 children. The main themes should at least incorporate some idea of Greece's geography, the influence of the sea and its legacy as a seafaring nation. It should also acknowledge some of the complexity, and the fact that there was no single country as such and that sometimes the small city states were at war with each other. It must incorporate powerful knowledge about key ideas and language, such as geography, classical architecture and ideas of beauty, and philosophers such as Plato and Aristotle, who continue to be cited by modern scholars. Greek culture, home life, food and clothes should also be included.

Finally, some time must be spent on the enduring aspects of myths, legends, gods and beliefs.

However enduring Viking culture has been, it is demonstrably less than the legacy of the Ancient Greeks, because the topic contains so much powerful and enduring knowledge. The following list of ideas is in roughly chronological order, but the case has already been made that this unit should not concentrate too much on time. It was previously noted that there is the potential for obvious and powerful cross-curricular links which could, theoretically, double the amount of content taught in the same half-term period. Alternatively, several elements could be combined for a termly project.

- Who were the Ancient Greeks? The obvious starting point is to begin with mapping exercises, ancient and modern, including an identification of the main settlements, city states, islands and proximity to other countries, such as Egypt, Israel and Italy. The link with geography is obvious. The National Curriculum 2014 requires a continent study of Europe and a region within a European country (DfE, 2013, p. 186). Thus, the Ancient Greeks could be studied alongside a focus on modern Greece. Although a non-chronological approach has been recommended, it would be necessary to discuss that this topic begins 5,000 years ago (3000 BC/BCE) and ends about the time of Jesus Christ, 2,000 years ago.
- Greek gods: The origins of the Greek gods are both very ancient and elusive, and continue to be researched and debated, but irrespective of chronology, it is arguably an ideal starting point for engaging children's interest. As a former Key Stage 2 teacher, when I taught this element within the Ancient Greeks topic, I created small teams to work on a specific Greek god or legend, which culminated in a brief presentation and combined display. It would be an ideal opportunity to develop early research and teamwork skills as well as making clear links with religious education (virtually all locally agreed syllabuses contain a requirement to study other belief systems), art work and mapping skills to find places associated with the Greek gods, such as Mount Olympus, Knossos or Corfu.
- Poetry, myths and legends: This element is equally ancient. Indeed, some scholars think that the origins of the epic poems are around 10,000 years old, and therefore possibly too challenging or abstract for some children. However, it would link very closely with the requirement for English, and introduce many of the main stories associated with the Greeks. It should include Homer and the many narrative elements associated with Troy. Other possibilities would include the *Odyssey* and the trials of Odysseus, the labours of Heracles, Jason and the Argonauts or the battle of Marathon. Abridged versions of these stories have been produced, and of course a suitable conclusion could be getting groups of children to write a play based on a Greek myth or legend.

- Home life of the Ancient Greeks: Latitude would be necessary to accommodate 3,000 years of history in one teaching element, but this approach lends itself to a themed day roughly half-way through the topic. It could include clothes (a day or morning dressed in Greek fashions), food (and naturally food tasting), the lives of women and children, and possibly broader elements such as the Greek alphabet and modern English words appropriated from Ancient Greece.
- The 'golden age' of Athens: This could be more teacher directed and include a longer teaching input. The key focus should be on the *substantive, first-order* concept of democracy (refer to the discussion in Chapter 2), and its links with citizenship and British values (DfE, 2014). Differentiation could be achieved through introducing an element of interpretation and challenging the extent to which Athens was truly democratic. The role of women and other non-citizens could be investigated, and the fact that Athenian society and its economy relied on a slave class.
- Art and architecture: The Athenian focus could continue with an examination of the enduring power of Greek ideas concerning architecture and sculpture. A study of the Parthenon is an obvious choice, and this could incorporate ideas such as the golden section, which has informed a lot of current thinking about the mathematics and proportions behind human ideas about beauty. It could also be an opportunity to make connections with art and design technology through children's own projects and designs.
- Sport and pastimes: Depending on the cycle of the modern Olympic movement, this could be linked to a forthcoming Olympic Games. It needs little introduction and has been one of the most commonly taught elements of the Ancient Greek topic. Nevertheless, there are some important teaching points. The Olympic Games were not the only tournaments. Children could research the Nemean, Ishmian and Pythian Games as a research project and then consider the question of why one became much more famous than the others. There are also citizenship themes around the role of women and non-citizens and how attitudes to sport have changed.
- Sparta: If the first session introduced the idea of a federation of small states, this would be the opportunity to study not only the second most renowned Greek state, but one that offers a clear contrast with Athens. The tough, militaristic upbringing for children, both boys and girls, would add something that Year 3s could relate to, and it should also include a very brief account of the Peloponnesian wars and the end of the 'golden period'.
- Macedonians and Alexander the Great: Not only would this be chronologically the right place to end the topic, it would also act as an appropriate coda with the last great figure from Ancient Greek history. It would be an opportunity to look at the Macedonian region,

and a return to map work and geography, and to consider the extent of Greek influence and empire in the classical world.

- What do we owe to the Ancient Greeks? A reflective ending might include time to recap and digest the legacy of the Ancient Greeks. While no list is definitive and would vary depending on planning decisions, it would probably include:
  - The Pantheon of the gods
  - The idea of democracy
  - Poetry and plays
  - Sporting tournaments and the Olympic Games
  - Philosophy and key thinkers
  - Words we still use
  - The start of history – Thucydides and his account of the Peloponnesian war
  - Great leaders
  - Architecture, sculpture and enduring ideas of beauty.

NON-EUROPEAN SOCIETY: MAYAN CIVILISATION CIRCA AD/CE 900 - YEAR 3

GENERAL CONSIDERATIONS

The requirement to study a 'World history' topic in previous iterations of the National Curriculum (DfEE, 1999, p. 107) resulted in most schools choosing to cover either the Ancient Egyptians or the Aztec civilisation – in that order of popularity. In the interests of accuracy, the Aztecs were part of the compulsory Core Study Unit 6, 'Exploration and Encounters 1450–1550' in the first iteration of the National Curriculum (DES, 1991a, p. 28), but became optional after this. Both of these units still can be chosen, although the Egyptians would now be placed in the early civilisation section, and so the decision to discuss the Mayan civilisation has been intentionally made to broaden perspectives and to consider alternative approaches. The Mayan civilisation is a fascinating topic for study, with several points of contrast alongside examples of parallel development with European culture. It offers engaging teaching and learning ideas. That stated, there is not as much knowledge to cover as there is for the Ancient Greeks, where the challenge is what to omit. Thus, irrespective of double counting time, lower-junior teachers ought to consider combining this topic with a geography focus on the Americas (DfE, 2013, p. 186), or possibly echoing the original 'Exploration and Encounters' study unit and extending it to include European exploration and colonisation of the Americas.

The peak of the Mayan civilisation is not ancient either. The 'classical' period lasted roughly from 200 AD/CE to 900 AD/CE, placing it within 'early history', although contemporary archaeological research is questioning the accuracy of both the start and finish dates. However, this does mean that if it is taught in Year 3, the timescales are not overly challenging, with most events paralleling the Anglo-Saxon and Viking periods in the British Isles.

WHAT TEACHERS OUGHT TO KNOW – 'BIG PICTURE' THINKING

One of the ways in which the Mayan topic can be extended, in terms of both knowledge and intellectual challenge for more curious or able children, is to provide a contextual discussion about the first people in the Americas. During the height of the Cold War, it was frequently pointed out that if one avoided the Eurocentric view of the globe, the former USSR and the USA were only separated by a narrow sea, the Bering Strait, rather than the breadth of the Atlantic Ocean. In an exact analogue with Doggerland and the land bridge between Britain and Europe, during the last cold spell the lower sea levels created a land bridge or connection geologists have termed 'Beringia'. This bridge allowed people to travel from the west coast of Asia into the Americas. The date of the first arrivals continues to be hotly debated (Worrall, 2018), with estimates ranging from 20,000 to 40,000 years ago, but there is general agreement that the peak was around 16,000 years ago (14,000 BC/BCE) and the final migration was 12,000 years ago (10,000 BC/BCE), essentially because rising temperatures and sea levels resulted in the loss of the land bridge. Intriguingly, according to Worrall (2018), there is archaeological evidence in the form of distinctive stone axes that some immigrants may have brought with them as they crossed the ice sheets from Europe. Nevertheless, at the point when Columbus and Cortez 'discovered' the Americas in the fifteenth and sixteenth centuries, the thousands of tribes and cultures that inhabited virtually the whole of the Americas had, and still have, similar ancestry to contemporary Asians.

Patterns of development varied quite considerably. In the north, the tribes tended to be nomadic and did not develop either writing or metallurgy (other than working with soft metals). They could therefore be accurately, if patronisingly, described as existing in the Stone Age, although other aspects of their culture and society were advanced. In the middle Americas, Meso-America (which is technically part of the continent of North America) and in some regions of South America, there were examples of full metallurgy, including smelting, as well as written language and advanced forms of mathematics. The economist Paul Krugman's famous quote, 'productivity isn't everything, but in the long run it is almost everything' (1994, p. 11), is relevant to the study of ancient societies for, as mentioned previously, it is only when a society has developed a system of farming that produces an agricultural and economic surplus, and developed a system of organisation through settlement, that talented individuals can be freed to develop their skills and make technical advances. In short, several Meso-America societies, including the Aztecs and Mayans, developed sufficiently productive agricultural systems, which allowed aspects of their culture, technology and knowledge to flourish. What is fascinating with the Mayans is that their developments, and interpretations of their society, have been so varied.

So, who were the Mayans? Their civilisation can be mapped against modern countries such as south-eastern Mexico and all of Guatemala and Belize, and so technically they were part of the continent of North America in a hot and fertile region. Since the mid-1980s (Hammond, 1986; Bower, 2013) there has been increasing archaeological evidence that the distinctive aspects of the Mayan civilisation began a little sooner than was first thought, and so the starting point has been shifted downwards to around 200 AD/CE. Archaeological evidence has also identified the first settlement in the region dating back 10,000 years (8000 BC/BCE), to roughly the same period as settlement in the British Isles, and the influence of the earlier Olmec society.

Nevertheless, the Mayan civilisation grew quickly around a series of city states (Hernandez, Ballonga and Escofet, 1992). What is unusual about the Mayans is that they left behind substantial stone buildings, which European explorers subsequently found covered by dense undergrowth. Such extensive evidence has not only ensured an enduring sense of mystery, but has also enabled later scholars to analyse Mayan culture and technology. The buildings and cities were created despite the lack of any form of metallurgy, so the Mayans had to use stone tools to quarry and shape the blocks of stone. Many of the ceremonial buildings were pyramidal, and up to 70 metres tall. Of course, an African culture had built much larger pyramids 3,000 years earlier (roughly 2500 BC/BCE), but the fact that an American society had developed similar architecture resulted in speculation about parallel cultural development.

Politically, each city state was a separate kingdom and so it was a federation of smaller states sharing common beliefs and language. It was initially thought that the Mayans had developed in a harmonious and non-aggressive way, but this has since been refuted. Mayan society was hierarchical, with a clear aristocracy, some evidence of a middle class, and a free farming peasant society supported by slaves. There is evidence of cooperation between the peasants, with each family having a small patch of land and an obligation to work on shared projects. Food production was largely vegetarian, although some hunting was carried out. The main crops were maize, vegetables such as squash, beans and cocoa. Clothing tended to be cotton-based weaving, with loincloths for men and tunics for women supplemented by leather and fur for shoes and more durable clothing, etc.

Mayan gods totalled around 150, and the principal ones were associated with fertility and farming, such as the Sun, Maize and Rain gods.

Some beliefs continued after the fall of the Mayan civilisation, but equally scholars have been able to work out some aspects of worship because the Mayans developed a complete writing system, supplemented by extensive stone carvings, which have been deciphered. Unfortunately, only four complete books are extant, and they are very like early European texts in that they were bound and written on a form of paper. The four copies are the only ones to survive both the decline in the Mayan civilisation and later European attempts to destroy what they viewed as a form of idolatry.

Equally impressive were Mayan mathematical discoveries (Hammond, 1986). In parallel with the Aztecs, they developed a base 5/20 system, including place value. Historians of mathematics assume base 10 has commonly emerged due to humans having five digits on each limb rather than the efficacy of 10, due to its lack of factors. However, the Mayans used only three symbols: zero, represented as a shell shape; one, represented as a dot; and five, represented as a bar (Brink, 2011). Again, this was viewed as another example of parallel human development. There has been increasing discussion about the importance of the discovery and the spread of zero. In brief, it was developed in India around the same time as the Mayan culture, eventually arriving in Europe, via Arabia, around 1200 AD/CE (Weiss, 2017). Take a moment to think about this: neither the Ancient Greeks nor the Romans, for all their other achievements, had developed the concept of a number to represent nothing and to act as a place holder. One can understand how exciting this discovery was in the annals of archaeology and early history. Equally impressive were the sophisticated and accurate calendar systems the Mayan astronomers had developed (Hammond, 1986).

In conclusion, the Mayans may have lacked metallurgy, but they had developed a highly organised and efficient agricultural system, advanced city states, a complete writing system, and a sophisticated system of mathematics. So why did they disappear so quickly? And how has their society been viewed by historians and ethnographers? The first thing to state is that the people themselves did not disappear, although there have been estimates that the population fell from 3,000,000 to 450,000 in a relatively short period of time (Crist and Paganini, 1980). They simply returned to a simpler way of life based on some aspects of Mayan society, and their ancestors can still be found in Belize and Guatemala. As Crist and Paganini (1980) summarised, it was a challenging question for researchers to answer, but as so often in history, there is no single cause. What seems likely is that the decline was not quite so precipitous as first thought, and involved overpopulation, periods of drought (Haug et al., 2003) and extensive crop failures. Additionally, there is evidence, not least from the situation that the first Spanish explorers witnessed, that 16 rival states were still in a period of conflict. So, far from being a bucolic ideal, Mayan society almost certainly experienced a breakdown of cooperation into an extended period of conflict. As Fash (1994) concluded, there has been a tendency on behalf of European intellectuals to initially overstate the achievements of the Mayans, followed by a revisionist phase which was overly negative. However, there remains a consensus of informed opinion that the Mayan intellectual achievements were impressive and tell us something about the emergence of parallel forms of human cultural development.

IDEAS FOR A HALF-TERMLY PLAN

Given the complexity of aspects of Mayan history, it would be preferable to focus on the more accessible domestic and cultural aspects of their civilisation with a Year 3 class, but the challenge could be extended if taught with older pupils.

- Who were the Mayans? This would allow a common entry point for both history and geography. Mapping exercises and a brief introduction to the countries of Central America could be discussed. While the complexity of the time periods is challenging, it would be helpful to discuss the first Americans and when and how they arrived in the Americas, possibly including an account of Beringia and the first settlers. This might also include the megafauna of the Americas, such as woolly mammoths and sabre-tooth cats. The timescales, including parallel developments from the British Isles, could be included in a timeline activity.
- Cities, buildings and pyramids: Since Mayan buildings and cities are the most obvious part of their legacy, an opportunity to look at the growth of Mayan cities would be informative (Hernandez et al., 1992). The parallels with Ancient Egypt could be made, and links with design technology are possible through a pyramid-making project.
- Gods and beliefs: The short account in this chapter cannot do justice to the full range of Mayan gods and beliefs. These would include some of the rituals, such as the rubber ball game pok-a-tok.
- Mayan home life: This might be spread out over several lessons and include farming, food, clothes and buildings. It could lead to a themed day and an opportunity to try Mayan food. Many schools have adapted planning around a chocolate theme and so the importance of cocoa beans in Mayan culture should be covered.
- Mayan achievements: This could include an input on writing, mathematics and astronomy.
- What happened to the Mayans? Although the disappearance of the city states has been satisfactorily explained by recent research, it is still mysterious, and children will almost certainly be drawn into the mystery in the same way historians and archaeologists responded a century ago. It would be a good opportunity to examine the evidence

and look at recent interpretations. A challenging activity would be to provide the main evidence and to allow children to create their own explanation.

- Mayans today: This would be the point at which the topic could transform into a geography unit of study.
- The history of chocolate: Many schools have developed cross-curricular themes linked to chocolate or the rainforest, with the Aztecs or Mayans as part of the overall theme (refer to Chapter 11 for more details on history and cross-curricular links).
- European exploration: Finally, aspects of European exploration and conquest of the Americas, especially the Spanish and Portuguese in the Americas, could be included.

THE ACHIEVEMENTS OF THE EARLIEST CIVILISATIONS: ANCIENT SUMER - YEAR 4

GENERAL CONSIDERATIONS

Chapter 2 briefly accounted for the more esoteric aspects of the primary history curriculum. However, to recap: the National Curriculum 2000 (DfEE, 1999, p. 107) required a European focus on Ancient Greece and a 'World' study unit, with choices from 'Ancient Egypt, Ancient Sumer, the Assyrian Empire, the Indus Valley, the Mayans, Benin, *or* the Aztecs'. This provided considerable latitude, but also relatively limited coverage. The fact that schools are now required to teach *both* a non-European society and an early civilisation topic, along with Ancient Greece, is arguably closer to the first iteration of the National Curriculum (DES, 1991a, p. 32), which required Key Stage 2 children to study Ancient Greece, 'Exploration and Encounters' (which included the Aztecs), and additionally a supplementary study unit chosen from Ancient Egypt, Mesopotamia (which includes the Sumer), the Assyrians, the Indus Valley, the Maya or the Benin (DES, 1991a, p. 32). One of the themes of this book has been the high levels of National Curriculum continuity, but this element of the National Curriculum does reflect politicians' belief in important knowledge and the value of history.

The argument for placing the Early Civilisation unit of study in Year 4 is that it acts as a precursor for the Ancient British history, but this does result in extended and ever more complex timeframes. The selection of the Ancient Sumer as an example was informed by the importance of citizenship themes and broadening children's minds away from a solely European or western perspective. As Adams (1994) noted during what is now termed the 'first gulf war', the way the west interprets Arabic countries like Iraq, principally as barbaric and culturally backward, is deeply ironic given that Iraq and Kuwait can fairly be described as the cradle of civilisation. There is an argument, therefore, for studying the Ancient Sumer to challenge and modify some of these beliefs. A similar case can be made for studying the Shang dynasty from China, especially given the fact that children educated in primary schools in the early twenty-first century will probably live long enough to witness China becoming the world's dominant state.

WHAT TEACHERS OUGHT TO KNOW – 'BIG PICTURE' THINKING

The term 'big picture' thinking is not original and has recently been adopted by Graeber and Wengrow (2018, p. 7) in their meta-analysis of research findings from palaeontology as well as archaeology. Indeed, this is the point to mention that discussion of the first people transcends history and archaeology and moves into the physical sciences. And yet this topic introduces the true start of history because it incorporates the development of written language.

Most educated people are familiar with the idea that the very first modern humans, early hominids and later *Homo sapiens*, emerged from Africa. Equally, it is important to note that new discoveries and research findings are demonstrating that the full story is far more complex than the initial accounts suggested, although it is generally agreed that the earliest ancestors of modern humans, *Homo erectus*, emerged about 1.8 million years ago. A landmark publication in *Nature* in January 1987 used mitochondrial DNA analysis to claim that all modern humans can be traced back to a small group of females in Africa roughly 140,000 years ago (Cann et al., 1987). As noted in Chapter 9, in geological terms this is very recent. Naturally, these early findings have subsequently been qualified, not least by evidence that there was an ebb and flow of *Homo sapiens* between Africa and Asia, and many scientists were disappointed that journalists tended to focus on the idea of a historical 'Eve' rather than the wider research findings. Yet the broad claims are still accepted. The migration to Europe from Africa occurred around 43,000 years ago and thus this can be compared with continuous settlement in the British Isles of approximately 11,000 years. Further analysis of bone remains suggests that these early Europeans interbred with Neanderthals and had dark skin.

The Sumer civilisation is important in this early human story because it was essentially the first modern society and the first place where incontrovertible evidence has been found of several crucially important human discoveries; and it can roughly be divided into three main periods. In terms of location, their settlements and land were part of the Euphrates river valley (the Euphrates flowed into the Persian Gulf in the southern part of greater Mesopotamia) and are now part of modern Iraq and Kuwait.

According to Mark (2011), the earliest archaeological evidence points to settlements as far back as 5000 BC/BCE (7,000 years ago). These early settlers were known as the Ubaidians and were likely to have developed the first cereal crops for cultivation. Archaeologists have termed this the Ubaid Period. I have already quoted Paul Krugman's words about productivity, but clearly the movement from hunting to farming had important consequences. It is not only that more food is produced; it also requires cooperation and organisation, and the idea of settlement – hence the first towns and cities. This became the Early Dynastic Period (2900–2334 BC/BCE), or second period in Sumerian history (Mark, 2011). As writers such as Graeber and Wengrow (2018, p. 20) have argued, a detailed analysis of the evidence from throughout the world does not support a sudden change, or revolution, into farming and settled communities. Nevertheless, archaeological evidence such as sickles, hoes and methods of irrigation around this time are clear evidence that in the Early Dynastic period, Sumerians had adopted an agrarian way of life. The first settlements emerged around 3600 BC/BCE (5,600 years ago), and Urek has a strong claim to be the world's oldest city. The first ruler, Etana of Kish, from 3000 BC/BCE was an avatar, or priest-king, and responsible for the success of the harvests.

Key Sumerian inventions, or early adaptations, included the wheel (which, in contrast to the Mayan topic, was not developed anywhere in the Americas) and sailing boats. However, the most significant idea of all was the development of writing. The development of language has fascinated scholars through the centuries and continues to be debated, including archaeological evidence of the development of larynxes. Writing clearly began with the discovery of art, and the idea that the world and its objects could be represented through drawings. It takes a considerable intellectual leap to recognise that pictures can be formalised as hieroglyphs, then refined into graphemes (symbols) which can represent individual phonemes (units of sound) which can then be used to construct words and capture language and meaning. Yet this did happen, and it occurred in Ancient Sumer. The first writing is known as cuneiform (Harford, 2017), and according to Quenet (2005) was developed between 3300 and 2900 BC/BCE (up to 5,300 years ago). During the middle of the Dynastic Period of the Sumerian civilisation, the early priest-kings were replaced by a more hierarchical and modern concept of leadership, along with the development of a bureaucracy. Increasing food surpluses and wealth resulted in an expansion of administration and trade, which in turn promoted the use of writing and record keeping.

The last period in Sumerian history (2047–1750 BCE) has been termed the Sumerian Renaissance (Mark, 2011) because of the impressive list of further achievements. These included tools, technology, legal codes, schools, music and mathematics. Essentially, the Sumerians developed a sexagesimal counting system which was based on six lots of 10. The explanation for why there are 60 seconds in a minute, 60 minutes in an hour or 360 degrees in a full rotation (six multiples of 60) is because of the Sumerians. Its wide adoption and persistence ultimately defeated subsequent attempts to create a decimal system for time and rotation. The Sumerians also divided day and night into two lots of 12, hence 24 hours in a full day. This is a contemporary example of their inventiveness and enduring legacy to the world.

The end came rather abruptly in 1750 BC/BCE (almost 4,000 years ago) with the sacking of Sumerian cities by the Elam and Amorites, despite the construction of a very long wall to keep them out. The language was lost, but not cuneiform writing. Arguably, their greatest legacy was to set the template for the modern world. All social forms of living imply a form of social compact, as Enlightenment philosophers such as Jean Jacques Rousseau, Thomas Hobbes and John Locke argued. The division of labour may well have sown the seeds of inequality, but it also implies a duty of common care. Both Kennedy (2014) and Keys (2014) reported on an exhibition that featured early British archaeological finds. One example of fine gold metalworking on a sword scabbard required such close focusing – the strands of gold were thinner than a human hair – that optometrists have calculated that it could only have been done by children, and that it would have eventually led to functional blindness. The point is that whoever carried out this work knew that they would eventually go blind and therefore require the support of their tribe for the rest of their lives.

There is also a tendency for modern humans to patronise people from the past. However fast people may think evolution happens, as Claude Lévi-Strauss observed, 'early Homo sapiens were not just physically the same as modern humans, they were our intellectual peers as well' (quoted in Graeber and Wengrow, 2018, p. 19). The initial discovery that if certain rocks were heated to about 250 degrees Celsius, liquid tin could be extracted, may have been accidental. To mix tin with copper to produce bronze requires superheating of over 1,000 degrees Celsius, and this can only be achieved through a bellows system, which is not accidental. People from early history were just as intelligent and resourceful as modern humans, and hopefully thinking through ideas such as the development of writing will demonstrate to children that we should not patronise people from the past

IDEAS FOR A HALF-TERMLY PLAN

If this unit is taught in Year 4 there will be challenges to cover the time periods accurately and with comprehension. Against that, it arguably does make sense to tell the 'out of Africa' story as a precursor to the Ancient British topic covered in Chapter 9. Additionally, it does offer the contrast and the strangeness that many lower-junior age children may find fascinating and inspiring.

- Who were the Sumerians? As with every unit discussed so far, this unit should ideally start with map work and timelines demonstrating the 'big picture' of human history and how recent civilisation is compared to geological and evolutionary time. Links could be made with geography, not least the Euphrates as part of a river study. The continent of Asia is theoretically part of the Key Stage 3 curriculum, but schools could incorporate a study of modern Arab countries in parallel with the Ancient Sumer.

- Farming: The invention of farming has featured heavily in the two Key Stage 2 chapters. The cultivation of barley, wheat and other cereals resulted in a food surplus, the beginning of settlements, and the consumption of foods such as bread, pastries and beer that are still widely consumed. This could be extended into a broader mini topic on the first foods and the importance of agriculture. Few children are now connected to life on the land, yet they still have school holidays linked to the farming seasons.
- Cities: This could include specific early Sumerian cities like Urek, but could also be opened out to include the idea of settlement and transport links.
- Sumerian discoveries: This would obviously include the development of writing and mathematical discoveries. It would be an interesting challenge to get children to think about the invention of writing, and how pictures became stylised and simplified and eventually represent parts of speech. Given that the National Curriculum requires children to identify and know all the phonemes in English (roughly 43) and how they can be represented by graphemes (26 in the case of English, not including blends), this might help them to reflect on one of the great achievements of early civilisations like the Sumer and Mayans.
- Home life: Initial archaeological and historical enquiries about the Sumer tended to concentrate on political and technological questions. Aspects of everyday life, such as food, were only considered much later. However, the richness of archaeological and textual information has resulted in detailed knowledge of these aspects of Sumerian culture. In short, they tended to favour barley to make flat bread. Higher quality breads tended to be mixed with fats and spices. They brewed beer, and although wine was produced, it was rarer. Poorer Sumerians ate a largely vegetarian diet. Animals were kept for meat and milk, the latter of which was also used for cheese production. Naturally, this could lead to a themed day with extensive food tasting.
- The role of women and children: Stol (1995) considered this question and claimed that there is considerable evidence about the lives of women and children, especially for the wealthier middle classes. It could be combined with ideas of housing, the first schools and the work that women and children carried out.
- Other civilisations: If teachers struggled to find enough material for a half-term plan, depending on the availability of local museums or suitable teaching resources, then the topic could be expanded to include other early civilisations from the recommended list.

- Time: Chapter 3 introduced the metaphor of the history of the Earth being compressed into the span of a year. This could be a very rewarding activity as part of this topic, possibly as a coda linked to mathematics. If 4.54 billion years are divided by the number of seconds in a year, and this could become both a calculator-based challenge and a recap of the units of time which are part of the Sumerian legacy, then the result is that each second would represent 144 years. At this point some interesting further calculations could be made, using the following links to check (both are reputable sources):
    - www.oum.ox.ac.uk/thezone/fossils/history/calendar.htm
    - https://biomimicry.net/earths-calendar-year-4-5-billion-years-compressed-into-12-months/
- It is possible to calculate that dinosaurs disappeared around the end of Christmas day, the first hominids walked around 11.30 am on New Year's Eve, *Homo sapiens* appeared at 23:36, the Sumerians discovered farming at 23:59, and finally, the Victorian age would be at its zenith at one second to midnight.

ASPECT OR THEME IN BRITISH HISTORY BEYOND 1066

The final aspect of the Key Stage 2 curriculum to consider is the 'British history beyond 1066' element. The full wording, with non-statutory suggestions, is as follows:

> A study of an aspect or theme in British history that extends pupils' chronological knowledge beyond 1066
>
> Examples (non-statutory)
>
> - The changing power of monarchs using case studies such as John, Anne and Victoria
> - Changes in an aspect of social history, such as crime and punishment from the Anglo-Saxons to the present or leisure and entertainment in the 20th Century
> - The legacy of Greek or Roman culture (art, architecture or literature) on later periods in British history, including the present day
> - A significant turning point in British history, for example, the first railways or the Battle of Britain. (DfE, 2013, p. 191)

GENERAL CONSIDERATIONS

It was previously noted that the addition of the 'theme' or 'aspect' beyond 1066 was probably included to acknowledge the fact that experienced primary practitioners were not going to omit aspects of British history that had been taught successfully for decades. The wording of the National Curriculum presented above can be interpreted in several ways. There is a general sense that the thematic and analytical aspects are important and very different from the continuation of a 'topic'-based approach. For example, a unit covering World War II would probably not fit the remit unless it had a clear link to a theme such as 'turning points' in British history, as suggested. The importance of timescales should be considered as well as the necessity of finding a theme or aspect that engages children's interest.

The prominence of historical knowledge is re-emphasised by the suggestion to examine the legacy of classical history, although given the amount of early history in the Key Stage 2 curriculum, it would be more than understandable if schools felt that a fresher approach would be preferable. The further suggestion to cover social history is encouraging given the importance of the PESRC formula discussed in detail in Chapters 2 and 3. However, there is arguably enough political history in the main history units, and the unit would present an opportunity to focus on science and technology through a detailed study of eminent British inventors and scientists and their impact on world history. Schools should also seriously consider themes linked to social history, including those that have the potential for feminist viewpoints. There is an understandable tendency for schools to choose themes or topics that are theoretically linked to boys' interests and this should not be accepted uncritically. For example, an aspect of social history might include clothes and fashion, which can introduce important questions about gender and cultural norms. If political history is preferred, then this might include citizenship themes, such as the development of democracy in the United Kingdom and the various struggles for the emancipation of the poor and women. Topicality, such as studying the Olympics Games or World Cups, is a further possibility, although the British focus should not be lost. Similarly, citizenship themes such as the promotion of women's sport could be included.

A final point is to consider combining an 'aspect or theme beyond 1066' with a locality study. For example, a unit covering the development of the first railways or transport in Britain since the nineteenth century could easily incorporate events in the locality. The small Northamptonshire town I live in once had two separate stations. Both lines and stations were closed after the 'Beeching' cuts in the early 1960s, leaving the town reliant on road connections, including a new by-pass and road-widening schemes. The proposed HS2 project is slated to be constructed near the town. The irony here, not lost on anyone who has studied railway history, is that the HS2 line replicates almost exactly the Great Central Line from the late nineteenth century, which was largely closed by the late 1960s. There are also canals, and two former Royal Air Force bases which are now private airfields and used for gliding, parachuting and private licence pilots. One would hope that a locality study would include more than just a transport theme; however, the two aspects, locality and the development of railways, could be studied simultaneously with perhaps geography taking the lead in the locality study, and the development of railways in Britain covering the history element combined with a local focus.

OVERVIEW OF KEY STAGE 2 HISTORY UNIT PLANNING

A key argument throughout this book has been the requirement to think carefully about the order and placement of the National Curriculum units. Table 10.1 follows the recommendations in this book. Year 3 would start with the accessible and contrasting European and non-European study units. Both can be taught successfully without reference to time, although some work on centuries and conventions of historical time would be advantageous. Year 4 would continue with an 'Aspect or Theme' from British history. Here the scope is very broad but, as suggested, could be combined with an overarching theme or a locality study. The placement of the 'Early Civilisation' topic would then act as a precursor for the Ancient British history unit. Years 5 and 6 would be retained for the chronological overview of British history. The argument has been that introducing this unit when pupils are older and have a more developed understanding of time and other key historical concepts, and in a more compressed two-year cycle, would result in more sophisticated and coherent learning outcomes.

Table 10.1 Suggested order of National Curriculum 2014 study units

Year Group	Unit One	Unit 2	Unit 3
Year 3	European Study – Ancient Greece (can be combined with geography)	Non-European Society (can be combined with geography)	
Year 4	Aspect or Theme in British History since 1066 (can be combined with geography and the Locality Study)	Achievements of the Earliest Civilisations (can be combined with geography)	
Year 5	Ancient British History	Roman Britain	
Year 6	Anglo-Saxon Invasion and Settlement	Viking Invasion and Settlement	Locality Study post-SATS (can be combined with geography)

Alternatively, subject coordinators and school leaders may feel that it is preferable to begin the British history chronology in Year 3. In this scenario the permutations are considerable. The example schedule in Table 10.2 retains some of the other arguments presented in this chapter, including the Ancient Greece topic in Year 3, but then moving the 'Early Civilisation' unit into Year 6 where it could be taught in a more intellectually rigorous and honest way.

Table 10.2 Alternative order of National Curriculum 2014 study units

Year Group	Unit One	Unit 2	Unit 3
Year 3	Ancient British History	European Study – Ancient Greece (can be combined with geography)	
Year 4	Roman Britain	Non-European Society (can be combined with geography)	
Year 5	Anglo-Saxon Invasion and Settlement	Aspect or Theme in British History since 1066 (can be combined with geography and the locality study)	
Year 6	Viking Invasion and Settlement	Achievements of the Earliest Civilisations (can be combined with geography)	Locality Study post-SATS (can be combined with geography)

CHAPTER SUMMARY

- This chapter introduced and discussed the remaining National Curriculum 2014 study units, including contextual knowledge from previous iterations of the National Curriculum and suggestions for placement in Years 3 and 4.
- The consistent place of the Ancient Greek topic was discussed, including why it is appropriate to place it in Year 3, and suggestions were made for the wide range of teaching and learning approaches that are appropriate for this unit. An overview of teacher subject knowledge was included as a suggestion for future research.
- The optional nature of the remaining history units was discussed, including suggestions for their placement in the lower juniors and ideas for combining these elements with geography and other subjects. Once again, suggestions for teacher subject knowledge teaching and learning ideas were provided.
- The chapter ended with two examples of overall curriculum planning for history in Key Stage 2.

FURTHER READING

In earlier chapters there were frequent suggestions to use online databases as a form of historical evidence and the starting point for enquiry, particularly with high-resolution scans of painting and objects. Google Arts and Culture has extended coverage to include databases of objects which can support the 'Early Civilisation' and 'Non-European' societies: https://artsandculture.google.com/project/openheritage

Burn, A.R. (1990) *The Penguin History of Greece*. London: Penguin.

As noted in the chapter, the Ancient Greece unit of study has been one of the consistent elements of National Curriculum history. Burn's text may be slightly dated, but it is easily available, highly informative and written in an engaging and accessible style.

McIntosh, J. and Twist, C. (2001) *Civilizations: Ten Thousand Years of Ancient History*. London: BBC Worldwide.

Given the considerable choice in the two non-European study units, no single text can be wholly relevant. This book, based on a successful BBC television series, is a good general introduction to the development of human civilisations.

CHAPTER 11

CROSS-CURRICULAR AND THEMATIC LINKS

What this chapter will cover

This chapter begins with a brief section examining definitions of cross-curricularity, concluding with an attempt to create some clarity and consistency over their use. This is followed by an equally brief overview of the arguments for cross-curricularity and curriculum flexibility, particularly the ability to double-count curriculum time, and these considerations are placed within the overall context of a broader debate about a creative curriculum. With specific reference to history, two models from my own research are discussed and further examples are provided, demonstrating how history works effectively as a lead subject and fits in well with many overarching curriculum themes.

INTRODUCTION

In brief, cross-curricularity can be interpreted as a sub-theme of the creative teaching and learning agenda (Craft, 2005). Perhaps unsurprisingly, there has been research that suggests that combining subjects does allow greater intellectual freedom and the promotion of children's learning than non-integrated methods. This was one of Barnes' (2011, pp. 1972–4) principal justifications for cross-curricular learning from his research into cross-curricularity.

Terms like 'cross-curricular' and 'thematic teaching' are often employed relatively indiscriminately, and therefore definitions and theoretical frameworks ought to be considered. It is possible to agree that the definitions of cross-curricularity can come across as a 'rather sterile debate'

(Rowley and Cooper, 2009, p. 2), but it still needs to be addressed. A review of the literature has produced surprisingly few models, and limited theoretical discussion, but some principles can be identified. 'Topic' work is certainly associated with the post-Plowden reforms in the UK (CACE, 1967), and is often associated with a 'key-word' starting point that is now largely associated with 'indiscriminate', 'superficial' and 'watered-down' teaching and learning (Laurie, 2011, pp. 128–9). In short, it was an uncritical approach that needed to be replaced by superior curriculum management models.

'Lead subject' cross-curricular approaches, which tended to be based around a specific subject or domain (Tyler, 1992), was the model favoured by Her Majesty's Inspectorate (HMI, 1985, 1989) and Ofsted (2002, 2007). It has been claimed that history is particularly suited to this role because of the natural links the discipline has with other subjects. By most definitions, 'cross-curricularity' refers to a teaching approach that combines the 'skills, knowledge and attitudes of a number of different disciplines' (Barnes, 2011, p. 53) within a single theme or lesson, and is therefore preferable as the overarching term. Thus, cross-curricularity is associated with the coverage of two or more subject domains within one lesson.

'Thematic' or 'integrated' approaches to teaching and learning are essentially the same, according to Barnes (2011, p. 10), but this claim does not fully stand up to scrutiny. It should be acknowledged that themes can vary enormously in duration, the number of subjects incorporated into the theme, and the extent to which the theme dominates teaching time in the classroom. It should also be admitted that logically a theme can unify several separately taught subjects without any examples of cross-curricularity at the level of individual lessons. In other words, each lesson can contain a single-subject focus within the overarching theme. Indeed, this was a belief shared by a head teacher in my own research.

However, thematic approaches require a little more analysis. A commonly held belief, articulated by Laurie (2011), is that there should first be a main theme of specific focus that reflects the lead subject. This might be history or another subject. Clearly, the implications for subject integrity depend quite heavily on whether history is the lead subject in the theme. A second argument, associated with Ofsted (2002), and therefore a quasi-official position, is that no more than two or three subjects should be combined within the theme. Perhaps more convincing because of its basis in his own extensive research, Barnes (2011, pp. 70–95) also argued that there should be a limitation on the number of disciplines combined within a theme.

To conclude, although this is a personal interpretation of the language used to describe cross-curricularity, and therefore cannot be considered in any sense definitive, the following distinctions can be made:

- Cross-curricular: This is most commonly used in planning, teaching and learning at the level of the classroom, where lesson objectives

for two or more subjects are combined into a single lesson. It is also used to represent the planning of several subjects around a 'lead subject', such as history.
- Thematic curriculum: This is mainly used for the integration of several subjects into an overarching theme. Each lesson may only contain learning objectives for a single subject discipline, but learning is organised around the theme.
- Integrated approaches: These are less useful because of the lack of definitional precision, but the term tends to be used, as Barnes (2011) indicated, as a synonym for thematic approaches.

ARGUMENTS FOR CROSS-CURRICULARITY AND THEMATIC LEARNING

One of the most powerful and commonly cited claims is that cross-curricularity fits more closely with how young children think and learn (Kerry, 2011). Similarly, it has been argued that subject disciplines should emerge gradually in the primary years to avoid 'fragmentation' and the creation of 'barriers' to learning (Pring, 1973, pp. 123–4). It has also been claimed that cross-curricularity develops and promotes children's reasoning skills (Chanda, 2007), and there is evidence that cross-curricular learning based on experiential approaches increases children's enjoyment and absorption of knowledge due to greater levels of independence, engagement and self-efficacy (for example, see Kelly's research; Kelly, 2013). Indeed, children's enjoyment of learning was an important consideration in the policy reviews from the late 1990s onwards.

There have also been claims that cross-curricular approaches support enquiry-based approaches to learning, and therefore independent learning in general. For example, Barnes (2011, pp. 1–2) has been an advocate of experiential learning, while Sayers (2011, p. 2) developed the concept of the 'mantle of [the] expert' in cross-curricular work to stimulate enquiry. Imagination, which is an important part of history (as discussed in Chapter 6), has long been associated with integrated approaches – for example, the work of the Nuffield Primary History Project (Fines and Nichol, 2009). Similarly, narrative, drama and oral approaches have been linked to cross-curricular work by Grainger (2005), also mirroring some of the important pedagogical approaches in history.

The third main argument is that of efficiency of coverage. Of course, combining subjects, especially within lessons, which theoretically allows the '*double-counting*' of curriculum time, is one of the most efficient ways of maximising time spent on learning, assuming that skills, knowledge and subject integrity are retained. Harnett (2000, p. 34) argued that 'as different subjects compete with each other for space on the timetable, linking subjects together has become more attractive'. Indeed, combining subjects was one of three strategies recommended by the Qualification and Curriculum Agency to alleviate curriculum overcrowding (QCA, 1998), but despite pronouncements that achieving both breadth and depth is possible in the primary school, each wave of curriculum reviews added yet more to the equation, a trend Jacobs (1989, pp. 3–4) termed the 'growth of knowledge' problem.

There is one final argument in favour of cross-curricularity – the importance of a *context* for learning. Given that primary-aged children are required to process mathematical data, carry out scientific experiments and, most commonly, produce written outcomes in several formats and genres, it makes sense to link these activities to subject content children have gained elsewhere in the curriculum. For example, producing information leaflets, non-chronological reports or imaginative essays can easily be linked to every aspect of historical knowledge. The counter-argument is even stronger: if English work outcomes are not linked to the broader curriculum, then time must be created in English lessons to provide the context and cover the content.

While English is the most obvious example, a similar case can be made for computing lessons, scientific experiments and even mathematics. As part of my research, I observed a Year 6 class conduct a cross-curricular 'mini-topic' on the *Titanic* which had a strong history focus. One of the principal work outcomes was a form of statistical analysis, which they presented using Excel spreadsheets and posters, of survival rates depending on social class, age, gender and position within the ship. It was a very powerful and effective work outcome, combining historical knowledge, enquiry and evidence with mathematics and computing. Without the information gained during the 'mini-topic', it would be challenging to find a context in which statistical data would have been equally engaging and relevant.

RESEARCH PROJECT: THE EFFICACY OF CROSS-CURRICULARITY AND PRIMARY HISTORY

To test the claims that cross-curricular approaches maximised learning time, engaged children's interest and provided a context for learning, while retaining subject integrity, and with a specific focus in history, I carried out a relatively large research project in four schools between 2011 and 2013. The research design, a multiple case-study enquiry which investigated cross-curricular approaches in four primary schools, can be accessed via the *SAGE Research Methods* online platform (Percival, 2017a). The research produced three models of cross-curricularity (Percival, 2018), although for brevity the two most effective examples are discussed in this chapter.

CASE STUDY 1: 'DISCIPLINED THEMATIC INTEGRATION'

The first and most important consideration when analysing Case Study 1, a small rural Oxfordshire school in an affluent area, was the fact this it was self-identified through discussion and interviews as providing a form of thematic integration, where National Curriculum subject disciplines were subsumed within overarching half-termly themes such as 'Fire and festivals' or 'Along the riverbank'. In some instances, the most obvious and least original example was the National Curriculum history unit on the 'Aztecs', in which history was dovetailed in a relatively crude way into the theme of 'Chocolate'. It was also evident that the degree of subject integration was variable and inconsistent, and there was an observable difference between the infants and juniors, where the single infant class adopted far higher levels of integration consistent with an Early Years' approach. In such a small school, containing only three classes (and five teachers due to job-sharing), this was almost certainly because of variables at the level of individual teachers and their personal attitudes and beliefs. Indeed, interviews and ethnographic conversations suggested that there were quite different interpretations of what subject integration meant. The level of integration for history was also dependent on the ease with which it could be incorporated into the theme, and clearly some themes, such as 'Conflict and resolution' and 'Built to last', had a more obvious historical element, while others were clearly more orientated to geography (for example, 'Islands') or science ('Flight').

Despite the clear identification of overarching themes, it was noted that the hierarchy between theme and subject discipline was sometimes uncertain, certainly variable, and that in some lessons the National Curriculum subject or unit seemed to be pre-eminent. This was the case with the 'Aztecs' and 'Chocolate', where the stand-alone history lessons seemed to have little genuine connection with the theme other than the very loose link of the cocoa bean in Aztec agriculture. Where the National Curriculum subject was pre-eminent the retention of subject integrity was easier to justify, but clearly this was at the cost of genuine thematic integration. However, in other observations and field notes it was clear that genuine subject integration had often been attained within a theme, and therefore the model is predominately based on this evidence. Moreover, it was highly scrutinised and considered as integration – hence the use of the term *Disciplined Thematic Integration* in this case study.

An important element in the level of discipline was school leadership. Due to the high turnover of individuals in this role from the time the school was identified as having serious weaknesses by Ofsted, but 'outstanding' at the time of the research project, the importance of leadership had clearly been embedded organisationally and culturally. Yet the analysis of interview data and observations revealed a highly tolerant and democratic school culture in which individual beliefs and practices flourished. Part of this was control of the planning process: out of the four schools researched, Case Study 1 had by far the most detailed and consistent medium-term planning, and the level of scrutiny was high. For example, when history was combined within a theme, its form and structure as a recognisable history study unit remained evident. The second aspect of leadership was the fact that in the observed history lessons the input was nearly always delivered in an authoritative way, and this frequently included high levels of subject knowledge and skill by the teacher. This was one of the defining features of this case study and arguably reflected the experience and confidence of the teachers.

CREATIVE APPROACHES AND THE CONTENT OF HISTORY

Interview data and ethnographic conversations revealed considerable variations in the underpinning philosophy, and this in turn indicated that personal belief was an important variable in understanding the school's approach to the curriculum. In an interview, a senior teacher who had been instrumental in transforming the school's curriculum during its challenging period indicated strongly that the underlying philosophy had been driven more by the creativity agenda than subject integration. Nevertheless, observations and field notes produced evidence that suggested that creativity was muted or absent in many lessons, and an axial code revealed tension between the desire to establish a creative curriculum and retaining teacher control and adherence to the National Curriculum.

The evidence therefore suggested lower levels of creativity, curriculum flexibility and enrichment, especially in the junior classes, than was claimed in all the research interviews. However, in terms of history teaching and learning, there was considerable evidence for experiential learning in terms of links with the locality, the proclivity of educational visits and visitors, and the use of artefacts and other historical evidence that resulted in powerful learning experiences which reinforced historical reasoning. Field work and observations identified many strong aspects of history knowledge and content, principally derived from the National Curriculum history units outlined above, and many worthwhile and justified links with other curriculum subjects, notably geography (through a local study focus), religious education, literacy and drama, but above all with art and design technology, possibly reflecting the strong association with a creative curriculum.

CONCEPT MAP FOR 'DISCIPLINED THEMATIC INTEGRATION'

The model of *Disciplined Thematic Integration* (Figure 11.1) includes many of the codes identified from observations and interviews. They illustrate well the tensions between creative and opportunistic learning constrained by the requirements of the National Curriculum and monitoring of the curriculum.

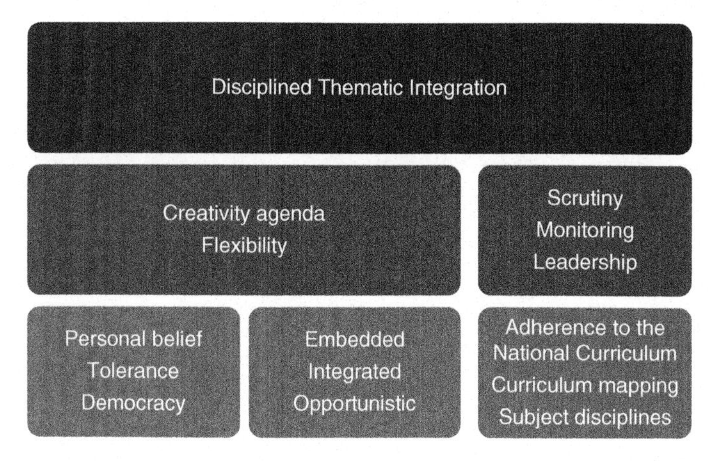

Figure 11.1 Concepts associated with 'Disciplined Thematic Integration'

Out of these tensions emerged a history curriculum that was frequently integrated with other subjects in a disciplined and justifiable way. Arguably, this resulted in many profound and deep-rooted learning experiences allied to teacher autonomy and professional judgement.

HOW THIS MIGHT WORK IN PRACTICE

An overarching theme, such as 'Rainforest' or 'Chocolate', could clearly be linked with the world and early history topics related to the Americas, namely the Aztec, Mayan or Inca civilisations, while also supporting a geographical focus on the continents of North or South America. It would also support art and design lessons and some aspects of the National Curriculum for music. English content around genre, stories from other cultures and several forms of writing would very obviously fit into such a theme.

Similar, a half-termly theme on 'Cities' or 'Civilisation' would create an opportunity to incorporate a study of the Ancient Sumer (or any other early civilisation). Geography could be linked through an area study of a city from the UK or elsewhere in the world, thus creating the opportunity to compare cities ancient and modern. The links with English, design technology, computing (in the form of research and creating databases) and religious education would all be feasible.

In both of these examples, other subjects, such as science or mathematics, might have some elements during a half-term that could be incorporated into the theme, but this is where the importance of disciplinary rigour, compared with 1970s-era 'topic work', is crucially important: subject disciplines should not be distorted to fit into a theme, and nor should the link be forced if it is not natural.

CASE STUDY 2: 'CONTROLLED IMMERSION' (OR 'LEAD SUBJECT INTEGRATION')

This module grew out of two schools: an initial pilot study, which was followed by Case Study 2. The pilot-study school was a medium-sized, two-form entry state school within an affluent area of an Oxfordshire market town. Interview data revealed that the impetus for developing cross-curricular links was the result of local initiatives and INSET sessions that challenged the school to adopt a more invigorating approach to the curriculum.

Most of the observations and field work data were drawn from the lower-junior classes, which were working on the 'Britain since 1930' history unit, with a focus on the home front. Activities included themed days, in which the children dressed up as evacuees, and extended literacy and design technology projects. It was evident that history was acting as the lead subject, and other curriculum subjects were adapting to the history content. The most noteworthy examples included letter- and report writing centred on evacuee experiences (although it was noted that the history content was sometimes weak and inaccurate) and measuring, which was linked to rationing and an investigation into how far a weekly ration of butter, jam and cheese could be translated into sandwiches and other meals. Once again, the history content was slightly traduced because metric measures were (arguably, rightly) used for the mathematics content, but without the historical and contextual understanding of the actual imperial measures used in 1940s rationing. The themed day centred on drama, literacy and design technology (model-making of gas masks and other home front items) and was clearly successfully planned and executed and generated high levels of enthusiasm from most of the children.

Overall the pilot study demonstrated strong links with the National Curriculum history content, providing notable examples of some historical concepts such as enquiry, evidence and imagination, but was weaker on chronology and interpretation. There were also examples where integration was weaker, echoing some of the earlier criticisms. For example, 'a soldier day', in which some children marched aimlessly around the school field in school clothes, did not address learning in either history or physical education; nor was this the only example of weak or forced subject links.

The school in Case Study 2 was a large, urban community school in a relatively deprived area of a large Oxfordshire town. Ofsted reports and interview data provided a clear narrative of a failing school, with new leaders, who had been encouraged to construct an extensive and creative curriculum to motivate pupils and move learning on. It also provided the clearest example of highly effective subject leadership out of the four research schools. Examples of the effectiveness of leadership of history included the instigation and coordination of the whole-school history week and several themed days, the creation of history skills ladders (the only research school where assessment of historical learning was routinely considered), and the close monitoring and promotion of history throughout the school.

The formal observations and field work days in every year group demonstrated that history was acting as the lead subject, predominately through National Curriculum-derived units of study. However, subject combinations were only made when the links could be justified. Outstanding examples included a strong combination with geography for a Year 4 local history topic; several art and design technology projects that linked with the history content; play writing followed by a whole-school performance based on tales from Greek mythology; and religious education, which also linked with the Ancient Greece unit. Overall, virtually all subjects were combined with history at some point throughout the whole school, but only when the link could be justified. It was also clear that the school leaders monitored this carefully. In terms of historical integrity, chronology was very strongly represented both in lessons and displays (timelines were visible in all junior classrooms), evidence and enquiry were very strongly represented, and only the concepts associated with historical reasoning were arguably under-represented.

The concept of *Controlled Immersion* was principally derived through analysis of the codes that demonstrated the fact that the National Curriculum study units, in this case history, provide the foci for learning rather than elevated themes associated with thematic integration. Therefore, children were 'immersed' into a disciplinary subject, or subjects in the case of a double focus (Barnes, 2011, pp. 66–7), and learning was directed by the content and elements linked to that discipline. It is specifically the integration of other National Curriculum subjects within the lead subject (history), hence the second-term, curriculum-based integration. It was the comparative weaknesses in the pilot study, notably unjustified links, termed 'shoehorning' and poorer subject leadership, that helped to identify the strengths of Case Study 2, particularly the consistently stronger links with other subject disciplines.

CONCEPT MAP FOR 'CONTROLLED IMMERSION'

The concept map (Figure 11.2) is introduced here with the addition of clusters of codes from discussions and interviews. It summarises well the hierarchy of coding, particularly those aspects associated with leadership and school culture, and the adherence to the elements of the National Curriculum. It is not possible to state whether this model works as well with other curriculum disciplines, but it does support Cooper's (2012) claim that history combines well with other subject disciplines and is well suited to adopt the lead subject role.

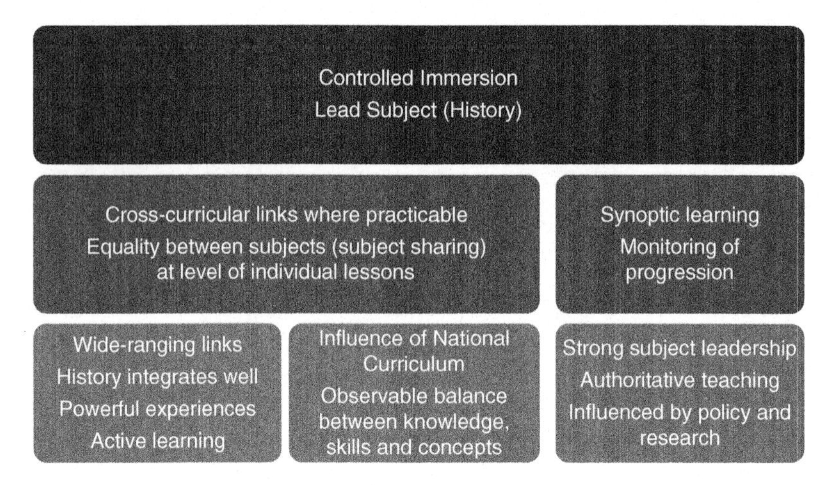

Figure 11.2 Concepts associated with 'Controlled Immersion'

In a sense, this model requires less discussion because of history's place as the lead subject, into which other subjects are combined with history if the link can be justified. However, it was noted that geography often acted as the co-lead subject, and this is where the distinction between lead subject and thematic approaches begins to break down in practice.

It should also be noted that in the research schools there was a conscious decision to alternate the lead subject from many of the other curriculum subjects, notably geography, science, art and music. The full research findings cannot be presented here, but the project produced evidence to support the natural and justifiable links between history units of study and elements of English, geography, art, design technology and religious education, and occasional links with music, mathematics and science. In this book, detailed examples of Ancient Greece in Chapter 6 illustrated how natural the connections can be, although Ancient Greece is particularly adaptable to take the lead subject role as it can include a wider range of subject domains, including physical education due to coverage of the Olympic Games. It should be noted that not all history topics are equally as suitable.

To provide one more example for consideration, let us take a topic on fashion and clothing as part of a 'Theme beyond 1066'. Quite apart from the lead subject focus on history – and this could be targeted at any period where there is a lot of evidence for fashion and clothing – the other subjects that could fit into this unit of study, leaving aside the omnipresent place of English, could include: design technology, with an activity to design and make clothes; art, with representations of clothes and fashion in art; technology, using software to aid design in computing; and PSHE, incorporating a (potentially) challenging focus on attitudes associated with clothes and gender.

A MODEL OF EFFECTIVE PRACTICE

The conclusion from the research project was that exemplary cross-curricular practice in history can be defined in terms of seven key concepts. These were most strongly associated with Controlled Immersion (Case Study 2), but were also present in some form in all four research schools.

INSPIRED AND INFORMED LEADERSHIP

All case-study schools demonstrated the importance of school leadership, but Case Study 2 demonstrated it both in terms of school leadership and in subject coordination.

PARITY (CURRICULUM BALANCE)

At the level of learning in the classroom, thoughtful and considered immersion and integration did not dilute the effectiveness of learning in the subsidiary subject, and very often genuine parity in teaching and learning was achieved. However, in less thoughtful settings (such as in the pilot-study school), the second subject was sometimes weakened.

EFFECTIVE HISTORICAL UNDERSTANDING

Content was generally balanced with enquiry and historical sources and a range of historical skills and concepts. All historical concepts identified in the earlier chapters of this book were observed at least once, so overall coverage was strong.

JUSTIFIABLE AND STRONG SUBJECT LINKS

History combines well with several subject disciplines. Literacy, geography, art, design technology, computing and religious education are the most obvious examples, while justifiable and workable links can be made with science, mathematics (especially data handing) and music. Physical education can be linked through the strand of dance or the history of sport. In nearly all examples, integration at the level of the classroom was usually limited to history combined with one other subject. Links were also carefully managed and monitored, and established only when they were justified.

ENGAGEMENT AND ENJOYMENT

Pupils and teachers alike appear to welcome the extra time and focus on history. This was strongly associated with an emphasis on creativity.

CURRICULUM COVERAGE AND EFFICIENCY

Immersion and integration allowed for considerably more time spent on the content and concepts of history due to the double-counting of curriculum time.

TEACHER EXPERTISE

To teach history well requires knowledgeable and enthusiastic teachers, and arguably this is even more necessary when two or more subjects are combined. There were many examples of effective teaching practice observed for this project, and they were usually associated with detailed and informed planning.

It is important to note that although many of these concepts were evident in the two case studies that adopted a thematic approach, the following categories associated with 'Disciplined or Extended Thematic Integration', which arguably weakened their effectiveness, were also identified:

1. Shoehorning – In the weakest cases the dovetailing of history into the overarching theme was crude and forced, and achieved little genuine integration.
2. Uncertain vision – It was observed that either some aspects of thematic integration lacked clarity (Case Study 1 overlapped with a creativity agenda) or there was an observable gap between the vision of the head teacher and the reality of practice. Examples were the extended themes that often reflected National Curriculum disciplinary units rather than being more original and genuinely overarching (Case Study 3; not discussed here, but see Percival, 2017a).
3. Uncertain thematic hierarchy – It was observable that in Case Studies 1 and 3 many of the themes were associated with a lead subject or National Curriculum unit, therefore suggesting elements of lead-subject integration which tended to undermine the notion that themes were unifying and overarching and stood above curriculum subjects.

There was an additional category, most closely associated with the pilot study, that resulted in the judgement that lead subject cross-curricularity did not in itself guarantee successful integration, therefore illuminating the challenge of balancing cross-curricularity and high standards of teaching and learning:

4. Trivial subject links – There were examples of links between history and other subjects that were forced rather than natural, and arguably placed experience over disciplinary rigour.

CHAPTER SUMMARY

- The arguments for cross-curricularity and thematic learning can be viewed as an aspect of the broader question of the creative curriculum, which emerged in the late 1990s as a response to subject overload following the introduction of the National Curriculum.

- A theoretical distinction can be made between thematic, integrated and cross-curricular approaches to curriculum management, but the terms have often lacked precision and the differences often break down when analysing practice.
- History seems ideally suited to the 'lead subject' role and can often fit into broader learning themes. However, it requires careful planning and skilful teaching approaches to ensure that subject integrity is retained.
- Two models from research have been briefly presented, and further examples have been discussed, to demonstrate how this might work in practice.

FURTHER READING

Barnes, J. (2015) *Cross-Curricular Learning 3–14* (3rd edn). London: Sage.

Barnes' research into cross-curricular teaching and learning has been highly influential. History is not his principal focus, but he provided many examples of how to plan and teach in an effective way, and his models of cross-curricularity have helped to shape the debate and have added intellectual rigour.

Cooper, H. (ed.) (2013) *Teaching History Creatively*. Abingdon: Routledge.

This edited book by Britain's most eminent writer on primary history contains many chapters that discuss thematic and cross-curricular approaches. It is strongly supportive of the claim in this chapter that this topic is an important element in the broader question of the creative curriculum and of history's specific and important place in this debate.

CHAPTER 12

ASSESSING HISTORICAL UNDERSTANDING

What this chapter will cover

This final chapter outlines several ways children's progress in history can be monitored. The argument presented here is that children's attitudes towards history should be recorded. The retention of historical knowledge can be assessed through informal tasks, such as online quizzes. Evidence for progress in historical skills and understanding is far more challenging, and a case is made for assessing children against the principal historical concepts that have underpinned this book.

INTRODUCTION

It is unquestionably true that the single biggest challenge of undertaking meaningful assessment in the humanities subjects is simply finding the time to carry out useful and productive assessment activities, given the pressure of planning and teaching the whole primary curriculum. This has been increasingly the case following the greater emphasis on mathematics and literacy from the late 1990s onwards, and the high-stakes pressure of the end of key stage tests. That stated, irrespective of the inspection framework, teachers still must report to parents on their child's progress in all the curriculum subjects and therefore assessment in history cannot be completely ignored.

It is worth recounting the background to the significant changes that occurred in the 1990s. An aspect as revolutionary as the new curriculum and assessment levels was the decision to test children in order to provide National Curriculum levels alongside teacher assessments. Two trends quickly emerged from this important decision: teacher assessments were soon downgraded compared with the hard data provided by formal tests; and the time demands placed on teachers meant that testing was quickly reduced to the core subjects of English, mathematics and science.

Strange though it may now appear, and seemingly almost forgotten, draft test materials for the foundation subjects, including history, were created and sent to key individuals and institutions for evaluation. In many respects, the draft materials were unworkable, partly because of the enormous time constraints, and partly because of the complex and extensive nature of the key concepts found in history and other subjects. So what emerged, particularly after the trimmed-down content of the revised National Curriculum (DfE, 1995) and National Curriculum 2000 (DfEE, 1999), was an overall statement for each child based on a single Attainment Target and level descriptors were developed for all foundation subjects, including history. Thus, what began as an ambitious, if overly complex, desire to assess each child against a range of skills, concepts and knowledge, quickly became an almost valueless exercise in which children were crudely and often haphazardly levelled on the National Curriculum scale between 1 and 6 for the whole of the primary years. It is little wonder that attempts to find an overall National Curriculum level were discarded by overworked professionals.

Nevertheless, as noted in the Introduction, the new Ofsted framework for school inspections (Ofsted, 2019) has a clear focus on the whole curriculum, including children's progress. In their most recent pronouncement, this clarification was provided:

> The curriculum is also distinct from pedagogy, which is how the curriculum is taught. Furthermore, it is distinct from assessment, which is a means of evaluating whether learners are learning/have learned the intended curriculum, although of course the curriculum and assessment need to work hand in hand. In so doing, the curriculum becomes the progression model. (Ofsted, 2019)

Therefore, in common with the CHATA project (introduced in Chapter 5), it is the intention of this chapter to explain how this progression in historical knowledge and understanding might be measured. The approach throughout the book has been to focus on the key underpinning historical concepts, and these are certainly more suited to assessing progression in historical understanding. Ofsted have also commented on the importance of considering learners' attitudes, and so the chapter will begin with some broader considerations.

ATTITUDES AND KNOWLEDGE

A child's attitude towards a subject is important. Few children will become academic historians – or research scientists, professional athletes or novelists for that matter – and therefore it is important that they enjoy a subject for its own sake and feel that they have learned something important. A theme in this book has been that research shows that history is a popular subject with primary children, but obviously there will be variations within any classroom and depending on the history topic. Therefore, it is reasonable to report on a child's enthusiasm, engagement and willingness to carry out extra research at home.

Another key theme in this book has been the neo-liberal reforms and concern for knowledge. It is reasonable to guess that this has been influenced by politicians' personal experiences of the private school sector. It is surely relevant that written outcomes, specifically writing at length in geography and 'written narratives and analyses' (DfE, 2013, p. 188) in history, are stated aims for the humanities subjects. The case for using history as a context for written outcomes in English has been made in Chapter 11, and so summative writing tasks can be used as an opportunity to assess both writing skill and historical understanding.

It would be reasonable to assume that Michael Gove probably had in mind end-of-term tests, which are still used in many private schools. This should not be dismissed without consideration. While formal tests principally assess retention rather than understanding and, as the History Working Group (DES, 1990) noted, historical knowledge is non-cumulative, tests and quizzes can also be designed in fun and engaging ways, which may motivate some children. For example, online systems such as 'Classmarker', which can be carried out at the end of a week or unit of study, can be used, and some quizzes can be organised and displayed through an interactive white board. If nothing else, the information gained will provide some feedback on the overall retention of knowledge at the end of the unit of work, or a summation of the whole topic, and which parts were largely forgotten.

CONCEPTS TO ASSESS HISTORICAL UNDERSTANDING

As a summary of the previous chapters, which outlined the concepts linked to historical understanding, and to delineate some of the elements that are suitable for assessment without the overwhelming detail contained in the CHATA project, this section provides a summary of the most useful assessment points (see also Table 12.1).

Table 12.1 Key historical concepts

Key Concept	Subordinate Concepts and Skills
Enquiry and evidence	Ability to frame and ask questions Ability to access information about the past from a range of historical evidence: • Objects and buildings (artefacts) • Documents and written sources • Images, including pictures and photographs • Oral evidence
Chronology (time)	Ability to sequence objects or images Development of a 'sense of time' Understanding and interpreting a range of historical timescales
Interpretation and understanding	Understanding that history can be represented in different ways Distinguishing between fact and opinion Understanding the connectedness of historical events (colligation) Developing historical 'judgement'

ENQUIRY AND EVIDENCE

The two key assessment points should centre on children's ability to carry out genuine historical research using a variety of forms of evidence and, equally important, their understanding that history should be an evidence-based subject discipline. In many respects, this is the most significant concept linked to the assessment of historical understanding because it identifies the crucial separation between the common-sense idea of history as a body of knowledge and history as a way of understanding and approaching the world as a systematic study of the past.

The key skill of being able to frame questions essentially rests upon opportunities for children to create and ask questions with visitors, people in the locality and educational officers. These can be assessed by either collecting or reviewing examples of questions, and children's ability to collect and interpret data from the responses to their questions. There should also be the opportunity to frame questions linked to drama activities, such as hot-seating, conscience alley, freeze-frame, etc. (see Chapter 6, p. 97).

In terms of using and understanding the importance of historical data, the key attributes children should demonstrate begin with observational skills (which can be easily linked with art and drawing) and the ability to make statements based on observations linked to primary evidence such as images, artefacts or oral testimony (see above). In this way, early forms of historical reasoning based on deductive forms of reasoning can be demonstrated. For example, archaeological finds such as flint spearheads indicate that Stone Age people hunted or defended themselves with weapons.

The next stage would be a child's increasing use of higher-order thinking skills, such as inferential reasoning (thus going beyond statements of fact or simple deductive reasoning). For example, Neolithic weapons for defence suggest that early Britons would have mostly eaten meat, especially during winter and spring when plants would have been much less available, and then tribes may have fought for land and resources.

The final stage during the primary years would be some pupils' ability to demonstrate an increasing understanding of the nature and form of historical evidence, and a burgeoning understanding of the way in which history is created from evidence. This will include an awareness of the gaps in documentation. For example, the lack of written records prior to the Roman invasion of the British Isles means that the only evidence available consists of the artefacts and bones that ancient Britons left behind. See Table 12.2 for a synopsis.

Table 12.2 Progression in historical enquiry

Assessment for progression in enquiry
Evidence for the increasing sophistication, refinement and independence of question framing, and the ability to identify and answer enquiry questions.
Principally, the movement from knowledge and observational statements, to deductive reasoning (thus demonstrating the ability to reason in logical steps), to inferential reasoning and the beginning of insight and historical judgement.

The schema that emerged from the CHATA project ought to be introduced at this point. The most complete model of progression is summarised in Table 12.3 (Lee and Shemilt, 2004, p. 12). It outlines six stages of understanding historical evidence, ranging from 'pictures of the past' or 'copy theory of history' to 'evidence in context'.

Table 12.3 Progression in ideas about evidence from the CHATA Project

Progression in ideas about evidence	
Pictures of the past	A simplistic copy notion of the past which is viewed as though it was the present. Questions do not arise. Stories are taken at face value.
Information	The past is viewed as fixed and presented as authoritative. Evidence is treated uncritically as information.
Testimony	The past is reported to us by people living at the time, like modern eyewitnesses. Questions about how we know are viewed as sensible. Conflicts over accounts are settled by personal responses. No understanding of bias, exaggeration or omission.
Scissors and paste	Collingwood's term. The past can be understood from multiple sources which are selected and rearranged. Notions of bias and lies are beginning to be understood.

Progression in ideas about evidence	
Evidence in insolation	Statements about the past can be inferred from sources of information. Questions can be formed that would not have been considered at the time. Evidence can be found from unlikely sources.
Evidence in context	A source only yields evidence when it is understood in its historical context. It is important to know what a source meant for those by and for whom it was produced – its context. Contexts vary across time and place and thus a sense of period is important.

It was previously mentioned in Chapter 5 that the CHATA project was designed for children aged between 7 and 14, and so falls out of the primary age range, but as also noted, one of the key findings was the seven-year differential of understanding in any classroom. This means that some upper juniors will be working at Key Stage 3 levels. This is true of any subject of course, and part of the challenge of effective primary practice.

TIME AND CHRONOLOGICAL UNDERSTANDING

In terms of assessment activities for chronological understanding, the obvious starting point is for children to demonstrate the ability to sequence objects, images or both combined, and then to be allowed time to explain their decision making. Discussion points, promoted by probing questions, can be directed towards materials, design, condition and usage. Discussion can centre on the comparison between pristine older objects (or facsimiles) and worn, newer objects, or comparisons between monochrome and colour illustrations. As noted in Chapter 3, Stow's (1999) research demonstrated that children tend to assume that all monochrome images are older, and these questions can illuminate the sophistication of a child's sense of time.

The other main assessment activity is the understanding, interpretation and production of timelines. This can begin towards the end of the Foundation Stage and the start of Key Stage 1 with a personal timeline based on life history events. Although some practitioners feel this may be an unwarranted intrusion into personal history, this was the suggested approach in the first iteration of the National Curriculum, and it is one aspect of a young child's life in which they demonstrate an ability to sequence events. Alternative approaches may be linked to literacy (story sequencing) or science (growth). In Key Stage 2, timelines may be extended to include the periods of history under review and can also be orientated towards the dimensions of history, such as political (Anglo-Saxon kings), technological (history of weaponry) or social (changes in clothing materials and design). Timescales may also extend beyond early British history and incorporate a theme beyond 1066 or be based on a theme from world history. The emphasis on assessment should be on the increasing independence in selecting and using timelines, but more obviously on the production (singly or in pairs) of timelines throughout any history theme or unit of work. This may also include the use of ICT to frame and create timelines. There are several commercial software packages that are now available (for example, TimeToast) for this purpose.

Table 12.4 provides a synopsis of methods for assessing progression in understanding historical time.

Table 12.4 Progression in understanding historical time

Assessment for progression in the understanding of historical time
Ordering and sequencing: evidence for sequencing a series of historical objects and images with increasing accuracy.
Evidence for the increasingly accurate use of historical timeframes, including pre-history and geological timescales, linked to an increasingly sophisticated 'sense of time' and reference to historical periods.
Increasing accuracy and independence in interpreting timelines; increasing independence in the creation of timelines, including identifying the historical timeframe and accuracy with historical dates.

INTERPRETATION AND UNDERSTANDING

Historical interpretation, discussed in considerable detail in Chapter 4, is arguably the most controversial aspect of the humanities curriculum, and certainly one of the most challenging and sophisticated concepts children are introduced to in the primary years (McAleavy, 2000). It is therefore equally challenging for teachers to assess. At its heart is the idea that history is created rather than discovered, and that historical accounts of the past are subject to change and revision, depending on the emergence of new evidence (thus reinforcing the importance of enquiry), changing theoretical perspectives and the lack of a direct relationship with the past.

Fortunately for teachers, the National Curriculum recognised the challenges surrounding the concept of interpretation, so in Key Stage 1 the suggestion was that children should be introduced to the idea of the contingency of historical knowledge by understanding that history can be represented in different ways. This can be as straightforward as introducing children to stories, paintings, drama and music about the past. As children's understanding develops, representations of the past, for example films or artwork, can be compared, analysed and critically assessed for historical accuracy.

Children are also challenged to distinguish between historical fact and opinion, and there is a case for stating that due to the democratic power of web-based information, and the removal of publishers and editors to filter the knowledge children can gain access to, this ability is more important than ever before. Again, the important link is with the historical record and evidence. Children should be encouraged to understand the limits of historical knowledge and therefore understand that there is simply a lot about the past that is unknown. For children at the start of Key Stage 2, the distinction between fact and opinion might be introduced by sorting prepared historical statements; by the end of Key Stage 2, more able children should be beginning to identify the various elements of fact and opinion in history texts. Most recent children's texts are generally clear when they introduce opinions or judgements about the past.

It can be argued that if the construction of historical knowledge is the essential nature of history, then children's own 'judgement' – arguably a form of empowerment or ownership of historical knowledge – is the most significant outcome. It is also an outcome linked to several other historical concepts discussed in this book, including cause and effect, change and continuity, similarity and difference, and significance (what is worth knowing in history). Given the immense time pressures on primary practitioners, it would be unrealistic to expect yet more assessment targets for primary history, but these concepts are listed in the revised National Curriculum (DfE, 2013, p. 188). Historical judgement can also be thought of as the ideal way of providing a summative assessment of children's understanding following a unit or topic of work. A workable proposal would be to use several written outcomes as a way of assessing overall understanding. It is possible that this was what the original framers of the National Curriculum had in mind when written narratives and analyses were included as learning outcomes for history.

However, it may also be thought that a child's ability to explain what it is they have now learnt from their work may be equally and more realistically conducted orally, and this can also be carried out individually, in pairs or in small groups. As children mature, this form or assessment can also take the form of a viva voce interview, in which the teacher poses challenging questions and probes children's understanding in a way written outcomes cannot do. Examples might include key questions such as 'Can you tell me three important facts about the Celtic tribes in the British Isles?' (Years 3 and 5), 'Can you explain why the Roman civilisation ended in the British Isles?' (Years 4 and 6), or 'Was the Battle of Hastings really an invasion of England?' (Year 6). All these questions require an element of interpretation, but the last question is very strongly linked to a more probing approach to history because it challenges the common misconception that the Norman conquest was an invasion of England, when in fact it was ostensibly a battle of succession between Danish and Saxon rulers who would have had a limited concept of England or France as sovereign states.

Table 12.5 provides a synopsis of methods for assessing progression in historical understanding.

Table 12.5 Progression in historical understanding

Assessment for progression in historical understanding
Understanding that the past can be represented in different ways, leading to an increasing understanding that historical knowledge is created from evidence. Eventually this should lead to an understanding that historical knowledge is contingent and liable to change.
Increasing ability to distinguish between historical facts and opinions about the past, leading to analysis of historical texts for accuracy and opinion.
Orally, or in writing, explaining key information and understanding of the past linked to evidence and study and being able to answer questions about the unit of study; increasing ability to link historical understanding to concepts such as causality, change and significance, etc.
Demonstrating an understanding of the connectedness of historical events and periods – colligation.
Summarising, orally or in writing, their personal interpretation and judgement on a historical unit of study.

A GENERAL MODEL OF PROGRESSION

One of the best-known theoretical models that children's historical reasoning can be measured against is Bloom's taxonomy, in which he suggested

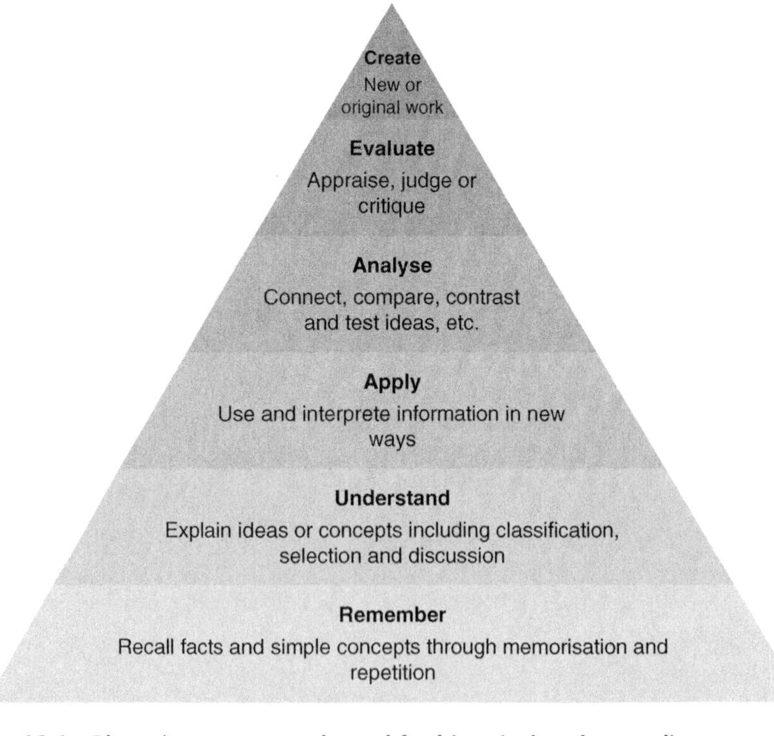

Figure 12.1 Bloom's taxonomy adapted for historical understanding

progression through six levels. The example provided in Figure 12.1 is based on the revised version produced by Anderson and Bloom (2001). Naturally, Bloom's taxonomy should not be accepted without question, but at the very least it does demonstrate that a focus on knowledge and recall is not likely to extend children's historical understanding or generic reasoning skills, although important knowledge may be a foundation for higher forms of learning. By contrast, the most challenging historical concepts, such as explanation, comparison, causality and interpretation, are likely to move children's reasoning towards the higher levels, from level 2, *understanding*, to level 4, *analysis*. This chapter has argued that *judgement* should be the ultimate outcome in primary history, and so while it would be unrealistic to expect primary-aged children to create original knowledge about the past, the attainment of level 5, *evaluation*, might be possible with high-achieving Year 5 and 6 pupils.

CHAPTER SUMMARY

- The revised Ofsted framework for inspection (Ofsted, 2019) shall to place more scrutiny on children's progress throughout the whole curriculum. Irrespective of this point, teachers have a professional duty to report on children's attainment and progress in history.
- A key claim is that reporting should include attitudes, historical knowledge and historical understanding.
- Historical understanding is much more demanding and time-consuming to assess. To make it manageable, therefore, a case has been made to assess children against the key concepts that have underpinned this book, namely enquiry and evidence, an understanding of historical time (chronology) and the range of concepts associated with overall understanding, including historical interpretation.
- A case has also been made that 'judgement' is the ultimate outcome of historical enquiry.

FURTHER READING

Hoodless, P. (2008) *Teaching History in Primary Schools*. Exeter: Learning Matters.

One of the few general texts to consider the assessment of primary history in a practical and detailed way.

Lee, P.J. and Shemilt, D. (2004) A Scaffold, Not a Cage: Progression and Progression Models in History. *Teaching History*, 113: 13–23.

Arguably the best and most concise summary of the main findings from the CHATA project and a key source for this chapter.

REFERENCES

Abrams, F. (2012) *Cultural Literacy: Mr Gove's School of Hard Facts*. Available at: www.bbc.co.uk/news/education-20041597.

Adams, J. (1998) 'Read all about it': Using Newspapers as an Historical Resource in an Infant Classroom. In P. Hoodless (ed.), *History and English in the Primary School*. Abingdon: Routledge, pp. 179–91.

Adams, R.M. (1994) Ancient Sumer, Modern Iraq. *Scientific American*, 271: 112.

Alexander, R. (2004) *Towards Dialogic Teaching: Rethinking Classroom Talk*. London: Dialogos.

Alexander, R., Armstrong, M., Flutter, J., et al. (2010) *Children, Their World, Their Education*. Abingdon: Routledge.

Anderson, L.W. and Bloom, B.S. (2001) *A Taxonomy for Learning, Teaching, and Assessing: A Revision of Bloom's* [Taxonomy of educational objectives]. New York: Longman

Anionwu, E.N. (2005) *A Short History of Mary Seacole: A Resource for Nurses and Students*. London: Royal College of Nursing.

Arthur, J. (2000) What are the Issues in the Teaching of History? In J. Arthur and R. Phillips (eds), *Issues in History Teaching*. Abingdon: Routledge, pp. 1–9.

Ashby, R. (2004) Developing a Concept of Historical Evidence: Students' Ideas about Testing Singular Factual Claims. *International Journal of Historical Learning, Teaching and Research*, 4(2): 1–12.

Ashby, R. (2011) Understanding Historical Evidence: Teaching and Learning Challenges. In I. Davies (ed.), *Debates in History Teaching*. Abingdon: Routledge, pp. 137–47.

Bage, G. (1999) *Narrative Matters: Teaching and Learning History through Story*. London: Falmer.

Bamford, P. (1970) Original Sources in the Classroom. In M. Ballard (ed.), *New Movements in the Study and Teaching of History*. Bloomington, IN: Indiana University Press, pp. 205–11.

Banham, D. (2000) The Return of King John: Using Depth to Strengthen Overview in the Teaching of Political Change. *Teaching History*, 99: 22–31.

Barnes, J. (2011) *Cross-Curricular Learning 3–14*. London: Sage.

Barnes, J. (2015) *Cross-Curricular Learning 3–14* (3rd edn). London: Sage.

Barnham, K. (2002) *Florence Nightingale: The Lady of the Lamp*. London: Hodder Wayland.

Berlin, S.I. (1960) History and Theory: The Concept of Scientific History. *History and Theory*, 1: 1–31.

Bloch, M. (1954) *The Historian's Craft*. Manchester: Manchester University Press.
Blyth, J. (1988) *History 5 to 9*. London: Hodder & Stoughton.
Blyth, J. (1989) *History in Primary Schools*. Buckingham: Open University Press.
Blyth, J. and Hughes, P. (1997) *Using Written Sources in Primary History*. London: Hodder & Stoughton.
Boffey, D. (2013) Historians attack Michael Gove over 'Narrow' Curriculum. *The Guardian*, 16 February.
Booth, M.B. (1983) Skills, Concepts and Attitudes: The Development of Adolescent Children's Historical Thinking. *History and Theory*, 22: 101–17.
Booth, M.B. (1987) Ages and Concepts: A Critique of the Piagetian Approach to History Teaching. In C. Portal (ed.), *The History Curriculum for Teachers*. Lewes: Falmer, pp. 245–57.
Bostridge, M. (2008) *Florence Nightingale: The Woman and Her Legend*. London: Viking.
Bourdillon, H. (1994) On the Record: The Importance of Gender in Teaching History. In H. Bourdillon (ed.), *Teaching History*. Abingdon: Routledge, pp. 62–75.
Bower, B. (2013) Maya Civilization Rooted in Ritual. *Science News*, 183: 12.
Brace, S., Diekmann, Y., Booth, T.J., et al. (2019) Ancient Genomes Indicate Population Replacement in Early Neolithic Britain. *Nature Ecology & Evolution*, 3(5): 765–71.
Braudel, F. (1980) *On History*. London: Weidenfeld & Nicolson.
Braudel, F. and Reynolds, S. (1972) *The Mediterranean and the Mediterranean World in the Age of Philip II*. New York & London: Harper & Row.
Briggs, H. (2018) Lost History of Brown Bears in Britain Revealed. *BBC Science and Environment*, 4 July. London: BBC.
Brink, D. (2011) Incan and Mayan Mathematics. In *Encyclopaedia of Mathematics and Society*. New York: Salem Press, pp. 493–6.
Bruner, J. (1960) *The Process of Education*. Cambridge, MA: Harvard University Press.
Bruner, J. (1996) *The Culture of Education*. Cambridge, MA: Harvard University Press.
Burn, A.R. (1990) *The Penguin History of Greece*. London: Penguin.
Burns, J. (2012) Overhaul School History, Urges Report by MPs and Peers. *BBC Family and Education*, 10 December. London: BBC.
Butterfield, H. (1957) *The Origins of Modern Science, 1300–1800*. London: Bell & Hyman.
CACE (Central Advisory Council for Education) (1967) *Children and their Primary Schools: A Report* (Plowden Report). London: HMSO.
Cann, R.L., Stoneking, M. and Wilson, A.C. (1987) Mitochondrial DNA and Human Evolution. *Nature*, 325: 31–6.
Cannadine, D. (2013) The Future of History. *The Times Literary Supplement*, 13 March.
Cannadine, D., Keating, J. and Sheldon, N. (2011) *The Right Kind of History: Teaching the Past in Twentieth-Century England*. Basingstoke: Palgrave Macmillan.
Card, J. (2010) Printed Pictures with Text: Using Cartoons as Historical Evidence. *Primary History*, 56: 10–12.
Carr, E.H. and Evans, R.J. (1961/2001) *What is History?* Basingstoke: Palgrave.
Cavendish R. (2005) Julius Caesar's First Landing in Britain. *History Today* 55.

Chanda, J. (2007) Learning from Images: A Source of Interdisciplinary Knowledge. *International Journal of Education through Art*, 3: 7–18.

Chapman, A. (2003) Camels, Diamonds and Counterfactuals: A Model for Teaching Causal Reasoning. *Teaching History*, 112: 46–53.

Chapman, A. (2011) Historical Interpretations. In I. Davies (ed.), *Debates in History Teaching*. Abingdon: Routledge, pp. 96–108.

Chapman, T. (1993) Teaching Chronology through Timelines. *Teaching History*, 73: 25–9.

Clark, S. (1985) The Annales Historians. In Q. Skinner (ed.), *The Return of Grand Theory in the Human Sciences*. Cambridge: Cambridge University Press, pp. 177–98.

Collingwood, R.G. (1925) The Nature and Aims of a Philosophy of History. In W. Debbins (ed.), *Essays in the Philosophy of History*. Austin, TX: University of Texas Press.

Collingwood, R.G. (1939) *An Autobiography*. Oxford: Oxford University Press.

Collingwood, R.G. (1946) *The Idea of History*. Oxford: Oxford University Press.

Coltham, J.B. and Fines, J. (1971) *Educational Objectives for the Study of History* (Historical Association Pamphlet 35). London: The Historical Association.

Cooper, H. (1995) *History in the Early Years*. Abingdon: Routledge.

Cooper, H. (2007) Thinking through History: Story and Developing Children's Minds. *Primary History*, 45: 26–9.

Cooper, H. (2012) *History 5–11: A Guide for Teachers*. Abingdon: Routledge.

Cooper, H. (ed.) (2013) *Teaching History Creatively*. Abingdon: Routledge.

Cooper, H. (2018) *History 5–11: A Guide for Teachers* (3rd edn). London & New York: Routledge.

Copeland, T. (1998) Constructing History: All *Our* Yesterdays. In M. Littledyke and L. Huxford (eds), *Teaching the Primary Curriculum for Constructive Learning*. London: David Fulton.

Coughlan, S. (2017) What Does Post-Truth Mean for a Philosopher? *BBC Family and Education*, 12 January. London: BBC.

Counsell, C. (2000) Historical Knowledge and Historical Skills: A Distracting Dichotomy. In J. Arthur and R. Phillips (eds), *Issues in History Teaching*. Abingdon: Routledge, pp. 54–71.

Counsell, C. (2004) Looking through a Josephine-Butler-Shaped Window: Focusing Pupils' Thinking on Historical Significance. *Teaching History*, 114: 30–6.

Counsell, C. (2011) What Do We Want Students to Do with Historical Change and Continuity? In I. Davies (ed.), *Debates in History Teaching*. Abingdon: Routledge, pp. 109–23.

Counsell, C. (2012) Disciplinary Knowledge for All, the Secondary History Curriculum and History Teachers' Achievement. *Curriculum Journal*, 22: 201–25.

Cox, C. and Hughes, P. (1998) History and Children's Fiction. In P. Hoodless (ed.), *History and English in the Primary School*. Abingdon: Routledge, pp. 87–102.

Craft, A. (2005) Changes in the Landscape for Creativity in Education. In A. Wilson (ed.), *Creativity in Primary Education*. Exeter: Learning Matters, pp. 7–18.

Crane, N. (2012) *Coast: Our Island Story: A Journey of Discovery around Britain's Coastline*. London: BBC.

Crist, R.E. and Paganini, L.A. (1980) The Rise and Fall of Maya Civilization. *The American Journal of Economics and Sociology*, 39: 23–30.
Croce, B. (1960) *History: Its Theory and Practice*. New York: Russell and Russell.
Culpin, C. (1994) Making Progress in History. In H. Bourdillon (ed.), *Teaching History*. Abingdon: Routledge, pp. 126–52.
Cunningham, R. (2001) Teaching Pupils How History Works. *Teaching History*, 102: 14–19.
Dearing, R. (1994) *The National Curriculum and its Assessment: Final Report* (The Dearing Review, December 1993). London: School Curriculum and Assessment Authority.
DES (Department of Education and Science) (1982) *Education 5 to 9: An Illustrative Survey of 80 First School in England*. London: HMSO.
DES (Department of Education and Science) (1988a) *History from 5 to 16: Curriculum Matters 11* (An HMI Series). London: HMSO.
DES (Department of Education and Science) (1988b) *Education Reform Act*. London: HMSO.
DES (Department of Education and Science) (1989) *National Curriculum: History Working Group – Interim Report*. London: HMSO.
DES (Department of Education and Science) (1990) *National Curriculum: History Working Group – Final Report*. London: HMSO.
DES (Department of Education and Science) (1991a) *History in the National Curriculum (England)*. London: HMSO.
DES (Department of Education and Science) (1991b) *Geography in the National Curriculum (England)*. London: HMSO.
DfE (Department for Education) (1995) *History in the National Curriculum (England)*. London: HMSO.
DfE (Department for Education) (2013) *The National Curriculum in England: Key Stages 1 and 2 Framework Document*. London: HMSO. Available at: www.gov.uk/government/publications/national-curriculum-in-england-primary-curriculum
DfE (Department for Education) (2014) *Promoting fundamental British values as part of SMSC in schools: Departmental advice for maintained schools*. London: HMSO.
DfE (Department for Education) (2017) *Statutory framework for the early years foundation stage: Setting the standards for learning, development and care for children from birth to five*. London: HMSO.
DfEE (Department for Education and Employment) (1999) *The National Curriculum: Handbook for Primary Teachers in England: Key Stages 1 and 2*. London: HMSO.
Dixon, L. and Hales, A. (2014) *Bringing History Alive through Local People and Places*. Abingdon: Routledge.
Du Garde Peach, L. and Kenney, J.P. J. (1959) *David Livingstone*. Loughborough: Ladybird Books.
Edgar, D. (2013) The British History New Citizens Must Learn: No Radicals, No Homosexuals, No Holocaust. *The Guardian*, 11 March.
Egan, K. (1992) *Imagination in Teaching and Learning*. Abingdon: Routledge.
Egan, K. (1997) *The Educated Mind*. Chicago, IL: University of Chicago Press.
Elton, G. (2002) *The Practice of History*. Oxford: Blackwell.

English, C. (2015) "Not a Very Edifying Spectacle": The Controversial Women's 800-Meter Race in the 1928 Olympics. Available at: https://ussporthistory.com/tag/iaaf/

English, C. (2015) 'Not a Very Edifying Spectacle': The Controversial Women's 800-Meter Race in the 1928 Olympics. *In Sport in American History*. Word Press.

Evans, R.J. (1997) *In Defence of History*. London: Granta Books.

Evans, R.J. (2013) Michael Gove's History Wars. *The Guardian*, 13 July.

Farmer, A. and Cooper, C. (1998) Story Telling in History. In P. Hoodless (ed.), *History and English in the Primary School*. Abingdon: Routledge, pp. 35–51.

Fash, W.F. (1994) Changing Perspectives on Maya Civilization. *Annual Review of Anthropology*, 23: 181–208.

Ferguson, N. (1997) *Virtual History: Alternatives and Counterfactuals*. London: Pan Books.

Fines, J. (1980) Trainee Teachers of History and Infants as Learners. *Teaching History*, 26: 3–5.

Fines, J. (1987) Making Sense out of the Content of the History Curriculum. In C. Portal (ed.), *The History Curriculum for Teachers*. London: Falmer Press, pp. 103–15.

Fines, J. (1994) Evidence: The Basis of the Discipline. In H. Bourdillon (ed.), *Teaching History*. Abingdon: Routledge, pp. 122–5.

Fines, J. and Nichol, J. (1997) *Teaching Primary History – Nuffield Primary History Project*. Oxford: Heinemann Educational.

Fischer, D.H. (1970) *Historians' Fallacies: Toward a Logic of Historical Thought*. New York: Harper Perennial.

Furness, H. (2014) CBBC Sketch 'Inaccurately' Painted Florence Nightingale as Racist, BBC Trust Finds. *The Daily Telegraph*, 30 September.

Gove, M. (2009) What is Education For? Speech by Michael Gove MP to the Royal Society of Arts, 29 June. London: RSA.

Graeber, D. and Wengrow, D. (2018) How to Change the Course of Human History. *Eurozine*, 2 March. Available at: www.eurozine.com/change-course-human-history/

Grainger, T. (2005) Oral Artistry: Storytelling and Drama. In A. Wilson (ed.), *Creativity in Primary Education*. Exeter: Learning Matters, pp. 33–43.

Green, A. and Troup, K. (1999) *The Houses of History* (A Critical Reader in Twentieth-Century History and Theory). Manchester: Manchester University Press.

Griffin, J. and Eddershaw, D. (1996) *Using Local History Sources: A Teachers' Guide for the National Curriculum*. Abingdon: Hodder & Stoughton Educational.

Guyver, R. (1997) National Curriculum History: Key Concepts and Controversy. *Teaching History*, 88: 16–20.

Guyver, R. (2001) Working with Boudicca Texts – Contemporary, Juvenile and Scholarly. *Teaching History*, 103: 32–5.

Haigh, C. (1985) *The Cambridge Historical Encyclopaedia of Great Britain and Ireland*. Cambridge: Cambridge University Press.

Hake, C. and Haydn, T. (1995) Stories or Sources? *Teaching History*, 78: 20–2.

Hall, S. (2001) *The Penguin Atlas of British and Irish History*. London: Penguin.

Hammond, N. (1986) The Emergence of Maya Civilization. *Scientific American*, 255: 106–15.

Harford, T. (2017) How the World's First Accountants Counted on Cuneiform. *BBC News/Business*, 12 June. London: BBC.

Harnett, P. (1993) Identifying Progression in Children's Understanding: The Use of Visual Materials to Assess Primary Children's Learning in History. *Cambridge Journal of Education*, 23: 137–54.

Harnett, P. (1998) Children Working with Pictures. In P. Hoodless (ed.), *History and English in the Primary School*. Abingdon: Routledge, pp. 69–86.

Harnett, P. (2000) Curriculum Decision-Making in the Primary School: The Place of History. In J. Arthur and R. Phillips (eds), *Issues in History Teaching*. Abingdon: Routledge, pp. 24–38.

Harris, P.L. (2000) *The Work of the Imagination*. Oxford: Blackwell.

Harrison, S. and Woff, R. (2004) Using Museums and Artefacts. *Primary History*, 37: 18–20.

Haug, G.H., Gunther, D., Peterson, L.C., et al. (2003) Climate and the Collapse of Maya Civilization. *Science, New Series*, 299: 1731–5.

Hawkes, A. (1996) Objects or Pictures in the Primary Classroom? *Teaching History*, 85: 30–5.

Haydn, T. (1995) Teaching Children about Time. *Teaching History*, 81: 11–12.

Haydn T, Arthur J and Hunt M. (2001) *Learning to Teach History in the Secondary School*. Abingdon: RoutledgeFalmer.

Hellemans, A. and Bunch, B. (1988) *The Timetables of Science: A Chronology of the Most Important People and Events in the History of Science*. New York & London: Simon & Schuster.

Hernandez, X., Ballonga, J. and Escofet, J. (1992) *A Mayan Town through History*. Hove: Wayland.

Hexter, J.H. (1971) *Doing History*. London: George Allen and Unwin.

Hicks, A. and Martin, D. (1997) Teaching English and History through Historical Fiction. *Children's Literature in Education*, 28: 49–59.

Hill, J., Collins, G.S., Avdis, A., et al. (2014) How Does Multiscale Modelling and Inclusion of Realistic Palaeobathymetry Affect Numerical Simulation of the Storegga Slide Tsunami? *Ocean Modelling*, 83: 11–25.

Hirsch, E.D. (1988) *Cultural Literacy: What Every American Needs to Know*. New York: Vintage Books.

Hissey, J. (1986) *Old Bear*. London: Hutchinson Children's.

Historical Association (2011) *The Historical Association – Primary History Survey (England) History 3–11*. London: Historical Association.

HM Inspector of Schools (1978) *Primary Education in England: A Survey by HM Inspectors of Schools*. London: HMSO.

HMI (Her Majesty's Inspectorate) (1985) *History in the Primary and Secondary Years: An HMI View*. London: HMSO, Publication Series 65.

HMI (Her Majesty's Inspectorate) (1989) *The Teaching and Learning of History and Geography* (Aspects of Primary Education). London: HMSO, Publication Series 41.

Hobsbawm, E. (1997) *On History*. London: Abacus.

Hodgkinson, K. (1986) How Artefacts can Stimulate Historical Thinking in Young Children. *Education 3–13*, 14: 14–17.

Hodkinson, A. (2007) The Usage of Subjective Temporal Phrases within the National Curriculum for History and its Schemes of Work – Effective Provision or a Missed Opportunity? *Education 3–13*, 31(3): 28–34.

Hoodless, P. (2002) An Investigation into Children's Developing Awareness of Time and Chronology. *Curriculum Studies*, 34: 173–200.

Hoodless, P. (2004) Spotting the Adult Agendas: Investigating Children's Historical Awareness Using Stories Written for Children in the Past. *International Journal of Historical Learning, Teaching and Research*, 4: 66–75.

Hoodless, P. (2008) *Teaching History in Primary Schools*. Exeter: Learning Matters.

Hughes-Warrington, M.T.E. (2012) *How Good an Historian Shall I Be?* Exeter: Imprint Academic.

Hunt, M. (2000) Teaching Historical Significance. In J. Arthur and R. Phillips (eds), *Issues in History Teaching*. Abingdon: Routledge, pp. 39–53.

Husbands, C. (1996) *What is History Teaching?* Maidenhead: Open University Press.

Husbands, C. and Pendry, A. (2000) Thinking and Feeling: Pupils' Preconceptions about the Past and Historical Understanding. In J. Arthur and R. Phillips (eds), *Issues in Teaching History*. Abingdon: Routledge, pp. 125–36.

Jacobs, H.H. (1989) *Interdisciplinary Curriculum, Design and Implementation*. Alexandria, VA: Association for Supervision and Curriculum Development.

Jeal, T. (1973) *Livingstone*. London: Heinemann.

Jeal, T. (2007) *Stanley: The Impossible Life of Africa's Greatest Explorer*. London: Faber & Faber.

Jenkins, K. (1991) *Re-Thinking History*. Abingdon: Routledge.

Jenkins, S. (2011) English History: Why We Need to Understand 1066 and All That. *The Guardian*, 1 September.

Jobling, I. (2006) The Women's 800 Metres Track Event Post 1928: Quo Vadis? *Journal of Olympic History*, 14: 43–7.

Keating, J. and Sheldon, N. (2011) History in Education: Trends and Themes in History Teaching. In I. Davies (ed.), *Debates in History Teaching*. Abingdon: Routledge, pp. 5–17.

Kelly, L. (2013) Why Use a Cross-Curricular Approach to Teaching and Learning? In L. Kelly and D. Stead (eds), *Enhancing Primary Science: Developing Cross-Curricular Links*. Milton Keynes: Open University Press, pp. 1–13.

Kennedy, M. (2014) Stonehenge: Children Revealed to be the Metal Workers of Prehistoric Britain. *The Guardian*, 18 September.

Kerry, T. (ed.) (2011) *Cross-Curricular Teaching in the Primary School*. Abingdon: Routledge.

Kettle, M. (2012) The English, Bereft of History, Have Lost Their Self-Respect. *The Guardian*, 13 December.

Keys, D. (2014) Stonehenge's Most Intricate Archaeological Finds were 'Probably Made by Children'. *The Independent*, 17 September.

King, C. (1963) *Stig of the Dump*. Bath: Chivers.

Knight, P. (1989a) A Study of Children's Understanding of People in the Past. *Educational Review*, 41: 207–19.

Knight, P. (1989b) Empathy: Concept, Confusion and Consequences in a National Curriculum. *Oxford Review of Education*, 15: 41–53.

Krugman, P.R. (1994) *The Age of Diminished Expectations: U.S. Economic Policy in the 1990s*. Cambridge, MA & London: The MIT Press.

Lane, M. (2011) The Moment Britain Became an Island. *BBC Magazine*, 15 February. London: BBC.

Lang, S. (1993) What is Bias? *Teaching History*, 73: 9–13.

Lang, S. (2003) Narrative: The Under-Rated Skill. *Teaching History*, 110: 8–17.

Laurie, J. (2011) Curriculum Planning and Preparation for Cross-Curricular Teaching. In T. Kerry (ed.), *Cross-Curricular Teaching in the Primary School*. Abingdon: Routledge, pp. 125–41.

Lee, P.J. (1991) Historical Knowledge and the National Curriculum. In R. Aldridge (ed.), *History in the National Curriculum* (Bedford Way Series). London: Institute of Education, University of London, pp. 39–65.

Lee, P.J. (1994) Historical Knowledge and the National Curriculum. In H. Bourdillon (ed.), *Teaching History*. Abingdon: Routledge, pp. 41–52.

Lee, P.J. (1998) 'A Lot of Guess Work Goes On': Children's Understanding of Historical Accounts. *Teaching History*, 92: 29–35.

Lee, P.J. (2011) History Education and Historical Literacy. In I. Davies (ed.), *Debates in History Teaching*. Abingdon: Routledge, pp. 63–72.

Lee, P.J., Dickinson, A.K. and Ashby, R. (1996a) Children Making Sense of History. *Education 3–13*, 24: 13–19.

Lee, P.J., Dickinson, A.K. and Ashby, R. (1996b) Concepts of History and Teaching Approaches in Key Stages 2 and 3: Children's Understanding of 'Because' and the Status of Explanation in History. *Teaching History*, 82: 6–11.

Lee, P.J., Dickinson, A.K. and Ashby, R. (1997) 'Just Another Emperor': Understanding Action in the Past. *International Journal of Educational Research*, 27: 233–42.

Lee, P.J. and Shemilt, D. (2004) A Scaffold, Not a Cage: Progression and Progression Models in History. *Teaching History*, 113: 13–23.

Lévi-Strauss, C. (1962) *The Savage Mind* (*La Pensée Sauvage*). London: Weidenfeld & Nicholson.

Lévi-Strauss, C. (1963) *Structural Anthropology*. Harmondsworth: Penguin Books.

Levstik, L.S. (1995) Narrative Constructions: Cultural Frames for History. *Social Studies*, 86: 113–17.

Levstik, L.S. and Barton, K.C. (1996) 'They Still Use Some of Their Past': Historical Salience in Elementary Children's Chronological Thinking. *Journal of Curriculum Studies*, 28: 531–76.

Levstik, L.S. and Barton, K.C. (2011) *Doing History: Investigating with Children in Elementary and Middle School*. Abingdon: Routledge

Lewis, C.S. (1950) *The Lion, the Witch and the Wardrobe: A Story for Children*. London: Geoffrey Bles.

Little, V., Thorne, A., Llewellyn, M., et al. (2007) Historical Fiction and Children's Understanding of the Past. *Education 3–13*, 24: 3–9.

Loader P. (1993) Historically Speaking. *Teaching History*, 71: 20–22.

Lomas, T., Burke, C., Cordingley, D., et al. (1996) *Planning Primary History for the Revised National Curriculum*. London: John Murray.

Low-Beer, A. (1989) Empathy and History. *Teaching History*, 55: 6–12.

Low-Beer, A. and Blyth, J. (1990) *Teaching History to Younger Children*. London: Historical Association.

Lowenthal, D. (1985) *The Past is a Foreign Country*. Cambridge: Cambridge University Press.

Lowenthal, D. (2007) The Past of the Future: From the Foreign to the Undiscovered Country. In K. Jenkins, S. Morgan and A. Munslow (eds), *Manifestos for History*. Abingdon: Routledge.

Lynn, S. (1993) Children Reading Pictures: History Visuals at Key Stages 1 and 2. *Education 3–13*, 21: 23–9.

Mahoo, S. and Yalden, D.W. (2000) The Mesolithic Mammal Fauna of Great Britain. *Mammal Review*, 30: 243–8.

Mark, J.J. (2011) Sumer. *Ancient History Encyclopedia*. Accessed at: https://www.ancient.eu/sumer/

Markland, E. (2010) 'Doing History' with Objects: A Museum's Role. *Primary History*, 54: 31–3.

Marwick, A. (1981) *The Nature of History* (2nd edn). Basingstoke: Macmillan.

Marwick, A. (2001) *The New Nature of History*. Basingstoke: Palgrave.

Masalski, K.W. (2001) Examining the Japanese History Textbook Controversies. *Japan Digest*, November.

May, T. and Williams, S. (1987) Empathy – A Case of Apathy? *Teaching History*, 49: 11–16.

McAleavy, T. (1993) Using the Attainment Targets in Key Stage 3: AT2, Interpretation of History. *Teaching History*, 72: 14–17.

McAleavy, T. (2000) Teaching about Interpretations. In J. Arthur and R. Phillips (eds), *Issues in Teaching History*. Abingdon: Routledge, pp. 72–82.

McIntosh, J. and Twist, C. (2001) *Civilizations: Ten Thousand Years of Ancient History*. London: BBC Worldwide.

McKie, R. (2018) Cheddar Man Changes the Way We Think about Our Ancestors. *The Guardian*, 13 February.

Moore, R. (1982) History Abandoned? The Need for a Continuing Debate. *Teaching History*, 32: 26–28.

Morgan, K.O. (1988) *The Oxford History of Britain*. Oxford: Oxford University Press.

Nagel, E. (1960) Determinism in History. In P. Gardner (ed.), *The Philosophy of History*. Oxford: Oxford University Press, pp. 187–215.

NCC (National Curriculum Council) (1993a) *Teaching History at Key Stage 1*. York: NCC Inset Resources.

NCC (National Curriculum Council) (1993b) *Teaching History at Key Stage 2*. York: NCC Inset Resources.

NCC (National Curriculum Council) (1993c) History at Key Stage 2: An Introduction to the Non-European Study Units. York: National Curriculum Council.

Nichol, J. (2010) Difficult and Challenging Reading: Genre, Text and Multi-Modal Sources – Textbreaker. *Primary History*, 56: 8–10.

Nuffield Primary History (2009) *Cross-Curricular Learning*. 2012. Historical Association. Available at: www.history.org.uk/resources/primary_resource_3638,3653_130.html

Oakeshott, M. (1933) *Experience and Its Modes*. Cambridge: Cambridge University Press.

Oakeshott, M. (1962) The Activity of Being a Historian. In T. Fuller (ed.), *Rationalism in Politics and Other Essays*. Indianapolis, IN: Liberty Press.

Oakeshott, M. (1972) Education: The Enjoyment and the Frustration. In T. Fuller (ed.), *The Voice of Liberal Learning: Michael Oakeshott on Education*. New Haven, CT: Yale University Press, pp. 89–109.

Oakeshott, M. (1983) *On History and Other Essays*. Indianapolis, IN: Liberty Press.

Oakeshott, M. and Fuller, T. (1989) *The Voice of Liberal Learning: Michael Oakeshott on Education*. New Haven, CT & London: Yale University Press.

Ofsted (Office for Standards in Education) (1999) *Primary Education: 1994–98: A Review of Primary Schools in England*. London: HMSO.

Ofsted (Office for Standards in Education, Children's Services and Skills) (2002) *The Curriculum in Successful Primary Schools*. London: Ofsted Publications Centre.

Ofsted (Office for Standards in Education, Children's Services and Skills) (2007) *History in the Balance: History in English Schools 2003–7*. London: HMSO.

Ofsted (Office for Standards in Education, Children's Services and Skills) (2009) *Twenty Outstanding Primary Schools – Excelling Against the Odds*. London: HMSO.

Ofsted (Office for Standards in Education) (2011) *History for All: History in English Schools 2007/10*. London: HMSO.

Ofsted (Office for Standards in Education, Children's Services and Skills) (2018) *HMCI commentary: Curriculum and the new education inspection framework*. London: Her Majesty's Inspectorate Gov.UK, webpage.

Ofsted (Office for Standards in Education, Children's Services and Skills) (2019) *Consultation outcome: Education inspection framework 2019: Inspecting the substance of education*. 29 July. London: Her Majesty's Inspectorate Gov.UK, webpage.

Olalde, I., Brace, S., Allentoft, M.E., et al. (2018) The Beaker Phenomenon and the Genomic Transformation of Northwest Europe. *Nature*, 555: 190.

Partington, G. (1980) *The Idea of an Historical Education*. Windsor: NFER Publishing.

Pedley, J.G. (1993) *Greek Art and Archaeology*. London: Cassell.

Pendry, A., Atha, J., Carden, S., et al. (1997) Pupil Preconceptions in History. *Teaching History*, 86: 18–20.

Percival, J.W. (2012) Developing Chronological Understanding through the Use of ICT. *Primary History*, 62: 22–4.

Percival, J.W. (2017a) A Multiple Case-Study Design in Education to Investigate Historical Integrity and Curriculum Management in Three English Primary Schools. *SAGE Research Methods*, 23 January. London: Sage.

Percival, J.W. (2017b) Investigating Narrative Forms of History Pedagogy in Primary Teacher Education in England. *International Journal of Historical Learning, Teaching and Research*, 15: 160–72.

Percival, J.W. (2018) History and Its Links Across The Curriculum. *Education 3–13*, 46: 712–27.

Percival, J.W. (2018) History and its Links across the Curriculum. *Education 3–13*, Special Edition: 1–16.

Phillips, R. (1998) *History Teaching, Nationhood and the State: A Study in Educational Politics*. London: Cassell.

Phillips, R. (2000) Government Policies, the State and the Teaching of History. In J. Arthur and R. Phillips (eds), *Issues in the Teaching of History*. Abingdon: Routledge, pp. 10–23.

Phillips, R. (2002) Historical Significance – the Forgotten 'Key Element'? *Teaching History*, 106: 14–19.

Piaget, J. (1946) The Child's Conception of Time. In H.E. Gruber and J.J. Voneche (eds), *The Essential Piaget*. Abingdon: Routledge & Kegan Paul, pp. 547–75.

Piaget, J. (1954) *The Construction of Reality in the Child*. New York: Basic Books.

Piaget, J. and Inhelder, B. (1963) Mental Images. In H.E. Gruber and J.J. Vonechc (eds), *The Essential Piaget*. Abingdon: Routledge & Kegan Paul, pp. 652–84.

Popper, K.R. (1966) *The Open Society and its Enemies*. Abingdon: Routledge & Kegan Paul.

Portal, C. (1987) Empathy as an Objective for History Teaching. In C. Portal (ed.), *The History Curriculum for Teachers*. London: Falmer Press, pp. 89–102.

Preston, R. (2013) Horrible Histories: 20 years of Entertaining Children. *The Daily Telegraph*, 21st February.

Pring, R. (1973) Curriculum Integration. In R.S. Peters (ed.), *The Philosophy of Education*. Oxford: Oxford University Press, pp. 123–49.

QCA (Qualifications and Curriculum Agency) (1998) *Maintaining Breadth and Balance at Key Stages 1 and 2*. Coventry: Qualifications and Curriculum Agency.

QCA (Qualifications and Curriculum Agency) (2007) *National Curriculum 2007 – History* (Programme of Study for Key Stage 3 and Attainment Target). Coventry: Qualifications and Curriculum Agency.

Quenet, P. (2005) The Diffusion of the Cuneiform Writing System in Northern Mesopotamia: The Earliest Archaeological Evidence. *Iraq*, 67: 31–40.

Redfern, A. (1998) Voices of the Past: Oral History and English in the Primary Curriculum. In P. Hoodless (ed.), *History and English in the Primary School*. Abingdon: Routledge, pp. 52–68.

Rincon, P. (2014) Prehistoric North Sea 'Atlantis' hit by 5m Tsunami. *BBC Science and Environment*, 1 May. London: BBC.

Rincon, P. (2018a) Ancient Britons 'Replaced' by Newcomers. *BBC Science and Environment*, 21 February. London: BBC.

Rincon, P. (2018b) Cheddar Man: DNA Shows Early Briton Had Dark Skin. *BBC Science and Environment*, 23 February. London: BBC.

Roberts, A. (2004) *What Might Have Been: Leading Historians on Twelve 'What Ifs' of History*. London: Weidenfeld & Nicolson.

Rogers, P.J. (1984) The Power of Visual Representation. In A.K. Dickinson, P.J. Lee and P.J. Rogers (eds), *Learning History*. London: Heinemann Educational Books, pp. 154–67.

Rogers, P.J. (1987) History – The Past as a Frame of Reference. In C. Portal (ed.), *The History Curriculum for Teachers*. London: Falmer Press, pp. 3–21.

Rowley, C. and Cooper, H. (2009) Cross-Curricular Learning and the Development of Values. In C. Rowley and H. Cooper (eds), *Cross-Curricular Approaches to Teaching and Learning*. London: Sage, pp. 1–16.

Ryle, G. (1949) *The Concept of Mind*. London: Penguin Books.

Salway, P. (1981) *Roman Britain*. Oxford: Clarendon Press.

Salway, P. (1993) *The Oxford Illustrated History of Roman Britain*. Oxford: Oxford University Press.

Sampson, J., Grugeon, L. and Yiannaki, E. (1998) Learning the Language of History: Teaching Subject-Specific Language and Concepts. In P. Hoodless (ed.), *History and English in the Primary School*. Abingdon: Routledge, pp. 143–56.

Sayers, R. (2011) The Implications of Introducing Heathcote's Mantle of the Expert Approach as a Community of Practice and Cross-Curricular Learning Tool in a Primary School. *English in Education*, 45: 2–35.

Scanlon, M. (2011) History beyond the Academy: Humor and Horror in Children's History Books. *New Review of Children's Literature and Librarianship*, 16: 69–91.

Scanlon, M. and Buckingham, D. (2002) Popular Histories: 'Education' and 'Entertainment' in Information Books for Children. *Curriculum Journal*, 13: 141–61.

Schama, S. (2000) *A History of Britain, Volume 1: At the Edge of the World? 3000BC–AD1603*. London: BBC Books.

Schwab, J.J. (1964) The Structure of the Disciplines: Meanings and Significances. In G. Ford and L. Purgo (eds), *The Structure of Knowledge and the Curriculum*. Chicago, IL: Rand McNally.

Scieszka, J. and Smith, L. (1989) *The True Story of the 3 Little Pigs*. New York: Viking Kestrel.

Scott, B. (1994) A Post-Dearing Look at Hi.2: Interpretations of History. *Teaching History*, 75: 20–6.

Seacole, M., Alexander, Z. and Dewjee, A. (eds) (1857/1984) *Wonderful Adventures of Mrs. Seacole in Many Lands*. Bristol: Falling Wall Press.

Seacole, M. and Salih, S. (2005) *Wonderful Adventures of Mrs Seacole in Many Lands*. London: Penguin.

Sellgren, K. (2013) Historians Split Over Gove's Curriculum Plan. *BBC Family and Education*, 27 February. London: BBC.

Sheldon, N. (2009a) Interview with Denis Shemilt (3 July). History of Education Project. Available at: www.history.ac.uk/history-in-education/browse/interviews/interview-denis-shemilt-3-july-2009.html

Sheldon, N. (2009b) Interview with David Sylvester (7 July). History in Education Project. Available at: www.history.ac.uk/history-in-education/browse/interviews/interview-david-sylvester-7-july-2009.html

Sheldon, N. (2009c) Interview with Jon Nichol (3 August). History in Education Project. Available at: www.history.ac.uk/history-in-education/browse/interviews/interview-jon-nichol-3-august-2009.html

Sheldon, N. (2011) The National Curriculum and the Changing Face of School History 1988–2010. *Journal of Curriculum Studies*, 42: 693–723.

Shemilt, D. (1980) *Evaluation Study: Schools Council History 13–16 Project*. Edinburgh: Holmes McDougall.

Skinner, Q. (1976) Motives, Intentions and the Interpretation of Texts. In J. Tully (ed.), *Meaning and Context: Quentin Skinner and His Critics*. Cambridge: Polity Press, pp. 68–78.

Slater, J. (1991) History in the National Curriculum: The Final Report of the History Working Group. In R. Aldridge (ed.), *History in the National Curriculum* (Bedford Way Series). London: Institute of Education, University of London, pp. 8–38.

Small, H. (1998) *Florence Nightingale: Avenging Angel*. London: Constable.

Smith, L. and Holden, C. (1994) I Thought it was for Picking Bones out of Soup: Using Artefacts in the Primary School. *Teaching History*, 76: 6–9.

Smith, R. (2016) Ancient Roman IOUs Found Beneath Bloomberg's New London HQ. *National Geographic*, 1 June. Washington, DC: National Geographic Society.

Standford, P. (2012) Tony Robinson Launches Series of History Books for Children. *The Daily Telegraph*, 28th April.

Stanford, M. (1986) *The Nature of Historical Knowledge*. Oxford: Basil Blackwell.

Starkey, D. (2005) History in British Education: What History Should We be Teaching in Britain in the 21st Century? Institute of Historical Research Conference, University of London, 14th and 15th April.

Stenton, F.M. (1971) *Anglo-Saxon England*. Oxford: Clarendon Press.
Stephens, W.B. (1977) *Teaching Local History*. Manchester: Manchester University Press.
Stol, M. (1995) Women in Mesopotamia. *Journal of the Economic and Social History of the Orient*, 38: 123–44.
Stone, L. (1987) *The Past and Present – Revisited*. Abingdon: Routledge & Kegan Paul.
Stow, W. (1999) Time and Period: Investigating Primary School Children's Understanding of Chronology. *Curriculum*, 20: 175–84.
Stow, W. and Haydn, T. (2000) Issues in the Teaching of Chronology. In J. Arthur and R. Phillips (eds), *Issues in History Teaching*. Abingdon: Routledge, pp. 98–112.
Sylvester, D. (1994) Change and Continuity in History Teaching 1900–93. In H. Bourdillon (ed.), *Teaching History*. Abingdon: Routledge, pp. 9–23.
Taylor, A.J.P. (1961) *The Origins of the Second World War*. London: Hamilton.
Taylor, A.J.P. (1983) *A Personal History*. Philadelphia, PA: Coronet Books.
Thornton, S.J. and Vukelich, R. (1988) Effects of Children' Understanding of Time Concepts on Historical Understanding. *Theory and Research in Social Education*, XVI: 69–82.
Tolkien, J.R.R. (1937) *The Hobbit: Or There and Back Again*. London: George Allen and Unwin.
Tosh, J. (1991) *The Pursuit of History* (Aims, Methods and New Directions in the Study of Modern History). London: Longman.
Tosh, J. and Lang, S. (2006) *The Pursuit of History*. Harlow: Pearson Longman.
Trivizas, E. and Oxenbury, H. (1993) *The Three Little Wolves and the Big Bad Pig*. London: Heinemann.
Turner-Bisset, R. (2005) *Creative Teaching: History in the Primary Classroom*. London: David Fulton.
Tyler, K. (1992) Differentiation and Integration of the Primary Curriculum. *Journal of Curriculum Studies*, 24: 563–7.
Vallance, E. (2009) *A Radical History of Britain: Visionaries, Rebels and Revolutionaries: The Men and Women Who Fought for our Freedoms*. London: Little, Brown.
Van der Dussen, J. (1994) Editor's Introduction. In J. Van der Dussen (ed.), *The Idea of History*. Oxford: Oxford University Press, pp. ix–xlviii.
Vass, P. (1992) Overwhelming Evidence: Written Sources and Primary History. *Teaching History*, 66: 21–6.
Vass, P. (1993) Have I got a Witness? Considerations of the Use of Historical Witnesses in the Primary Classroom. *Teaching History*, 73: 19–24.
Vass, P. (2004) Thinking Skills and the Learning of Primary History: Thinking Historically through Stories. *International Journal of Historical Learning, Teaching and Research*, 4.
Vass, P. (2005) Stories about People: Narrative, Imagined Biography and Citizenship in the KS2 Curriculum. *Primary History*, 41: 13–16.
Vass, P., Galloway, R. and Ullathorne, N. (2003) After the Sirens Sounded: Event Framing and Counterfactuals. *Primary History*, 33: 18–19.
Verrier, R.L. (2007) A Classroom Museum. *Primary History*, 45: 13–17.
Vianna, E. and Stetsenko, A. (2006) Embracing History through Transforming It. *Theory and Psychology*, 16: 81–108.

Visram, R. (1994) British History: Whose History? Black Perspectives of Gender in Teaching History. In H. Bourdillon (ed.), *Teaching History*. Abingdon: Routledge, pp. 53–61.

Vygotsky, L.S. (1978) *Mind in Society* (The Development of Higher Psychological Processes). Cambridge, MA: Harvard University Press.

Walsh, W.H. (1951) *An Introduction to Philosophy of History*. London: Hutchinson's University Library.

Weiss, I. (2017) Nothing Matters: How the Invention of Zero Helped Create Modern Mathematics. *The Conversation*. Accessed at: http://theconversation.com/nothing-matters-how-the-invention-of-zero-helped-create-modern-mathematics-84232

West, J. (1978) Young Children's Awareness of the Past. *Trends in Education*, Spring: 8–15.

West, J. (1981a) Time Charts. *Education 3–13*, 10: 48–50.

West, J. (1981b) Primary School Children's Perception of Authenticity and Time in Historical Narrative Pictures. *Teaching History*, 29: 8–10.

West, J. (1986) The Development of Primary School Children's Sense of Time. In R. Fairbrother (ed.), *Greater Manchester Primary Contact, History and the Primary School*. Manchester: Didsbury School of Education.

White, H. (1978) *Tropics of Discourse: Essays in Cultural Criticism*. Baltimore, MD: Johns Hopkins University Press.

White, H. (1999) *Figural Realism: Studies in the Mimesis Effect*. Baltimore, MD: Johns Hopkins University Press.

White, R. (1997) Time for History: Some Ideas for Teaching Chronology in Year 2. *Teaching History*, 89: 22–5.

Williams, R. and Davies, I. (1998) Interpretations of History: Issues for Teachers in the Development of Pupils' Understanding. *Teaching History*, 91: 36–40.

Wood, M. (2014) Travelling in Time. *Your Manchester Magazine*, September 2014: pp. 18–19.

Wood, S. (1995) Developing and Understanding of Time – Sequencing Issues. *Teaching History*, 79: 11–14.

Woodcock, J. (2011) Causal Explanation. In I. Davies (ed.), *Debates in History Teaching*. Abingdon: Routledge, pp. 124–36.

Worrall, S. (2018) When and how did the First Americans arrive? It's complicated. *National Geographic*, 9 June. Washington, DC: National Geographic Society.

Wrenn, A. (1998) What If ... What If ...: What If We Had All Been Less Sniffy about Counterfactual History in the Classroom? *Teaching History*, 92: 46–48.

Wrenn, A. (2002) Equiano – Voice of Silent Slaves. *Teaching History*, 107: 13–19.

Wrenn, A. (2011) Significance. In I. Davies (ed.), *Debates in History Teaching*. Abingdon: Routledge, pp. 148–58.

Wright, M. (1996) *The Really Practical Guide to Primary History*. Cheltenham: Stanley Thornes.

Young, M.F.D. (2008) *Bringing Knowledge Back In: From Social Constructivism to Social Realism in the Sociology of Education*. Abingdon: Routledge.

Young, M.F.D. (2011) The Return to Subjects: A Sociological Perspective on the UK Coalition Government's Approach to the 14–19 Curriculum. *The Curriculum Journal*, 22: 265–78.

INDEX

Page numbers in *italics* refer to figures and tables.

Printed in Great Britain
by Amazon